# The Cinema of Wang Bing

# The Cinema of Wang Bing

Chinese Documentary between History and Labor

Bruno Lessard

Hong Kong University Press
The University of Hong Kong
Pok Fu Lam Road
Hong Kong
https://hkupress.hku.hk

© 2023 Hong Kong University Press

ISBN 978-988-8805-77-8 (*Hardback*)

All rights reserved. No portion of this publication may be reproduced or transmitted in any form or by any means, electronic or mechanical, including photocopying, recording, or any information storage or retrieval system, without prior permission in writing from the publisher.

British Library Cataloguing-in-Publication Data
A catalogue record for this book is available from the British Library.

Digitally printed

# Contents

Acknowledgments   vi
Editorial Note   vii
Introduction   1

**Part One: The Labor of History**

Chapter 1. The Great Leap Forward: Famine and the Oral History Film   27
Chapter 2. *Fengming, a Chinese Memoir*: The Embodied Archive   43
Chapter 3. *The Ditch*: Techniques of Creative Repetition   61
Chapter 4. *Dead Souls*: Documenting Human and Nonhuman Survivors   77

**Part Two: The History of Labor**

Chapter 5. Observing the Workers: Chinese Governmentality and Critical Realism   97
Chapter 6. *West of the Tracks*: Embracing a Lost Social Totality   110
Chapter 7. *Coal Money*: Tracking an Energy Commodity in the Chinese Anthropocene   131
Chapter 8. *Bitter Money*: The Spatial Politics of Migrant Labor   144
Conclusion   161
Bibliography   165
Index   174

# Acknowledgments

This monograph on Wang Bing's cinema is the culmination of several years of research, teaching, and writing during which I have benefitted from the invaluable support and insightful feedback of many. First, I would like to express my gratitude to the graduate students who participated in the seminars in both the Documentary Media and the Communication and Culture programs at Toronto Metropolitan University (formerly Ryerson University) where I first shared some of my ideas on Wang Bing's cinema. Their constructive criticism prompted me to refine my approach to the films. I also wish to thank audiences at the Film-Philosophy Conference (University of Brighton) and the XXVI Visible Evidence Conference (University of Southern California), both held in 2019, where several attendees encouraged me to complete this monograph. At the University of Nottingham-Ningbo, I am grateful to Corey Kai Nelson Schulz for allowing me to present on Chinese documentary at the "100 Years of Chinese Film & Screen" Conference in 2021. For their research assistance, I owe a special thanks to graduate students Chris Hugelmann and Neal Rockwell. I also wish to acknowledge the financial support of the Social Sciences and Humanities Research Council (SSHRC). I am also thankful to the editorial staff at Hong Kong University Press for their helpful guidance. Finally, I would like to dedicate this publication to my lovely wife, Joëlle, for her love and patience during the writing of this book.

# Editorial Note

This book follows the convention for Chinese names according to which the surname precedes the given name (for example, Wang Bing, Ai Xiaoming). The Chinese pinyin system is used for the romanization of Chinese names. Unless otherwise noted, translations from the French, Italian, and Chinese are mine.

# Introduction

The Chinese documentary filmmaker at the heart of this study is Wang Bing 王兵, who was born in Xi'an, the capital of Shaanxi Province, in 1967. Associated with independent documentary filmmaking, Wang Bing's cinema offers a sustained political engagement with Chinese history (especially the Maoist period), the tranformation of labor practices since the early 2000s, and the everyday life of the Chinese in all its multifaceted forms. The lives that Wang has documented over the past twenty years refract the challenges that China has faced as a nation and the uneven development and rising inequalities that invariably emerge when such large-scale societal changes happen over a brief period. Attending to the dispossessed and the marginalized, the documentarian has tirelessly investigated the legacy of China's Maoist past in the present and the country's spectacular economic growth in the twenty-first century, as well as its impact on labor practices and the workers themselves.

A significant portion of Wang's practice bears witness to the social impact that the economic reforms launched by Deng Xiaoping in 1978, better known as the "Reform-and-Opening" (*gaige kaifang*) era, have had on those who have not benefitted from the economic progress signaling China's rise to the rank of international superpower. The economic accomplishments of the last four decades have seen millions of Chinese lifted out of poverty because of the transition from the rural economic model based on collectivized farming, state-owned and collectively owned enterprises, and socialist planning to the market-oriented economic reform indicating the country's move toward privatization, corporatization, and foreign investment, culminating in China's accession to the WTO in 2001. China's "growth miracle" has been characterized as "the biggest, fastest, longest, and overall most dramatic transformation of an economy in history."[1] This unprecedented transition marked the end of the Maoist model of economic isolation that had been in place for decades and launched China's effort to modernize and implement a mixed economy combining socialism and capitalism. After forty years of wide-scale social and economic transformations at home and opening internationally, China has profoundly changed the face that it presents to the world.

Economists have noted that many have been in favor of the implementation of the "Reform-and-Opening" measures.² However, several of Wang Bing's films have sought to show the other side of the coin of China's rapid economic progress. Indeed, they document those dissatisfied with the Chinese Communist Party (CCP)'s policies and what they have entailed for them. Those who have not benefitted from the reforms make up an important segment of the Chinese population whose experiences of the post-Reform era are not featured in the state-controlled media, and their living conditions certainly do not reflect the much-publicized increased standard of living. As many scholars have noted, there seem to be a number of rising inequalities in China's post-socialist brand of neoliberalism.³ For example, the shift from public to private ownership has revealed one of the most alarming inequalities: "As a result, while in 1978 about 70 percent of national wealth was public and 30 percent private, in 2015 the proportions are reversed: 30 percent of national wealth is public and 70 percent private. China used to be a communist country and is now a mixed economy."⁴

As many now realize, China's economic success since 1978 has come at a price: rural unemployment, massive internal migration, environmental degradation, income disparities (the rural-urban divide), bureaucratic corruption, and Xi Jinping's brand of authoritarian politics, among others, are only a few of the issues that the Chinese face today. Delisle and Goldstein provide a succinct account of the situation: "Wide disparities have emerged between prosperous coastal regions and a lagging interior, between cities and the countryside, and within urban areas that are home to the world's first or second largest group of billionaires as well as recent migrants from the countryside who work in the informal economy and lack full access to China's modest social safety net and other publicly provided goods."⁵ Reacting to the CCP's quest to make China more prosperous and improve the living conditions of Chinese citizens, Wang Bing has focused on the silent majority whose socioeconomic future remains uncertain and has been ignored in mainstream media and official historical records. While millions of Chinese have been lifted out of poverty, countless others have yet to see the benefits of the reforms. They are the focus of Wang Bing's cinema.

Whether it be the closing of state-owned enterprises (SOEs) or migrant labor, Wang has relentlessly documented the darker side of China's post-Reform era. An astute observer of contemporary China, the filmmaker has remarked on the reification process taking place on a national scale: "The economy has kidnapped every one of us. In this sense, human relations today are essentially economic relations."⁶ As opposed to those who are quick to celebrate the great changes that China has undergone, Wang wishes to qualify that transformation and underline its false nature: "we all hope for a big change, but I think that contemporary society does everything it can to prevent this change."⁷ In a rare hyperbolic statement, he has remarked that "China is living the most catastrophic period of its history."⁸ Such statements orient this study of Wang Bing's cinema, which seeks to offer a fine-grained treatment of sociohistorical, political, economic, urban, cultural, and aesthetic issues by developing a *sociopoetics* of independent Chinese documentary. Given that the filmmaker's work reflects a profound engagement with what China has become since launching its campaign of openness and reform in 1978, I argue that it is crucial to pay closer attention to the variously interrelated social, historical, and economic issues that frame Wang's practice than has been the case so far.

Wang Bing's *West of the Tracks* (*Tiexi qu* 铁西区, 2003) first took the film-viewing public by storm by documenting yet-unseen spaces of labor in Shenyang, bearing witness to the end of SOEs in China and the uncertain fate of soon-to-be-unemployed workers.[9] Since then, Wang has documented the vestiges of the Great Leap Forward's famine years and Mao's Anti-Rightist Campaign through the words and life experiences of labor camp survivors in a thought-provoking trilogy (*Fengming, a Chinese Memoir* [*He Fengming* 和凤鸣, 2007]), *The Ditch* [*Jiabiangou* 夹边沟, 2010]), and *Dead Souls* [*Si linghun* 死灵魂, 2018]). Other notable films in Wang's oeuvre document coal industry workers (*Coal Money* [*Tongdao* 通道, 2008]), migrant workers in the textile industry (*Bitter Money* [*Ku qian* 哭钱, 2016]), abandoned children in the remote province of Yunnan (*Three Sisters* [*San zimei* 三姊妹, 2012]), psychiatric patients in a Yunnan asylum ('*Til Madness Do Us Part* [*Feng ai* 瘋愛, 2014]), ethnic refugees fleeing civil war at the Myanmar-China border (*Ta'ang* [*De'ang* 德昂, 2016]), and the final days of a disabled woman (*Mrs. Fang* [*Fang Xiuying* 方绣英, 2017]). Wang has made films destined for the movie theater, and he has also created photographic series and video installations for art galleries and museums such as the fourteen-hour-long *Crude Oil* (*Caiyou riji* 菜油日记, 2008), *Man with No Name* (*Wumingzhe* 无名者, 2009), the one-take, fifteen-hour-long *15 Hours* (*15 xiaoshi* 小时, 2017), *Beauty Lives in Freedom* (*Mei shi ziyou de xiangzheng* 美是自由的象征, 2018), which focuses on Anti-Rightist Campaign survivor, artist, and author Gao Ertai,[10] and *Scenes: Glimpses from a Lockdown* (2020), a performative installation in which the artist combined film and live performance for the first time. At the 2023 Cannes Film Festival, Wang presented two works: the 61-minute portrait *Man in Black* (*Heiyi ren* 黑衣人, 2023), about Chinese composer Wang Xilin, and *Youth (Spring)* (*Qingchun* 青春, 2023), which is his most recent documentary on migrant labor.

Numerous screenings, awards, exhibitions, and retrospectives around the world have cemented Wang Bing's reputation as one of the most significant documentarians of his generation. His films have been screened and have received major awards at prestigious film festivals such as the Venice International Film Festival, the Berlin Film Festival, the International Film Festival Rotterdam, and the Cannes Film Festival. His oeuvre has been the subject of major retrospectives at the Lincoln Center, the Museum of the Moving Image, the Harvard Film Archive, the Musée national d'Art moderne-Centre Georges-Pompidou, the Tate Modern, the Cinémathèque royale de Belgique, the Museo Nacional Reina Sofía / Filmoteca Española, and the Cinémathèque française, among others. His photographic series and video installations have been exhibited at art galleries in Paris, Zürich, Brussels, Geneva, and San Francisco, and at Documenta 14 in Kassel (2014) and Athens (2017). Wang Bing received the EYE Art & Film Prize (Amsterdam) for his body of work in 2017 and the CHANEL Next Prize in 2021.

In this book, I inquire into what it means for a filmmaker such as Wang Bing to take twenty-first-century China as an *object of cinematic thought*, and I attend to the audiovisual strategies used to represent his two obsessions: Maoist history and the evolution of labor practices in the twenty-first century, the latter having been described as the "very essence"[11] of Wang Bing's cinema. I am therefore interested in how Wang understands cinema as an *object of historico-political thought* regarding the representation of both history and labor more specifically. Needless to say, historico-political subjectivity takes various forms within independent Chinese documentaries as they deconstruct and reconstruct history to create an "alternative archive" of lives and events, as Berry and Rofel have described it.[12] Wang Hui has claimed that the "political subjectivity (*zhengzhi zhutixing*) of New China was established on the basis of the foundation of its own historical activity."[13] One hundred years later, I argue that Wang Bing makes documentaries that ground the historico-political subjectivity of twenty-first-century China in a sustained reflection on both the legacy of the Maoist era and Deng Xiaoping's neoliberal reforms whose multifaceted impact on labor and workers have been felt quite dramatically since the 2000s. Pickowicz and Zhang aptly capture Wang Bing's critical perspective when they state that twenty-first-century Chinese documentaries generally "stand in disquieting and jarring contradiction to a grand vision of China proudly marching forward as the world's second largest economy, a one-dimensional notion that is being propagated everywhere in official and commercial media in China."[14]

Building on the achievements of independent Chinese documentary scholarship, this monograph emphasizes the insightful role that social and economic histories can play in the close analysis of select films. For example, the analysis of Wang Bing's "Anti-Rightist" trilogy, examined in Part One, greatly benefits from the thorough integration of social and oral histories of Maoist China to make sense of what happened during the Great Leap Forward and the Great Famine. Similarly, the transformation of labor practices within twenty-first-century China at the heart of the documentaries analyzed in Part Two requires a profound understanding of SOEs and what led to their demise, the coal industry's transportation issues, and the spatial and gender politics of migrant labor within the textile industry. This study of Wang Bing's cinema seeks to demonstrate what is gained by more deeply contextualizing his practice and developing a sociopoetics of documentary film, which could be used to analyze the work of other Chinese documentarians.

## Situating a Documentary Practice

In the early 1990s, Wang Bing entered the Lu Xun Academy of Fine Arts in Shenyang, Liaoning Province, where he majored in photography and took classes in literature, art history, and painting. Upon graduation in 1995, he would go on to study at the Beijing Film Academy in the Cinematography Department. That is where Wang first saw films by Antonioni, Bergman, and Godard, major influences he still cites to this day. In addition to Tarkovsky, whom he regularly mentions as his favorite filmmaker, Wang also acknowledges Visconti for having taught him how to combine shots and sequences to make films "in a non-traditional way."[15] Noteworthy is that Wang had seen very few documentaries before he started making them. His first foray into documentary filmmaking was under the auspices of the state-run Production Studio for Information, Documentary, and Cinema (Xinwen Jilupian Dianying Zhipian Chang). At the time, Wang worked as a first assistant and director of photography on a state-produced documentary film about Zhou Enlai, who was Prime Minister of the Republic of China from 1949 to 1976, titled *Zhou Enlai waijiao fengyun* (The Diplomatic Charm of Zhou Enlai). Working on this documentary film allowed Wang Bing to have access to studio equipment, including a 35 mm camera, various cinema lenses, and 35 mm film, and get a sense of what film could accomplish as an artistic medium.

Describing the state studio as "the biggest communist propaganda machine,"[16] Wang soon felt dissatisfied creatively and reconsidered his career path after the Zhou Enlai documentary. In 1999, after a disastrous experience working on a fiction film, Wang decided to work independently. As he has stated numerous times, his documentaries have been shot without proper state authorization by the National Department of Radio, Cinema, and Television (Guojia Guangbo Dianying Dianshi Zongju), which approves the content of radio and television shows, as well as film scripts. Working independently of the studio system, Wang set out on a creative journey that would require his films to be funded by foreign bodies, which are mostly European in his case. To say that his work has been ostracized in China would be an understatement: his films have never been approved there and, therefore, cannot be shown publicly. On the screening of his films, Wang adds: "On the one hand, few spectators see my films because mainstream cinema occupies all the space. On the other hand, few spectators know of their existence because they are only available as pirate DVDs. One can thus say that in China my cinema doesn't exist, at least on the surface."[17] Wang's comment points to the idiosyncratic case of a Chinese film practice that relies primarily on European funds to exist and whose audience is mainly Western.

Wang's films have attracted a great deal of critical attention because of their stylistic choices, which are often associated with the notion of "slow cinema" within film studies. In various publications devoted to the Chinese filmmaker, authors systematically mention the exceptional length of his films.[18] Indeed, most last several hours and make extreme demands on spectators. For example, Wang's first film, *West of the Tracks*, clocked in at over nine hours. Favoring the long take and exploring the potential of cinema to offer an immersive experience over several hours, Wang has capitalized on the notion of duration to challenge the traditional, formatted filmic experience with its predictable plot lines and character arcs. Alongside documentary filmmakers such as Claude Lanzmann and Patricio Guzmán, Wang has developed a practice in the *longue durée*, a crucial aspect of his films that is often related to the slow cinema movement.

The author of the first monograph on Wang Bing, French film scholar Antony Fiant has introduced the notion of "subtractive cinema"[19] (*cinéma soustractif*) to discuss films associated with "slow cinema" in anglophone scholarship. The distinction between a cinema of subtraction and a cinema of slowness is an important one. While subtraction concerns the elements that are no longer present or privileged, slowness has to do with the pace of the filmic experience. The distinction is even more important in the case of a cinema such as Wang's because the filmmaker himself has drawn attention to the fact that his films are not *slow* per se: "Actually, I think that my films are long, it's true, but not slow."[20] He adds: "It's not that I like to shoot very long films . . . If one chooses a subject that hasn't been treated before, one is obligated to take one's time to present it."[21] On the subject of *Dead Souls*, Wang remarks: "The reason for the 8 hours and 15 minutes lies in the subject, in a very rich content that would have made it impossible to make a short film."[22] Wang's comment echoes what Nichols has said of time in observational cinema: "Though observational films are rooted in the present, they also take time, and such recurrences heighten the impression of narrative development, of transformation over time, as opposed to the alternative impression of an atemporal slice of selected scenes from a single moment in time."[23] In sum, Wang takes issue with the supposed slowness of his films, arguing that there is a crucial difference between slowness, which has to do with pace, and length, which he associates with duration. This clarification should make slow cinema scholars rethink the relationship between Wang's films and the trend in international art cinema with which they have too hastily associated his work.

More crucial than the discussion around "slow cinema" in the description of his sociopoetics is the filmmaker's relationship to the history of the present, that is, life in the late 1980s, and how it profoundly marked him and set him on his creative path. Reflecting on the Tiananmen incidents of June 1989, Wang notes: "I grew up in a politically stable period. The student movement showed me there could exist a relationship between politics and society, that society could change . . . My commitment dates back to that time."[24] As Berry has remarked, the tragic events at Tiananmen have acted as a "crucial structuring absence"[25] for many Chinese documentarians. Although Wang has not dwelt on June 1989 that much in interviews, masterclasses, or question-and-answer periods, it is instructive to read about the significance of the June 1989 events in terms of the development of his political subjectivity.

Wang Bing's political awakening is related to how he conceives of history. Indeed, the movements of Chinese history that Wang Bing would eventually document concern the subfield of historiography known as "microhistory." As he points out: "As far as I'm concerned, regarding History, spectacular events don't interest me. I prefer to film small things; it's the details that interest me."[26] In fact, Wang has articulated a vision of history unfolding that aligns with the radical rethinking historiography has undergone under the sign of microhistory and its emphasis on small-scale events and so-called minor actors who do not appear in official historical records. The emphasis on the personal is a cornerstone of Wang's revisionist understanding of the function of the event in documentary. He notes: "It's easy to explain how an event leads to another, but a real film should not be made of a succession of events. It's much more difficult to show the interior movements of a person that, of course, can also be expressed through concrete events."[27]

A central focus of Wang's historico-political perspective is what he has described as a case of "collective amnesia" regarding twentieth-century Chinese history, especially about Mao's Anti-Rightist Campaign of 1957. The documentarian's audiovisual act of performative rectification stands out as one of the richest in contemporary documentary practices. In the "Anti-Rightist" trilogy consisting of *Fengming, a Chinese Memoir*, *The Ditch*, and *Dead Souls*, Wang erects a visual monument to the victims of the regime and restores a certain collective memory at a time when the Chinese government seems unwilling to critically look at its past, especially the Mao era. It is no surprise that, reflecting on the work of his contemporaries associated with the "Fifth Generation" of filmmakers such as Chen Kaige and Zhang Yimou, Wang has remarked that "[t]here are a lot of films about antiquity and the imperial dynasties, or about the glorious past of the CCP, but very few films—actually, no films have focused on the short periods of Chinese history such as, for example, that of the reeducation camps that I address in *The Ditch*. Even though they are very short periods in the plurimillennial history of China, they are very important and very rich moments for the filmmaker."[28]

Wang's cinema thus focuses on the microhistorical, the marginalized, and the forgotten, and contains a philosophy of history that eschews major events to privilege small-scale details refracting dramatic changes in Chinese history. He notes: "I believe that cinema is meant to tell detailed things. People's lives are very real, our life is very true. Our own existence is really very precise; it lies in the details."[29] In the final analysis, Wang reverses the commonplace understanding of documentary's role, which still rhymes with capturing major events and their actors in many circles: "Generally speaking, I avoid telling political events. Rather, it's political events that emerge in my films."[30] Therefore, it is a documentary sociopoetics of refraction that lies within Wang's practice.

Veg has noted three characteristics that define how independent Chinese films deploy a historico-political perspective. He writes: "Each of the three characteristics is both an aesthetic principle that guides the visual representation and a methodological discourse that implicitly advocates a certain way of understanding society."[31] First, independent films would tend to emphasize the textures of everyday reality to the detriment of the notion of "ideology" or "theory," as had been the case before. Second, Veg argues that "independent cinema represents history as contingent time, breaking with the discourse of teleology that underpins not only visual and literary representations but also much of the historical or sociological work that is undertaken within the boundaries of Chinese academia and Marxist theory." Finally, independent film work, according to Veg, "focuses on characters envisaged as individuals rather than as 'representatives' of a class or a social group."[32]

Wang Bing's documentary sociopoetics reflects Veg's understanding of independent filmmaking in twenty-first-century China in terms of aesthetics and methodology. It is the contingent nature of his subjects' living conditions that Wang shows in his effort to feature the lives of those who had gone undocumented for decades. While one may argue that it is the collective destiny of twenty-first-century China that is at stake in his cinema, the subjects who appear in Wang's films do not speak on behalf of the nation or merely illustrate an ideology. As Veg puts it, "Marginality, contingency, and individuality are instead brought to the fore"[33] in this kind of independent cinema in which subjects address both the filmmaker and the spectator from the point of view of their own singularity as human beings in the context of their contingent conditions of existence.

### The Documentarian as *Minjian* Intellectual

In her 2003 book, *Documenting China: The New Documentary Movement in Contemporary China* (*Jilu Zhongguo: dangdai Zhongguo xin jilu yundong*), Lü Xinyu first brought attention to a surge of actuality-based visual productions since the 1990s by a group of filmmakers whose efforts, she argued, could be said to be homogenous enough to bear the name "New Documentary Movement."[34] Discussing the work of Wu Wenguang, Duan Jinchuan, Jiang Yue, and Zhang Yuan, among others, Lü showed how filmmakers were seeking a way of documenting China *independently*, that is, without the approval of the state, thus bypassing the official system and censorship. In films such as *Bumming in Beijing—The Last Dreamers* (*Liulang Beijing – zuihou de mengxiangzhe* 流浪北京——最后的梦想者, Wu Wenguang, 1991), *The Other Bank* (*Bi'an* 彼岸, Jiang Yue, 1993), *The Square* (*Guangchang* 广场, Duan Jinchuan and Zhang Yuan, 1994), and *No. 16 Barkhor South Street* (*Bakuo nanjie 16 hao* 八廓南街16号, Duan Jinchuan, 1996), the aesthetic approach eschewed socialist realism to adopt a critical stance favoring the everyday and the marginal within a rising market economy. In subsequent publications in Chinese and English, Lü has refined the portrait of the New Documentary Movement by addressing how Chinese filmmakers had been influenced by documentary photographers such as Zhang Xinmin and Sixth Generation filmmakers such as Jia Zhangke, and by attending to the work of a filmmaker such as Wang Bing in her well-known analysis of *West of the Tracks*.[35]

Before the emergence of the new documentary scene in the 1990s, documenting China was far from being a new practice in modern history. As is well known, the CCP had documented China in various forms for decades, from photojournalistic pieces to state-approved documentary films showing the life of the working class. In the post-1990 period, what significantly differed was the emergence of an independent documentary scene, which bypassed the need for state-approved productions. Prior to the rise of the filmmakers associated with the "New Documentary Movement," documentaries took the form of "special topic programs" (*zhuantipian*) broadcast on television, whose domineering voice-over narration was the hallmark of documentary productions up until the end of the 1980s. Lü has shed light on the underlying intention of such programming: "The special topic program is a product of the Chinese television industry, but its history dates back to the heyday of cinema in socialist China . . . Guided by the aesthetic of 'socialist realism,' the social function of these documentaries was to inspire socialist consciousness in the people and to serve the mainstream political ideology of the state using the Leninist method of 'political visualization.'"[36] Scripted programs meant to instruct the masses, such documentaries adopted a didactic tone and monologism whose purpose was to disseminate CCP ideology. Independent film production could not emerge in such an environment where the state owned the means of production and approved all scripts.

Wang Bing and other Chinese documentarians are indebted to a pioneering figure such as Wu Wenguang, who imparted a sense of immediacy and spontaneity in documenting unscripted everyday life in the early 1990s. For an emerging filmmaker such as Wu, what mattered was defining an independent (*duli*) stance toward both the official system and the interrelated activities of production, distribution, and exhibition that had fallen under the purview of the state. In the late twentieth century, documenting China independently signaled a shift toward an autonomous practice predicated on establishing a critical distance between the system and the idealized images of China that had been disseminated for decades in state-sanctioned media channels such as television and the press. As a result, documentary images of China shot by Wu tended to focus on the stories and subjects not covered by the mainstream media. Wu thus elevated the marginalized and the everyday to the rank of primary subject matter. As Pickowicz and Zhang have argued, Wu considered that independent documentary work "values the *grassroots* as its primary locus and the *everyday* as its foundational temporality."[37]

Before launching his career as an independent filmmaker, Wu worked in television on traditional documentaries. His breakthrough as a filmmaker working independently of the studio system took the form of a low-budget documentary, *Bumming in Beijing: The Last Dreamers*, for which he had to borrow a hand-held video camera. Eschewing voice-over narration and artificial lighting and adopting an observational point of view, Wu's film documents the lives of four Beijing-based artists working outside the state system (just like the filmmaker himself), using off-the-cuff interviews with subjects whose voices had never been heard before in China, let alone showing the difficult conditions in which they live. It is the degree of informality in capturing contemporary life and the everyday that Wu's film is perhaps most memorable for. Zhang Zhen has aptly summarized the attitude of Chinese documentarians such as Wu: "the contemporary filmmakers depart consciously from the more didactic tradition of Chinese cinema as a whole, be it critical realism or socialist realism, by taking up instead a more humble position of the witness who produces testimonials rather than epistles."[38] Wu's pathbreaking documentary would herald the new generation of Chinese documentary filmmakers, which demonstrated a new kind of independent production model and style associated with lightweight camera equipment, synchronized sound, in-person interviews, the long take, and "on-the-spot realism,"[39] which is also referred to as *xianchang* (现场 on-the-scene) in the literature.

Over the past decade or so, Western and Chinese scholars have thoroughly analyzed the films associated with the "New Chinese Documentary Film Movement" (*xin Zhongguo jilupian yundong*). These scholars have covered the history of the movement at length, and I will refer the reader to their comprehensive treatments, as it is not my intention to repeat their findings in these pages.[40] Rather, I wish to underline a certain critical development in the field of Chinese documentary studies. Indeed, in addition to the historical accounts of the New Documentary Movement, the publication of monographs and collections of essays on Chinese documentary that use specific notions and concepts have helped to better qualify the notion of independent cinema in China. For example, scholars have turned to the philosophical concept of contingency,[41] the notion of personal documentary,[42] activist documentary and alternative public sphere,[43] digital culture and subjects,[44] and first-person documentary[45] in order to push the boundaries of the field and establish meaningful connections with the notion of independence, which is at the center of most studies of Chinese documentaries. In this study, I build on the work of Chinese documentary scholars and propose to rethink how to conceptually frame a Chinese documentarian's practice such as Wang Bing's.

While the problematic issue of cohesiveness traditionally associated with artistic "movements" also concerns the New Chinese Documentary Film Movement, it is not the supposed unity of the movement or lack thereof that deserves closer attention, but its actual diversity in terms of authorial predilections, which concern shooting style, narrative structure, point of view, sound design, aesthetics, and the complex nature of the political within the films. Indeed, I argue that it is preferable to focus on how twenty-first-century Chinese documentarians such as Wang Bing, Wu Wenguang, Jiang Yue, Duan Jinchuan, Hu Jie, Ou Ning, Du Haibin, Zhao Liang, Xu Tong, Ai Weiwei, Zou Xueping, Zhang Mengqi, and Ai Xiaoming, among others, relate to the category of the sociopolitical in its various declensions instead of using labels such as the "Urban Generation," the "New Chinese Documentary Film Movement," or the "iGeneration," which tend to homogenize a diversified group of filmmakers and interests. I wish to further qualify the notion of independence in the case of Wang Bing and focus on how the sociopolitical unfolds within his cinema. I thus concur with Edwards and Svensson, who argue that "[t]he sheer diversity evident in Chinese film, in terms of filmmakers' ages, ethnicities, geographic locations, styles, commercial orientations and thematic concerns means that a generational understanding of Chinese film is no longer accurate or, we believe, critically useful."[46] Indeed, rather than address filmmakers and documentaries in terms of generational distinctions that act as sweeping generalizations, it is more useful to focus on the notion of independence and how the sociopolitical finds a means to express itself cinematically in the context of practices having to do with production and distribution. This corresponds to the approach adopted in this study of a single Chinese documentarian.

Chinese documentary scholars have argued that the notion of radical politics or leftist orientation must be reframed in a country such as China to account for the type of political involvement that filmmakers share. Indeed, if a defining feature of Chinese documentaries is "the absence of a radical leftist perspective or the expression of any commitment to radical sociopolitical transformation,"[47] then one should pay closer attention to what type of political content can be found in Chinese documentaries, if any. While it may be argued that within an ever-growing society of control and surveillance such as Xi's China the possibility for an activist tradition to emerge is unlikely, numerous Chinese documentaries nevertheless offer a critical take on the present. Edwards and Svensson have proposed a tripartite model to understand independent Chinese documentaries and their modes of political engagement. The first mode is "[m]aking visible people and identities that state-sanctioned representations hide, elide or gloss over"[48] such as migrant workers, queer individuals, and ethnic minorities. The second mode of engagement concerns "[b]earing witness to events and situations that are similarly hidden, or presented in a very particular manner, in state-sanctioned representations,"[49] which might include the lives of abandoned children whose parents have gone to work in large cities or the case of environmental pollution. Lastly, the third form deals with "[e]xploring memories and historical experiences which are otherwise unacknowledged or presented within a narrow range of interpretive parameters in state-sanctioned media."[50] Wu Wenguang's *1966—My Time in the Red Guards* (*1966 nian, wo de hongweibing shidai* 1966年——我的红卫兵时代, 1993), Wang Bing's "Anti-Rightist" trilogy (2007–2018), Zou Xueping's "Zoujiacun" series (2010–2014), Qiu Jiongjiong's *Mr. Zhang Believes* (*Chi* 吃, 2014), and Ai Xiaoming's *Jiabiangou Elegy* (*Jiabiangou jishi* 夹边沟祭事, 2017) exemplify this mode of engagement.

In addition to using Edwards and Svensson's modes of engagement, one of the major contributions of this monograph to Chinese documentary studies is to consider a filmmaker such as Wang Bing as a *minjian* intellectual. The word "*minjian*" (民间) literally refers to the state of being "among the people," and it is often translated as "unofficial," "popular," "grassroots," or "folk" (as in Wu Wenguang's "Folk Memory Project" ["Minjian jiyi jihua" 民间记忆计划] documenting village memories of the Great Famine). A "*minjian* intellectual" is an ordinary citizen seeking to build knowledge based on shared, firsthand experiences outside the political, media, or university system, or someone whose activities combine academic and professional work such as Ai Xiaoming's documentary practice. Veg elaborates on the outsider position of the *minjian* intellectual: "In everyday speech, minjian often refers to a combination, to different degrees, of three characteristics of people or institutions: independence from state income (self-funded), lack of approval by the state system (unofficial), and a low social marker (nonelite or grassroots)."[51] As the destiny of the Chinese nation recedes into the background, grassroots intellectuals such as citizen journalists, social activists, and documentarians reshift the conversation to privilege the everyday problems, concerns, and issues faced by the voiceless and the marginalized, and the neglected spaces in which they find themselves. Associated with the less derogatory term "*diceng*" (底层) (lower stratum or subordinate), the marginalized no longer merely reflect the class struggles of yesteryear or continous revolution, but the disenfranchised of today. In the case of Wang Bing, to the list of the dispossessed one should add survivors of Maoist labor camps, ethnic refugees, and migrant workers.

The figure of the grassroots intellectual, with which I associate a filmmaker such as Wang Bing, thus privileges issues of precarity, vulnerability, marginality, and disenfranchisement within post-Reform Chinese society. Adopting a defined critical stance, this kind of intellectual is the central focus of the "Silent Majority," which Wang Xiaobo has discussed in his well-known 1996 essay of the same name in which he criticizes the Chinese intelligentsia, from May Fourth literati to Maoist-era Marxists, and emphasizes the vulnerable groups (*ruoshi qunti* 弱势群体) composing the silent majority.[52] Veg notes: "Emphasizing the *minjian* status of intellectuals as part of a 'silent majority' suggests that society is not aligned along class lines but rather polarized between vested interests (including the political and economic elite) on the one hand and a mosaic of disenfranchised groups with diverging agendas on the other."[53] Wang Xiaobo's emphasis on vulnerability in his essay reflected the concern for a profoundly divided society in which the great majority of citizens belong to a marginalized group such as laid-off employees, sex workers, petitioners, migrant workers, or expropriated residents.

Since the Tiananmen events of June 1989 and the development of the market economy, the role of the intellectual in China has changed dramatically. At the time, a number of historians, sociologists, and filmmakers turned to the more vulnerable groups within Chinese society and, along the way, reconsidered what it meant to do intellectual work grounded in specific socioeconomic issues: "Although the pro-democracy movement had reached broad segments of society, many intellectuals, both critically self-reflecting on what had gone wrong and anticipating how to continue their work in a context of increased state control, took issue with the elitist bias of the democracy movement . . . Many now shifted their interests toward concrete problems, often associated with people situated not at the center but at the margins of society."[54] *Minjian* intellectuals' focus on everyday practices moved the conversation away from grand narratives (democracy, class, or the nation) to develop new objects of study and potential forms of intervention and memorialization. As filmmaker Hu Jie has succinctly noted: "Because the Chinese official authority does not want us to remember the history, we non-official people should remember on our own."[55] In the process, the role of public intellectual, so crucial to the May Fourth Movement and Marxist representations of society, has been redefined.

In the context of Chinese documentary studies, *minjian* has the advantage of representing an indigenous, epistemological concept framing both a filmmaking practice and a politics of knowledge with which to address post-Reform Chinese society without having recourse to Western theory or Marxist terminology, which remains the preferred frame of reference of the CCP. *Minjian* mobilizes a documentary methodology attuned to the plurality of everyday experiences within China and favors the individual, empirical study of the margins in terms of both spaces and individuals. It also has the advantage of bypassing theoretical debates associated with the New Left in China. Indeed, the grassroots intellectual is not the type of thinker who was associated with the "New Left" in the 1990s. Discourses of liberalism and democracy, the nascent public sphere, and the evolution of Chinese society in general are not the focus of grassroots intellectuals as they were for the New Left. On the contrary, the priority of *minjian* intellectuals has been the quotidian struggles of those who remain unseen and unheard in the mainstream media, or those whose sufferings have been ignored. In fact, and this is a key point to emphasize, the pain and misery of ordinary people have been at the heart of *minjian* intellectuals' concerns. As Wang Bing has emphasized: "To me, it is the lives of ordinary people that must be shown."[56] Rather than overemphasize the sufferings of the elites or intellectuals during Mao's tenure, as had been the case for decades, grassroots intellectuals have focused on the marginalization that many Chinese face in the post-Reform era. Given their focus on the *ruoshi qunti* and *diceng*, *minjian* intellectuals have been likened to the "subaltern intellectual" in the West, especially in terms of representation, and their activities have often been associated with "subaltern history" (*diceng lishi*).[57]

The socioeconomic concerns of *minjian* intellectuals echo those of an independent filmmaker such as Wang Bing. In fact, the notion of "independence" itself can be associated with *minjian* intellectuals. Veg writes: "The term 'independent' generally refers to films not produced, or at least not initiated, by a state studio or broadcaster, which are in this sense 'outside the system' and therefore also generally underfunded and in resonance with grassroots society."[58] Working independently has meant both focusing on the marginalized and living with them for extended periods of time, as is the case of Wang Bing, who has travelled around China to document the everyday lives of the most vulnerable segments of society and has captured the life experiences and oral histories of individuals whose living conditions in remote areas had not been the focus of mainstream media and documentaries.

## Rethinking *Xianchang*: Toward a *Minjian* Ethics

The wish of a *minjian* filmmaker such as Wang Bing to document labor camp survivors and marginalized workers requires a perspective that is quite different from that of his forebears who worked within the Chinese studio system. Indeed, abandoning the prescriptions associated with state-approved scenarios, *minjian* filmmakers engage contemporary Chinese society in a way that embraces the contingent aspects of both life and filmmaking, which Wu Wenguang referred to as *xianchang* ("on-the-spot" or "on-the-scene") in the early 2000s. *Xianchang* is more revealing in the original Chinese because it combines the notions of time or present (*xian*) and space in the form of the scene, site, or place (*chang*) where the filming occurred. Referring to both time and space, the etymological roots of *xianchang* thus suggest an embodied, phenomenological approach to capturing the real in the here and the now, which has meant closely following subjects, sharing their work or living spaces, and adopting more reflexive shooting methods associated with liveness and the contingency of events unfolding in real time. Zhang Zhen has thus captured what *xianchang* entails: "Xianchang thus constitutes a particular social and epistemic space in which orality, performativity, and an irreducible specificity of personal and social experience are acknowledged, recorded, and given aesthetic expression."[59]

Combining both time and space, *xianchang* functions as a potent philosophical concept containing an open-ended epistemological and ethical program. Edwards has remarked that *xianchang* is not only a visual style but also "a philosophical desire to engage with the prosaic, physical reality of China without the filter of an ideologically informed expositional interpretation to guide the viewer informed Chinese independent documentary making from its earliest days."[60] Associated with the documentation of contingent events, liveness and the long take function as perhaps the two most discussed traits of *xianchang*. No wonder film scholars have noted the influence of Frederick Wiseman's observational style on many independent filmmakers, considering the absence of voice-over narration, talking heads, and nondiegetic soundtrack. Rather, *xianchang* embraces the unpredictable and, by doing so, leads to ethical questions that only it could have generated: "*xianchang* becomes an ethical problem: narrative structures that make historical contingencies into necessities driven by a teleological vision of progress are rejected in favor of contingency and particularity."[61] The *xianchang* approach to documentary making reveals a complex practice combining aesthetic, epistemological, and ethical concerns that *minjian* filmmakers such as Wang Bing have confronted in reaction to post-Reform China.

Lü Xinyu has made a crucial intervention to reposition debates over *xianchang*,[62] as there seems to be critical fatigue with *de rigueur* discussions of *xianchang* within Chinese documentary studies. Braester explains: "The concept of *xianchang* no longer suffices to describe independent documentary in the twenty-first century. Lü's idea of self-ethics directs the conversation away from defining a profilmic subject—*diceng*, director, or otherwise—and notes how the director is transformed in the process of filming, most significantly as an ethical subject."[63] Braester goes on to argue that Wu Wenguang's notion of *xianchang*, that is, the documentation of an event at both the time and place of its occurrence, "ascribes to the filmmaker a relatively passive role. *Xianchang* takes both the filming and the filmed as givens, rather than focusing on the performative aspect of their interaction. Ethical engagement is of no explicit concern."[64] Noting that the "lack of self-reflection threatened to turn into self-indulgence"[65] within Chinese documentary practices, Braester welcomes the increasing attention paid to ethics in both Chinese documentary studies and filmmaking itself.

While Lü and Braester are correct to demand that greater attention be paid to the ethical stakes of documentary practices, I believe that in their accounts, the notion of "self-ethics" (*ziwo lunli*) remains undertheorized from a Western, Chinese, or global perspective. On the one hand, there is a crying need for more sustained engagements with the ethical stakes of *xianchang*, which is what Lü has implicitly proposed with the notion of self-ethics. On the other hand, while self-ethics may indeed "fill a glaring gap in theoretizing documentary cinema in the early twenty-first century,"[66] the Chinese documentary filmmaker, as an ethical subject, deserves closer attention. If indeed Lü's notion of self-ethics emphasizes "the critical process taking place within the filmmaker's consciousness,"[67] then more needs to be said about that process. The following chapters closely examine how Wang Bing's filmmaking choices and process reflect his self-ethics and artistic criticality.

## Overview

This book is divided into two parts. Building on the foundation laid in the Introduction, Parts One and Two concentrate on the two obsessions at the heart of Wang's films: Chinese history and labor. Part One, "The Labor of History," foregrounds the pain and exhaustion associated with the unfolding of historical events in Maoist China and turns to the collective trauma of the Great Leap Forward (1958–1962) and the Great Famine (1959–1961) as documented in Wang Bing's "Anti-Rightist" trilogy (*Fengming, a Chinese Memoir*, *The Ditch*, and *Dead Souls*), which was inspired by the fictionalized testimonies in Yang Xianhui's *Chronicles of Jiabiangou* (*Jiabiangou jishi*, 2002). More than a simple representation of past events and traumas, history is *put to work* in Wang Bing's films: it is asked to mediate and perform certain tasks to address the horrors of the Chinese past, especially the Maoist era, and the difficulty to remember. In the trilogy, the filmmaker confronts his country's historical amnesia and accomplishes the difficult task of historical rectification by creating an archive of his own.

In Part One, I show that, as a *minjian* filmmaker, Wang Bing engages the question of the archive in his own singular way with the resources of both documentary and fiction. Wang's "Anti-Rightist" trilogy functions as a fascinating case study for understanding the reconstruction of the Chinese past by audiovisual means in the context of unopened archives and the paucity of reliable documents. I argue that the filmmaker uses three distinct modes of archiving in the trilogy, each film addressing a specific issue pertaining to the creation of an archive. In the process of creating audiovisual archives for future generations, Wang Bing demonstrates how the oral history film and the fictionalized treatment of history need to walk the fine line between history and memory, on the one hand, and preservation and creation, on the other, with respect to archiving labor camp life and experiences.

In the first chapter, I draw on the work of social historians of China to contextualize the representation of survivors at the heart of Wang Bing's "Anti-Rightist" trilogy, which serves as a unique audiovisual archive of the legacy of Maoist China, especially the representation of the Great Leap Forward and the ravages of the famine of 1958–1962. Bridging the gap between social history and film studies, Chapter 1 seeks to provide a rich sociocultural background to Wang Bing's work. This introductory chapter reflects on the erasure of historical events in twentieth-century China such as the Great Famine and the role that documentary film can play. I pay special attention to forced labor and the prison camp (in both its *laogai* and *laojiao* forms) and touch on aspects of Chinese penology pertaining to Maoist camps such as Jiabiangou. Memoirs, microhistories, and scholarly studies mediate what remains of Maoist China and contextualize the films analyzed in subsequent chapters under the sign of oral history.

Chapter 2 examines the function of *Fengming, a Chinese Memoir* as an oral history film focusing on a single female survivor, He Fengming. I argue that, in the process of documenting He's life experiences over three hours, the *minjian* filmmaker turns his subject into an embodied archive with a specific affective and performative charge. Equally significant in *Fengming* is the exploration of intertextual resonances between three texts: He Fengming's published memoir, *Jingli: wo de 1957 nian*, Yang Xianhui's fictionalized account of the period in *Jiabiangou shiji*, and Wang's long-form interview with He herself in his 2007 film. These different media use three modes of archiving to retell a traumatic period in Chinese history. I show that one of the film's greatest contributions is to have implicitly challenged the binary opposition between oral testimony and archive in influential theories such as Paul Ricoeur's by emphasizing the primordial role of performance, affect, and trauma in what I describe as a nascent form of critical archive theory mediated by moving images.

The focus of Chapter 3 is on *The Ditch*, which is Wang Bing's only foray into feature-length fiction. I examine the second film in the "Anti-Rightist" trilogy and show how the recourse to fiction and reenactment raises important ethical issues about the representation of labor camp guards and survivors played by semi-professional and nonprofessional actors and about the recreation of the camps themselves. The chapter seeks to understand what kind of potential the *minjian* filmmaker saw in fiction to capture the experiences of the Great Famine that he had not explored before. I argue that the representational and ethical issues in the film depend on what I call "techniques of creative repetition," which correspond to how *adaptation* and *reenactment* allow for the creative repetition of past events and experiences. In the case of adaptation, the filmmaker returned to Yang Xianhui's fictionalized accounts, which appear in the collection discussed in the previous chapter on *Fengming*, and he used rare archival photographs of the camps to recreate the setting for his film. Finally, I draw on documentary scholars' writings on reenactment and Gilles Deleuze's reflections on repetition to argue that what Wang ultimately sought to accomplish in *The Ditch* was to find a new audiovisual strategy to represent historical events, and that the two techniques of creative repetition used in *The Ditch* make the spectator reconsider key moments in twentieth-century Chinese history concerning the horrors of labor camp life.

The last chapter of Part One, Chapter 4, turns to the third installment in the "Anti-Rightist" trilogy, *Dead Souls*, which focuses on the testimonies of several survivors of the Mingshui labor camp over eight hours. In this *film-fleuve*, which serves a decidedly archival purpose, Wang Bing alternates between long-form interviews with survivors and landscape sequences, aligning this film and the trilogy as a whole with the work of social historians who have emphasized the agency of survivors and the role of oral history to archive labor camp life experiences. Wang Bing's marked interest in the vivaciousness of the spoken word testifies to both his belief in the self-presence of the survivor in human form and the plastic nature of human memory as represented in the nonchronological treatment of the interviews. This chapter argues, perhaps most provocatively, that *Dead Souls* is equally interested in documenting *nonhuman* survivors, which take the form of remnants such as bones scattered across the land where the labor camps used to be. The nonhuman perspective of the film has not received any critical attention, even though the landscape sequences function as crucial markers of critical distance for the *minjian* filmmaker, who uses them to pause from heart-wrenching interviews with survivors. Yet these landscape sequences are no mere transitional moments in the film: they allow the spectator to understand landscape as both a view and a site in terms of ontological, epistemological, and practical considerations.

Part Two, titled "The History of Labor," turns to the second obsession at the heart of Wang Bing's cinema: the representation of Chinese labor and its transformation in the twenty-first century. In addition to what is Wang's most celebrated film, *West of the Tracks*, I examine works that have received less critical attention such as *Coal Money* and *Bitter Money*, and I assess how Wang Bing approaches the challenges faced by workers who have to find employment in other sectors such as the coal industry and textile manufacturing now that most SOEs are a thing of the past. As a *minjian* intellectual and artist, Wang Bing carefully documents the profound labor changes that China has undergone, going from the end of SOEs and its impact on Tiexi district in Shenyang to the predominance of migrant labor in coastal cities such as Huzhou.

Chapter 5 sets the stage for the study of *West of the Tracks*, *Coal Money*, and *Bitter Money* in Part Two. There are two central notions at the heart of this introductory chapter: Chinese governmentality and critical realism. Regarding the former, it is the transition from Maoist state planning to Chinese governmentality that signaled the transformation of worker identity in China. The new forms of societal organization under the sign of governmentality meant the adaptation of Western governmental practices to the Chinese context, which is to say understanding the enduring legacy of Maoism after the CCP turned to a mixed economy in its quest to transform the country. The CCP having vastly invested in the control of its population's conduct since the 1950s, the management of life that is at the center of Part Two concerns the socioeconomic and political behavior of workers facing the closure of SOEs and its aftermath, the transportation of energy commodities within the coal industry, and the emergence of textile workshops and the widespread reliance on migrant labor in the garment industry. The transition from the safety net of the *danwei* system to the worker as an entrepreneur of the self who is responsible for finding solutions to socioeconomic problems such as unemployment is a major concern of this chapter, as many of Wang Bing's subjects discuss how they can improve their living conditions.

The second concept at the heart of Chapter 5, critical realism, borrows from Allan Sekula's publications and artistic projects that focus on labor. More than a visual style, critical realism is a documentary method first and foremost, which can help to rethink how the notion of observation has been defined within documentary studies. Privileging labor and workers as the focus of its investigation, the critical realist method takes the everyday conditions of workers and the impacts of neoliberalism as the locus of sociopolitical struggles within society. Inspired by Sekula's work, this study develops a finer-grained account of Chinese workers and their struggles, from the positivity of employment to the negativity of unemployment and all the contingent moments in-between, including visual moments imbued with idleness and uncertainty. The critical realist method, as a visual research method, thus departs from socialist realism's efforts to monumentalize the working body in the representation of labor, as was the case in socialist art and revolutionary realism, to emphasize the dialectical understanding of the worker in terms of precarity and exploitation. The concept of critical realism accounts for both Wang Bing's observational tactics and the documentary records of Chinese labor found in *West of the Tracks, Coal Money,* and *Bitter Money.*

Chapter 6 turns to Wang Bing's breakthrough epic, *West of the Tracks*, which was shot in Shenyang (Liaoning Province) in northeastern China. This nine-hour-long visual journey carefully documents the end of a gigantic industrial complex, Tiexi, and points to the end of SOEs as the CCP transformed the planned economy and transitioned to the hybrid economic model in place today. The chapter argues that Wang Bing's interest in Tiexi was to document a decaying social totality, focusing on three key aspects corresponding to the three parts in the film: the material state of the factories themselves and the financial and psychological state of workers facing impending unemployment ("Gongchang"); the impact of the closure of SOEs on a Tiexi neighborhood and its youths and the challenges of forced relocation ("Yanfen jie"); and finally, a microhistorical perspective on a father-son relationship under difficult financial circumstances ("Tielu"). Wang Bing's desire for a totalizing view of labor in *West of the Tracks* explains the emphasis on working life within SOEs, the documentation of community life in a Tiexi neighborhood facing demolition, and the socioeconomic challenges facing a poor family unit. I argue that it is imperative to analyze all three parts of the film as interrelated components in this cinematic portrait of a disintegrating social totality. The film combines both macrohistorical and microhistorical perspectives on Chinese labor and the impact of Chinese governmentality on the population of Tiexi to paint an unforgettable portrait of the "urban poor" after the dismantling of the *danwei* system.

In Chapter 7, I examine a neglected film in Wang Bing's oeuvre, *Coal Money*, which documents China's coal industry, more specifically the extraction and transportation of coal and the working lives of those who, we can imagine, used to find employment in the type of SOEs archived in *West of the Tracks*. The film offers a meditation on the real price of coal and the human costs associated with it in such precarious employment within the Chinese Anthropocene. I argue that *Coal Money* makes a singular contribution to the environmental documentary genre and the representation of Chinese labor because the film frames the coal-related production, transportation, and negotiation activities defining the conditions of workers. The treatment of coal as a *transportable* and *negotiable* commodity brings to light the precarious labor that comes with the *movement* of coal and *negotiation* of coal prices. The chapter contextualizes this overlooked film by turning to the literature on the Chinese coal industry, highlighting some of the environmental challenges associated with the transportation of coal and analyzing how coal industry workers such as truck drivers and coal sellers are represented across various geographical areas and "minescapes."

In the final chapter, the wheel comes full circle with Wang Bing's *Bitter Money*, which addresses the current generation of rural migrant workers who move to the east coast to find employment in the textile and garment industry. While *West of the Tracks* marks the end of SOEs and a certain kind of social existence, *Coal Money* and *Bitter Money* make spectators reflect on the new industries that allow China to be a key player in a globalized world. Coming from provinces where jobs are scarce, the migrant workers in *Bitter Money* seek a better future in Zhejiang Province, where they hope to find employment in small family-run workshops, which is an underrepresented aspect of the Chinese textile industry. Painting a picture of the changing labor conditions in twenty-first-century China, Wang Bing focuses on social issues that reveal the spatial politics of migrant labor: mobility, labor exploitation, the dormitory labor regime, migrant subjectivity, and domestic violence. Wang Bing's unexpected focus on a struggling migrant couple and domestic violence in *Bitter Money* reflects a concern about female migrant subjectivity, gender, and power that had not been present to such an extent in his previous films.

## Notes

1. Barry Naughton, "China's Domestic Economy: From 'Enlivening' to 'Steerage,'" in *To Get Rich Is Glorious: Challenges Facing China's Economic Reform and Opening at Forty*, ed. Jacques Delisle and Avery Goldstein (Washington, D.C.: Brookings Institution Press, 2019), 32.
2. Jacques Delisle and Avery Goldstein, "China's Economic Reform and Opening at Forty," in *To Get Rich Is Glorious: Challenges Facing China's Economic Reform and Opening at Forty*, ed. Jacques Delisle and Avery Goldstein (Washington, DC: Brookings Institution Press, 2019), 6.
3. Thomas Piketty, Li Yang, and Gabriel Zucman, "Capital Accumulation, Private Property, and Rising Inequality in China, 1978–2015," *American Economic Review* 109, no. 7 (2019): 2472.
4. Piketty, Li, and Zucman, "Capital Accumulation, Private Property, and Rising Inequality in China, 1978–2015," 2480.
5. Delisle and Goldstein, "China's Economic Reform and Opening at Forty," 8.
6. Wang Bing, "Filming a Land in Flux," *New Left Review* 82 (2013): 133.
7. Wang Bing, "Premier dialogue avec le cinéaste. Entretien avec Wang Bing réalisé par Isabelle Anselme," in *Wang Bing. Un cinéaste en Chine aujourd'hui*, ed. Caroline Renard, Isabelle Anselme, and François Amy de la Bretèque (Aix-en-Provence: Presses universitaires de Provence, 2014), 38.
8. Wang Bing, *Alors, la Chine. Entretiens avec Emmanuel Burdeau et Eugenio Renzi* (Paris: Les Prairies ordinaires, 2014), 148.

9. Speaking of *West of the Tracks*, Wang has said: "I don't know if I have made a political film, but politics is part of life and I have filmed life." Wang Bing, "La memoria rimossa della Cina. Conversazione con Wang Bing," in *Wang Bing: Il cinema nella Cina che cambia*, ed. Daniela Persico (Milan: Agenzia X, 2010), 23.
10. See Er Tai Gao, *In Search of My Homeland: A Memoir of a Chinese Labor Camp*, trans. Robert Dorsett and David E. Pollard (New York: Ecco Press, 2009).
11. Elena Pollacchi, *Wang Bing's Filmmaking of the China Dream: Narratives, Witnesses and Marginal Spaces* (Amsterdam: Amsterdam University Press, 2021), 122.
12. See Chris Berry and Lisa Rofel, "Alternative Archive: China's Independent Documentary Culture," in *The New Chinese Documentary Film Movement: For the Public Record*, ed. Chris Berry, Lu Xinyu, and Lisa Rofel (Hong Kong: Hong Kong University Press, 2010), 135–54.
13. Wang Hui, *Dongxi zhijian de "Xizang wenti"* (Beijing: Shenghuo, dushu, xin zhi sanlian shudian, 2011), 105.
14. Paul G. Pickowicz and Yingjin Zhang, "Introduction: Documenting China Independently," in *Filming the Everyday: Independent Documentaries in Twenty-First-Century China*, ed. Paul G. Pickowicz and Yingjin Zhang (Lanham, MD: Rowman & Littlefield, 2017), 4.
15. Wang, *Alors, la Chine*, 91.
16. Wang, *Alors, la Chine*, 52.
17. Wang, *Alors, la Chine*, 146.
18. Pollacchi, *Wang Bing's Filmmaking of the China Dream*; Wang Bing, *Wang Bing—L'œil qui marche* (Paris: Le Bal / Delpire & Co., 2021); Antony Fiant, *Wang Bing: un geste documentaire de notre temps* (Laval: Warm, 2019); Caroline Renard, Isabelle Anselme, and François Amy de la Bretèque, eds., *Wang Bing. Un cinéaste en Chine aujourd'hui* (Aix-en-Provence: Presses universitaires de Provence, 2014); the special issue of the French journal *Images documentaires* (no. 77, 2013) devoted to Wang Bing; and Daniela Persico, ed., *Wang Bing: Il cinema nella Cina che cambia* (Milan: Agenzia X, 2010).
19. See Antony Fiant, *Pour un cinéma contemporain soustractif* (Paris: Presses Universitaires de Vincennes, 2014). I have explored the artistic ramifications of the notion of subtraction in Bruno Lessard, *The Art of Subtraction: Digital Adaptation and the Object Image* (Toronto: University of Toronto Press, 2017).
20. Wang, "Premier dialogue avec le cinéaste," 34.
21. Wang, "Premier dialogue avec le cinéaste," 34.
22. Wang Bing, Dominique Chateau, and José Moure, "Documentary as Contemporary Art—A Dialogue," in *Post-cinema: Cinema in the Post-art Era*, ed. Dominique Chateau and José Moure (Amsterdam: Amsterdam University Press, 2020), 363.
23. Bill Nichols, *Speaking Truths with Film: Evidence, Ethics, Politics in Documentary* (Berkeley: University of California Press, 2016), 41.
24. Wang, *Alors, la Chine*, 40.
25. Chris Berry, "Getting Real: Chinese Documentary, Chinese Postsocialism," in *The Urban Generation: Chinese Cinema and Society at the Turn of the Twenty-first Century*, ed. Zhang Zhen (Durham, NC: Duke University Press, 2007), 118.
26. Wang, "Premier dialogue avec le cinéaste," 23.
27. Wang, "La memoria rimossa della Cina," 26.
28. Wang, "Premier dialogue avec le cinéaste," 41.
29. Wang, "Premier dialogue avec le cinéaste," 24.
30. Wang, *Alors, la Chine*, 166.

31. Sebastian Veg, *Minjian: The Rise of China's Grassroots Intellectuals* (New York: Columbia University Press, 2019), 142.
32. Veg, *Minjian*, 142.
33. Veg, *Minjian*, 151.
34. See Lü Xinyu, *Jilu Zhongguo. Dangdai Zhongguo xin jilu yundong* (Beijing: Sanlian shudian, 2003).
35. See Lu Xinyu, "*West of the Tracks*: History and Class-Consciousness," in *The New Chinese Documentary Film Movement: For the Public Record*, ed. Chris Berry, Lu Xinyu, and Lisa Rofel (Hong Kong: Hong Kong University Press, 2010), 57–76.
36. Lu Xinyu, "Rethinking China's New Documentary Movement: Engagement with the Social," in *The New Chinese Documentary Film Movement: For the Public Record*, ed. Chris Berry, Lu Xinyu, and Lisa Rofel (Hong Kong: Hong Kong University Press, 2010), 16.
37. Pickowicz and Zhang, "Introduction: Documenting China Independently," 4, emphasis in original.
38. Zhang Zhen, "Bearing Witness: Chinese Urban Cinema in the Era of 'Transformation' (*Zhuanxing*)," in *The Urban Generation: Chinese Cinema and Society at the Turn of the Twenty-first Century*, ed. Zhang Zhen (Durham, NC: Duke University Press, 2007), 7–8.
39. In addition to his pioneering films, Wu has also edited a three-volume series titled *Xianchang* (English subtitle: "Document") in which one finds photographs, scripts, oral history, and interviews that document the new cultural moment in which liveness and contingency would fuel cultural productions. See Wu Wenguang, ed., *Xianchang* (Tianjin: Shehui kexueyuan chubanshe, 2000), Wu Wenguang, ed., *Xianchang 2* (Tianjin: Shehui kexueyuan chubanshe, 2003), and Wu Wenguang, ed., *Xianchang 3* (Tianjin: Shehui kexueyuan chubanshe, 2005).
40. For historical accounts of the New Documentary Movement, see Paul G. Pickowicz and Yingjin Zhang, ed., *From Underground to Independent: Alternative Film Culture in Contemporary China* (Lanham, MD: Rowman & Littlefield, 2006); Chris Berry and Lisa Rofel, "Introduction," in *The New Chinese Documentary Film Movement: For the Public Record*, ed. Chris Berry, Lu Xinyu, and Lisa Rofel, 3–13 (Hong Kong: Hong Kong University Press, 2010); Luke Robinson, *Independent Chinese Documentary: From the Studio to the Street* (London: Palgrave, 2013); Dan Edwards, *Independent Chinese Documentary: Alternative Visions, Alternative Publics* (Edinburgh: Edinburgh University Press, 2015); and Judith Pernin, *Pratiques indépendantes du documentaire en Chine: histoire, esthétique et discours visuels (1990–2010)* (Rennes: Presses universitaires de Rennes, 2015).
41. See Robinson, *Independent Chinese Documentary*.
42. See Wang Qi, *Memory, Subjectivity and Independent Chinese Cinema* (Edinburgh: Edinburgh University Press, 2014).
43. See Edwards, *Independent Chinese Documentary*.
44. See Zhang Zhen and Angela Zito, ed., *DV-Made China: Digital Subjects and Social Transformations after Independent Film* (Honolulu: University of Hawaii Press, 2015).
45. See Kiki Tianqi Yu, *'My' Self on Camera: First Person Documentary Practice in an Individualising China* (Edinburgh: Edinburgh University Press, 2020).
46. Dan Edwards and Marina Svensson, "Show Us Life and Make Us Think: Engagement, Witnessing and Activism in Independent Chinese Documentary Today," *Studies in Documentary Film* 11 no. 3 (2017): 167.
47. Edwards and Svensson, "Show Us Life and Make Us Think," 162.
48. Edwards and Svensson, "Show Us Life and Make Us Think," 164.
49. Edwards and Svensson, "Show Us Life and Make Us Think," 164.

50. Edwards and Svensson, "Show Us Life and Make Us Think," 164.
51. Veg, *Minjian*, 8.
52. Wang Xiaobo, "The Silent Majority," accessed May 20, 2022, https://media.paper-republic.org/files/09/04/The_Silent_Majority_Wang_Xiaobo.pdf.
53. Veg, *Minjian*, 252.
54. Veg, *Minjian*, 2.
55. Rui Shen, "To Remember History: Hu Jie Talks about His Documentaries," *Senses of Cinema* 35 (2005), https://www.sensesofcinema.com/2005/conversations-with-filmmakers/hu_jie_documentaries/.
56. Dufour, and Païni, "Entretien avec Wang Bing," 816.
57. On the subaltern intellectual, see the pioneering collection: Ranajit Guha and Gayatri Chakravorty Spivak, ed., *Selected Subaltern Studies* (Oxford: Oxford University Press, 1988).
58. Veg, *Minjian*, 124.
59. Zhang, "Bearing Witness," 20.
60. Edwards, *Independent Chinese Documentary*, 32.
61. Sebastian Veg, "Literary and Documentary Accounts of the Great Famine," in *Popular Memories of the Mao Era: From Critical Debate to Reassessing History*, ed. Sebastian Veg (Hong Kong: Hong Kong University Press, 2019), 134.
62. Lü Xinyu, "'Diceng' de zhengzhi, lunli yu meixue," in *Xueshu, chuanmei yu gonggongxing* (Shanghai: Huadong shifan daxue chubanshe, 2015), 244–57.
63. Yomi Braester, "For Whom Does the Director Speak?: The Ethics of Representation in Documentary Film Criticism," in *Filming the Everyday: Independent Documentaries in Twenty-First-Century China*, ed. Paul G. Pickowicz and Yingjin Zhang (Lanham, MD: Rowman & Littlefield, 2017), 40.
64. Braester, "For Whom Does the Director Speak?," 40.
65. Braester, "For Whom Does the Director Speak?," 40.
66. Braester, "For Whom Does the Director Speak?," 40.
67. Braester, "For Whom Does the Director Speak?," 40.

# Part One

# The Labor of History

# 1
# The Great Leap Forward

## Famine and the Oral History Film

If one were to characterize Wang Bing's obsession with Chinese history and wish to reclaim repressed memories of the Maoist era, one would be hard pressed to find a better starting point than the Anti-Rightist Movement (*Fan youpai yundong*) of 1957 and the Great Famine (*Da jihuang*) of 1958–1962. In a trilogy[1] comprising *Fengming, a Chinese Memoir* (*He Fengming* 和凤鸣, 2007), *The Ditch* (*Jiabiangou* 夹边沟, 2010), and *Dead Souls* (*Si linghun* 死灵魂, 2018), Wang erects a monument to the victims of Mao's policies and celebrates the fighting spirit of those who have survived to tell their stories, as he documents the tragedy of those who lost their lives in the forced labor camps. A cornerstone of Wang Bing's filmic production, the trilogy reconstructs a key period in the country's eventful twentieth century and the enforced amnesia that characterizes twenty-first-century China regarding the historical traumas of the past. The trilogy constitutes Wang's only departure from present-day Chinese politics and society, and its goal is to explore the vestiges of the Anti-Rightist Movement in the present.

As an oral history documentary, *Fengming* bears witness to the life story of a single woman, He Fengming, who was persecuted by the regime and whose husband died in a forced labor camp. Adopting a minimalist mise-en-scène, *Fengming* spends over three hours retelling one woman's life from the foundation of the republic in 1949 to her rehabilitation in the late 1970s. The second film in the "Anti-Rightist" trilogy, *The Ditch*, greatly departs from *Fengming* in terms of audiovisual strategies, and from Wang Bing's body of work in particular, as it is the filmmaker's only feature-length fiction film. The film offers a fictional representation of the sufferings of those sent to the Jiabiangou forced labor camp in the winter of 1960 and the extreme conditions that they faced there, leading to physical exhaustion, hunger, and death. The third film, the eight-hour-long *Dead Souls*, concerns the testimonies of numerous survivors in their eighties and nineties who bear witness to both their own horrific experiences during the Great Famine and to those who died of starvation in the labor camps.

A recurring issue in the literature on the Great Leap Forward and famine is that of the archives and their role in creating a new image of Maoist China. As numerous researchers have noted, the CCP's wish to keep central archives such as the Beijing Archives closed to the public has prevented many from coming to terms with the Great Leap Forward. Social scientists and historians have had to rely on provincial- and county-level archives and collections to tell the stories of individuals whose lives were dramatically altered in the 1950s and early 1960s. In his pioneering work in the archive, revisionist historian Frank Dikötter has used party archives and recently available documents to reconsider the Great Leap Forward and Mao's responsibility in an estimated 45 million deaths. While the historian appreciates the fact that more and more provincial archives are opening their doors to researchers, he nevertheless notes that "the entire record of the Maoist era, as reflected in official and internally published sources, is a skillful exercise in obfuscation and, as such, an inadequate basis for historical research."[2] Access to the archives has become paramount for researchers such as Dikötter, and the availability of documents cannot but appear as a primordial element in historical research. But what happens when archives and documents remain inaccessible or unavailable, or when the available documents are deemed unreliable? How can this crucial period of Maoist China be reconstructed for future generations?

In the case of *Fengming*, Wang Bing is interested in understanding how three interrelated texts—a memoir, a collection of short stories, and a film—can create unforeseen relations and generate unexpected insights into the life of one woman, He Fengming, and her experience of the Great Leap Forward and famine. In *The Ditch*, the filmmaker explores another kind of relationship with the past and the archive by turning to fiction filmmaking, reenactments, and techniques of "creative repetition" to recreate the experiences of the Jiabiangou labor camp, where He Fengming's husband, Wang Jingchao, died. The third film, *Dead Souls*, is a monumental effort to revisit the same historical period considering the filmmaker's dissatisfaction with fiction filmmaking and directing to explore the ways in which both human and non-human survivors can be documented in a single work over eight hours.

Wang Bing's Anti-Rightist trilogy offers a striking body of work whose purpose is to question the epistemological boundaries between history and memory and those between creation and preservation. Indeed, the trilogy walks the fine line between drawing on historical events and relying on the experiences of ordinary people caught in the web of socialist utopia such as He Fengming. The films also straddle the distinction between creation and preservation in Wang's quest to create an audiovisual archive of Maoist China and preserve the traumatic experiences of his interviewees. One could argue that the trilogy's distinct modes of archiving, supported by the type of observational realism that Wang has championed, make the spectator reflect on not only the Chinese past but also on the very possibility of bearing witness to the horrors of Maoist China and finding the appropriate filmic dispositif to do so. It would not be farfetched to claim that *The Ditch* acknowledges the limitations of the monologic, archival dispositif at the heart of *Fengming*, just like *Dead Souls* implicitly addresses the limitations of fiction filmmaking and acting in *The Ditch* to confront the complexity of the historical and sociocultural issues at the heart of this era. In the final analysis, the eight-hour-long *Dead Souls* acts as a documentary utopia trying to embrace a historical period and its actors once and for all, and it supplements both *Fengming* and *The Ditch* by acknowledging the potentialities and limitations of the previous two films' archival dispositifs in its documentation of human and nonhuman survivors.

In his quest to archive the testimonies and memories of those who survived the labor camps, Wang has reflected on the erasure of historical events such as the Great Famine within contemporary China and the fate of collective memory in the twenty-first century. According to the filmmaker, there are two main issues that deserve closer attention. The first concerns "the people who are old enough to address this period [who] do not always want to talk about it, and the way in which they understand the period is limited by the fact that back then they were quite young."[3] The second issue relates to education and the teaching of history in contemporary China: "My generation, for example, is quite ignorant of the Cultural Revolution and, more generally, Chinese history. Like so many others, I never learned anything about traditional culture, and I suffer from an inferiority complex in relation to those who received that kind of education."[4] Wang's trilogy can thus be considered an audiovisual supplement—an archive in the making, as it were—to Maoist historical records and the Chinese education system. The memoirs, oral histories, and scholarly studies that have appeared on the topic of the Great Leap Forward and the Great Famine, in addition to Wang's trilogy, bear witness to the failures of the Chinese education system to educate its population and face the horrors of the past.

In the three chapters making up Part One, I seek to understand how Wang Bing's "Anti-Rightist" trilogy offers a critical reflection on twentieth-century Chinese history and its fraught relationship with the archive. In these chapters, I examine how Wang's trilogy reconstructs Maoist history; how it calls upon survivors to remember and share their experiences and traumas for the camera; and what could explain the recourse to fiction in the second film. Wang uses two archival strategies to present the labor of history in the trilogy: the long-form interview (*Fengming* and *Dead Souls*) and reenactments (*The Ditch*). These two strategies complement one another in Wang Bing's audiovisual reconstruction of the Chinese past.

In Part One, I argue that the key locus for understanding the "labor of history" in Wang's trilogy is the forced labor camp, which took two distinct forms in Maoist China: the *laogai* and the *laojiao*. The prison camp is where rightists were exiled, and it is there that their forced labor could be said to redouble the labor of history. In the following chapters, I show that the significance of forced labor and the prison camp has been overlooked in studies of Wang Bing's trilogy, and that the experiences inside the camps are the driving force of the historical construction presented to the spectator. Documentary film plays no innocent role in providing the spectator with this historical reconstruction; it could be argued that documentary works hard to allow access to the Chinese past, laboriously seeking to tell the ultimate truth of an era without ever succeeding. The labor of history is also the labor of documentary: reeducation through labor parallels reeducation through documentary. History and pedagogy are thus intertwined in this story in a way that could be said to remedy some of the shortcomings that Wang Bing has identified regarding the Chinese education system.

In addition to the analysis of the trilogy, I also examine how the films complement the oral histories and scholarly studies published about the Anti-Rightist Movement's persecutions and the famine-stricken victims of the Great Leap Forward.[5] At the heart of Wang Bing's trilogy, which is based in oral history, one finds a sense of urgency about capturing the voices of aging survivors. As Berry and Rofel have noted: "More recently, some of China's alternative documentary filmmakers—perhaps aware that the generations who can remember revolutionary history are passing—have begun to make oral history films again."[6]

Wang Bing's trilogy makes an unforgettable contribution to the resurgence of oral history films that runs parallel to the work of social historians of Maoist China who are rewriting the history of this crucial period by paying attention to the famine, the forced labor camps, and the experiences and memories of survivors, and by drawing increasingly on oral accounts, both published and unpublished. Relying on the work of social historians and sociologists, I develop a sociocultural poetics of Chinese documentary, using the distinction that Montrose has made between "the historicity of texts and the textuality of histories."[7] By the "historicity of documentary texts," I refer to the sociopolitical and historical embeddedness of all modes of documentary making, as well as Wang Bing's observational realism. By the "textuality of documentary histories," I argue that we have no direct access to Maoist China, and, when we think we do, we only have access to the mediated vestiges of Chinese history in the form of, say, the words and memories of survivors. Wang Bing's trilogy reflects the tenets of this proposed sociopolitical approach because it eschews teleological history insofar as the films do not impose a particular interpretative framework on Maoist history or the interviewees, who are not shown as historical actors leading the country to its programmed utopia but the victims of the regime's ideology. On the contrary, the survivors' words and actions lead us to believe that it is only the beginning of a growing interest in revisiting China's troubled twentieth century.

China historian Felix Wemheuer has proposed a tripartite model to make sense of Maoist China. First, there is the notion of "social change," by which he refers to "the transformation of economic and ownership structures, urbanization, social mobility, state-directed and self-organized migration, rationing systems, and expansion and downsizing of the socialist welfare state and changes in family and gender relations."[8] The second area addresses the notion of classification and the following research questions: "How did the party-state structure society by assigning official labels or urban and rural under the household registration system? What was the impact of other labels—of class status, gender, and ethnicity—applied by the state to almost every Chinese citizen?" The final area that Wemheuer has identified concerns conflict: "Whether at the central or local level, the party-state played a crucial role in assigning labels and served as a 'gatekeeper' regulating social mobility. In this context, how the various levels of the CCP understood the state of Chinese society and interpreted its developments and conflicts becomes an essential question."[9] Considering these three foci—social change, classification, and conflict—helps to provide thicker descriptions of the sociopolitical issues at the heart of the trilogy, and brings to light a different picture in terms of the practices of everyday resistance in the films, which is an area to which scholars need to pay closer attention to establish a grassroots field of Chinese documentary studies.

There is a growing body of literature on Maoist China and the forced labor camps. Indeed, social historians have examined the emergence of the labor camp in terms of their goals and functions, which is to be distinguished from the concentration camp. As twentieth-century history has shown in both the West and Asia, concentration camps target individuals for who they are or what they believe in rather than for what they have done. Mühlhahn writes: "Persons are placed in such [concentration] camps often on the basis of identification with a particular ethnic or political group rather than as individuals and mostly without benefit either of indictment or fair trial. Concentration camps are thus not built for individuals, but rather for large groups and particular categories of non-criminal, civilian prisoner, members of an 'enemy' group."[10] The Maoist labor camps were built to hold those deemed anti-Rightists or counterrevolutionaries by the regime, which mainly concerned "intellectuals" such as journalists and teachers. Camps in Vietnam, North Korea, Cambodia, and China are only some of the most well-known sites where numerous counterrevolutionaries died in the twentieth century. In the Chinese context, reeducation through labor in *laogai* was a way for the CCP to implement ideological reform or "thought transformation" (*sixiang gaizao*) to ensure future loyalty. What is particularly striking in the Chinese case is the interrelation between thought transformation and corporeality. As Cai has noted: "the transformations of the intellectuals' thought are actually conducted through their body. Under pressure to eke out a bare existence, the Chinese intellectuals deserted their valued principles."[11] Forced labor, combined with the greatest man-made famine in history, would mark the Great Leap Forward as a chaotic, murderous era.

Wang Bing has reflected on the importance of returning to this crucial period in history to better understand what role the Maoist labor camp played in the

Great Leap Forward. Needless to say, Wang's main interest lies in archiving forms of human existence and trauma. According to the filmmaker, the Jiabiangou labor camp, located in Gansu Province, played an unsuspected role in modern Chinese history, which can explain Wang Bing's claim to the effect that "[t]he camp is very important for us in understanding our own past."[12] Up to 3,000 workers were at the Jiabiangou camp, Wang mentions, and, when it was decided to shut down operations in the early 1960s, "the rare survivors were sent back home to the four corners of China, and the event was forgotten. Yang Xianghui's book made me understand the extent of this moment in Chinese history."[13] It is the role of Wang Bing's films to provide the kind of mediation that is necessary to come to terms with twentieth-century Chinese history and its continuous impact on the present. In fact, one could argue that without films such as Wang's, the violence, power, and terror associated with the banishment that characterized the labor camps would remain quite abstract for twenty-first-century Chinese observers, a point that Wang Bing also makes when noting how such camps had been practically forgotten until the publication of Yang Jisheng's groundbreaking two-volume study, *Mubei: 1958–1962 nian Zhongguo da jihuang jishi* (*Tombstone: The Great Chinese Famine 1958–1962*), published in Hong Kong in 2008.[14] Absent from history books, labor camps such as Jiabiangou have now re-emerged in the studies of revisionist social historians of Maoist China and in the memoirs of those who survived the camps such as He Fengming, who published hers under the title *Jingli: wo de 1957 nian* (Experience: My 1957) at the beginning of the 2000s.

## Punishment with Chinese Characteristics

In the early 1950s, the CCP elaborated a complex penal system that laid the foundation for the prison camp system that is still in place to this day. Within this system, there are two central institutions: the *laogai* and the *laojiao*. *Laogai* is the contraction of *laodong gaizao* (reform through labor), which refers to the type of forced labor camp where prisoners would be sent to be thoroughly reformed. *Laojiao* (*laodong jiaoyang*) points to reeducation through labor. At the heart of both institutions lies the CCP's belief in labor's power to reinvent the dissident subject or counter-revolutionary by reform or reeducation. Punishment thus took a singular form in Maoist China insofar as political violence masqueraded as a pedagogical initiative meant to strike at the core of individuals' strong-held beliefs and change them in the process. Discipline and punishment were reinvented to establish a system wherein either reform or reeducation would replace punishment per se. At least, that was the ideal of the regime whose socialist penology integrated Marxism's emphasis on (forced) labor as an agent of social change and promulgated institutionalized forced labor on a national scale to help with public construction projects. Forced labor and prison camps have a perennial pedigree in China. As Williams and Wu have noted: "The corvée system of mandatory, unremunerated labor service to the state is deeply rooted in Chinese civilization, as is the sentencing of convicts to forced labor in camps, mines, and military posts."[15] The prison camp system and forced labor have thus functioned as crucial tools of the Chinese state, aiming to transform the subject into an instrument of the CCP. Reforming and remolding the Chinese subject's worldview were sine qua non conditions to achieve the communist utopia, and the prison system served as a crucial ideological state apparatus of power and indoctrination in that regard.

The transformative process at the heart of socialist penology was first enunciated in Mao's famous 1949 speech, "On the People's Democratic Dictatorship," in which he expressed the need to reform prisoners through forced labor and indoctrination. *Laojiao* inmates were incarcerated following an administrative decision, often made by the police, while *laogai* inmates were convicted in court and sentenced. Domenach estimates that prison camps held from four to six million inmates between 1949 and 1952, and that at least two million counterrevolutionaries died in the camps.[16] While Mao's *laogai* system was less deadly than Stalin's gulag, there remains the fact that the *laogai* is associated with forced labor, indoctrination, and famine.

Over the past decades, numerous survivors have shared their experiences of the *laogai* and *laojiao* in memoirs and prison fiction. The memorial imperative at the heart of these memoirs, diaries, letters, or short stories serves an archival purpose: "Camp inmates who survived especially harsh periods such as the great famine of 1959–62 have sometimes felt duty-bound to preserve the memory and succor the relatives of those wronged inmates who died or otherwise disappeared in the camps . . . Numerous former inmates have wanted to use their writings to shed light on the shadowy laogai system, most aspects of which have been shrouded in secrecy from ordinary PRC citizens and foreigners alike."[17] It is the living and working conditions within the camps that have marked the imaginations of readers not only in China but also in the West where numerous translations have been published. He Fengming's memoir offers a striking example of one woman's account of her experiences during the Great Leap Forward and famine, her time spent in a *laojiao*, and her husband's own experiences in the Jiabiangou *laogai*. Yang Xianhui's collection, *Jiabiangou jishi*, on which *The Ditch* is based, is another example of this kind of literature that delves into the harshness of the camps, especially during the famine years.

Wang Bing's trilogy functions as an original audiovisual supplement to the prison camp literature emerging out of China. In Wang's trilogy, it is the physical and psychological impact of the Great Leap Forward, the unprecedented famine, and the forced labor that is discussed or represented in films that emphasize the CCP's political violence on its own people and the trauma of internment. The films account for practices of the self—confession, self-examination, and self-criticism—that were employed to reform inmates. The profound ideological transformation sought by the regime was meant for inmates to reinvent themselves through labor. Documentary technology redoubles the *laogai* practices of the self in allowing a subject such as He Fengming to revisit difficult memories, thus enabling the subject to become an agent in the historical process while maintaining her status as a victim of the Maoist regime. It is this dialectical positioning that makes the various testimonies in *Fengming* and *Dead Souls* quite poignant.

## The Great Leap Forward and Famine

Wishing to transform China into an industrial society, the CCP launched its first "Five-Year Plan" in 1953. Based on the Soviet planned economy, the socioeconomic transformation would allow China to go from a predominantly agrarian society to an industrial nation within a matter of years. This would be a tall order for any government, but in the Chinese case the transition to state socialism meant the development of heavy industry and the creation of a national defense base, in addition to the other aspects associated with a state-planned economy such as the elimination of exploitation and profit-driven modes of ownership. This would inevitably lead to the elimination of capitalists and other "class enemies" of the regime.

In 1957, Mao launched another national program, the Great Leap Forward, meant to accelerate China's societal transformations. A key component of the Great Leap Forward was the "Hundred Flowers Campaign" (*Bai hua qifang*) of 1956–1957, which initiated a tumultuous period in Chinese history when intellectuals were encouraged to openly criticize the social and political shortcomings of the communist regime since the foundation of the republic in 1949 and begin the public voicing of criticisms directed at CCP rule. Upon witnessing worker and student strikes and rural unrest, that is, the inability of the campaign to bear the expected fruits, Mao launched a counterattack to identify and persecute the enemies of the party ideology. Mao's radical reaction reflected the fact that "[c]riticism from intellectuals had been much harsher than expected and had been directed not only against superficial problems, but also against the whole political system and even CCP rule in general."[18] Far from being the anticipated celebration of letting a "hundred flowers bloom, and a hundred schools of thought contend," the regime launched the "Anti-Rightist Campaign" to identify and purge intellectuals in various institutions and state apparatuses whose subversive voices were deemed unacceptable and therefore "rightist." Wemheuer writes that "[b]y the end of 1968, over 550,000 people had been officially labeled as 'rightists,' many of them innocent victims of a poisonous dynamic of denunciations and 'exaggeration.'"[19] Subsequently, hundreds of thousands of "rightists" would be sent to remote labor camps to be "reeducated" through work for many years. The Anti-Rightist Campaign would have a disastrous impact on the way criticism would be expressed in public for decades, as those working in the media, education, and government would think twice about voicing their critiques and remember the purges of the past when many were labeled enemies of the people.

It is important to stress the CCP's fixation on the relationship between reform and thought in the 1950s to better understand the creation of labor camps within the context of the Anti-Rightist Campaign. As Wemheuer has shown, the goal of imprisonment was not simply to punish and isolate socially undesirable individuals. Rather, "Not only was labor the only way to turn people into productive members of society, but, by experiencing the hardships and pleasures of creation through work, the former exploiter or criminal could come to understand the suffering of the masses and the 'parasitic' nature of their own former life. Forced labor was not simply punitive but also instructive."[20] Those whose crimes were deemed serious would be sent to forced labor camps (*laogai*). *Laogai* thus marked longer sentences and graver crimes. Wemheuer notes that "[b]y 1951, the new government had begun building a nationwide network of labor camps"[21] and that "[m]any of these camps were located in remote areas in western China. In some locations in the desert, no walls or fences were built to keep the inmates in, since conditions were so extreme that escape would mean almost certain death."[22]

In addition to the difficult living conditions in the labor camps, there arose a tension between thought reform, that is, the ideological reeducation of the prisoners, and increased production or work, which many have claimed is related to a given camp's own contradictory interest in exploiting the labor of inmates to profit the nation. After all, the goal of reeducation was to make inmates see the benefits of socialism, while the rest of the day their labor would be exploited by the camp in a perverse, ironic situation. It is reported that there were between 12 and 20 million camp prisoners by 1960.[23]

In these camps reigned a climate of fear and denunciation based on discipline, surveillance, and punishment. Wemheuer points out that "[p]rison brigades and individual inmates were ranked according to output and were required to supervise each other and report transgressions to the authorities. Under the 1954 laogai regulations, inmates could be kept inside even after their sentence had elapsed, meaning attachment to a labor camp could become essentially permanent."[24] Considering the great number of people who lived and survived the labor camps, it is difficult to believe that, prior to the surge of publications on the topic of thought reform and labor camp life, the Chinese knew very little about the actual lives of those who had to endure such treatment.

By 1958, the Great Leap Forward was underway as widespread governmental innovations such as modern industrialization, agricultural collectivization, and the establishment of the People's Communes (*renmin gongshe*)—described as "the most radical social revolution that Chinese villagers had ever experienced"[25]—had paved the way for the socialist utopia. As a sign of intellectual independence, Mao envisioned the Great Leap Forward as an alternative to the Soviet mode of planning that had privileged heavy industry to implement China's own indigenous plan that would be more in tune with the needs of the peasants based on more self-reliance and autonomy being accorded to the countryside. This took the form of decentralization and the recourse to provincial and local powers to implement the policies. The communes were responsible for agriculture, education, finance, and government, among others, at the local level. The success of the communes would show the world that China was well on its way to communism and that peasants were better integrated than they had been before.

As historians have noted, however, the socialist climate deteriorated quickly: by 1959 "a combination of poor harvests and misguided policy-making meant that some parts of the countryside were already experiencing the famine that would turn into a national catastrophe the next year."[26] The famine severely hit those living in the countryside, as peasants starved to death. The unprecedented crisis originated in the collapse of economic planning, which itself stemmed from "[a] mixture of genuine enthusiasm and political pressure from above [that] saw local cadres report soaring figures for grain and steel production. Soon, competition developed at the county and village level to announce increasingly implausible levels of output . . . Buoyed by this apparent success, the higher levels of government raised local quotas for steel and grain, which in turn placed even more pressure on cadres to inflate their figures. It was not until the onset of winter that Mao and the central leadership realized that many of the achievements they believed the Great Leap had delivered in fact existed only on paper. At this point, Mao called on cadres to report the real figures, but he refused to significantly reduce grain production quotas."[27]

The Great Leap Forward resulted in the destruction of China's agriculture and industry because of the regime's relentless drive toward industrialization and collectivization. Most importantly, it devastated China's countryside and its population because of the three-year famine that ensued. Depending on the source, it is reported that between 15 and 45 million Chinese died of starvation between 1959 and 1961, which is one of the worst man-made tragedies in world history.[28] These years are still referred to as a "natural disaster" in official documents in China even though the famine was the product of the ideologues in power. The Central Committee's 1981 "Resolution on Some Questions Concerning the History of the Party since the Founding of the People's Republic of China" does not mention the word "famine," preferring euphemisms such as "great economic difficulties" and "damage to the people," which were caused by natural disasters. The reasons that explain the Great Famine are multiple, and the hypothesis of a single great natural calamity impacting the Chinese has been discredited: "The decline in production was attributable to a number of factors: the chaos that accompanied the introduction of the larger communes; poor labor performance leading to reduced productivity; and general labor shortages in agriculture. Natural disasters and unfavorable climatic conditions also played a role, but no serious Western or Chinese scholars regards bad weather as the major reason for the famine."²⁹ It is the irony of history that most of the famine-related deaths were in the countryside, which is where grain and food came from, after all, and not in the industrial centers such as Beijing and Shanghai where rations were not as significantly cut as in the countryside. The regime's urban bias translated into a starving countryside, which is to say that the CCP decided who lived and who died in China's biopolitical experiment.

The societal problems associated with the Great Famine were compounded by the behavior of the officials and cadres who decided not to report starvation-related deaths to the central government authorities. Indeed, historians have claimed that local officials, remembering the purges of a few years prior, "covered up negative developments of any kind. Some reports about the famine did reach the central government, but until the autumn of 1960 these continued to underestimate the extent of the disaster."³⁰ As expected, when Mao and the CCP got wind of the struggles for survival in the countryside, local officials were blamed, and thousands were imprisoned for their incompetence and inability to report the actual number of starvation cases and death rates in their jurisdictions. In hindsight, it is difficult to believe that these officials decided to turn a blind eye on villagers eating "tree bark, grass and pets. Some resorted to slaughtering cattle owned by the People's Communes . . . In Henan, peasants attempted to survive on so-called 'Guanyin soil,' a kind of white clay named for the Buddhist goddess of mercy. All over China, many people died after eating inedible, indigestible or poisonous things."³¹ Far from being the "three years of hardship" (*san nian kunnan shiqi*) that the CCP euphemistically mentions in official historical publications, the period left deep scars and a host of traumatic memories. Wang Bing's "Anti-Rightist" trilogy has provided the audiovisual complement to the scholarly studies, oral histories, and memoirs on this dark period of Chinese history.

## Overturning Tombstones: The Oral History Film

Great Famine scholarship draws on a wealth of hitherto unavailable primary sources such as archives, ethnographic research, and oral histories, and, most importantly, such sources cast light on the experiences of rural residents for the first time. By doing so they began the hard work of creating "alternative histories of China's experiment with state socialism"³² that in turn would allow filmmakers to consider this period of Chinese history as a significant gap in historiography, departing from the concerns of the past that emphasized CCP decision-making, structures of governance, and Mao's role in the Great Leap Forward. The focus on villager resistance, state violence, and gender politics, among others, has signaled a shift in terms of scholarly interests, which greatly benefits from ethnographic reports, memoirs, and oral histories in a way that has rejuvenated research into not only the Great Leap famine but also the Cultural Revolution and Reform eras. These three periods—the

Great Leap Forward, the Cultural Revolution, and the beginning of the Reform and Opening era—all figure in He Fengming's published memoir and filmed testimony and in famine-related documentary films largely based on oral history. As a former journalist whose father died of starvation in the famine, Yang Jisheng has documented the state violence and the regime of terror in place in the provinces most affected by the famine, including Gansu Province where Wang Bing's *Fengming* and *The Ditch* were shot, in his study *Tombstone: The Great Chinese Famine 1958–1962*. What has emerged from books such as Yang's and the scholarship on the famine is that "[i]t was China's peasants, not intellectuals, who suffered the most during this period, whether from forced labour assignments or from the hunger that gripped most of rural China from 1959 into 1962 and even 1963."[33]

Wang Bing's *Fengming* belongs to a group of revisionist films that focus on the Mao years, especially the Great Leap Forward and famine. Alongside film projects such as Zou Xueping's "Zoujiacun" series (2010–2014), Qiu Jiongjiong's *Mr. Zhang Believes* (2014), and Ai Xiaoming's *Jiabiangou Elegy* (2017), Wang's trilogy and similar films have sought to create an archive of audiovisual and textual records of rural experiences during the Great Leap famine. Salvaging the rural memories of the famine has become a race against the clock as many of the survivors and first-hand witnesses are now in their eighties and nineties, and it is imperative to document their memories before they pass. Their accumulated testimonies form a local, grassroots history of the Great Famine. Consisting mainly of interviews, Great Leap famine documentaries mobilize the oral history film tradition and mix the various modes of address associated with observational cinema, participatory filmmaking, and performative documentary. The audiovisual archives created exemplify what form the grassroots approach to documenting unofficial histories can take in twenty-first-century China.[34]

There is a series of research questions that applies to the aforementioned oral history films dealing with the Great Leap famine, and these will guide the analysis of Wang Bing's trilogy. These questions include: Which are the favored film techniques (observational strategies, filming and editing techniques, etc.) in Wang Bing's trilogy? How does the filmmaker interact with the subject and to what ends? What is the filmmaker's understanding of a truthful account? What are the perspectives on the Great Leap Forward and famine that emerge from the trilogy? What are interviewees' strategies for remembering their own pasts and the historical events informing them? In the case of *Fengming*, what is the added value of asking a subject to repeat the contents of her published memoir for the camera? What kind of documentary film adaptation is it, and how do the textual and the audiovisual interact to form an entity greater than the sum of its parts? How does the interaction of documentary and fiction serve a greater understanding of Chinese history in *The Ditch*? In the case of the trilogy as a whole, what kind of historical reconstruction and understanding of Chinese history is offered to the spectator?

There are many elements that characterize the documentaries associated with such a revisionist take on the Chinese past. First, they do not focus on a particular event itself. Rather, they prefer to let time unfold and explore the memories of the interviewee as they emerge through dialogue (or monologue in the case of He Fengming). The counternarratives and unofficial historical records constructed by audiovisual means serve the purpose of rehabilitating everyday life experiences and generally eschew the use of archival footage of the Mao era evoking the Chinese past as something to be appropriated. This kind of history from below plays an important role, as Pernin describes it: "studies in film and media have revealed the importance of ordinary people's memories not only to unveil concealed historical facts, but also to act as an agent of change in contemporary societies."[35]

It is also important to bear in mind Walker's admonition to contextualize the oral testimony—and therefore the oral history film—and avoid idealizing the findings therein, as "an audiovisual testimony is always in some sense 'staged,' staged in that the interviewee would not be speaking if not for the occurrence of the filming, and staged in the sense of being put into a scene, a *mise-en-scène*."[36] This is not meant to deny the trauma that the survivors of the Great Leap famine have endured—having experienced the famine itself and then facing the impossibility of bearing witness to their suffering and that of others who died in the labor camps—but to caution the film viewer to carefully understand the various kinds of mediation in complex works such as Wang Bing's trilogy. This is especially important for the generation—as mentioned by the filmmaker himself—that was never taught the Great Leap Forward tragedies in school and that receives this information audiovisually. It is no exaggeration to claim that the construction of social memory and collective understanding of China's troubled past will be the result of the work of revisionist historians and sociologists, as well as that of the audiovisual constructions of documentarians such as Wang Bing, and that media education will be instrumental in the formation of twenty-first-century Chinese political subjectivity.

Oral history has played (and will continue to play) a crucial role in the reception of historical events in China. In the face of state propaganda, collective forgetting, and historical erasures, oral history (in the form of published memoirs, ethnographic reports, and oral history film projects) has helped to rescue portions of the past and create an unofficial archive of the famine and its survivors' lived experiences and memories. In Wu Wenguang's "Folk Memory Project," Ai Xiaoming's *Jiabiangou Elegy*, and Wang Bing's "Anti-Rightist" trilogy, one is struck by how oral history has been transformed into a singular form of audiovisual "history-writing" or "becoming-archive" informed by testimonies and lived experiences aimed at the rehabilitation of oral evidence in the process.

Wu's *minjian* project deserves closer attention, as it is the largest audiovisual project about the Great Famine and, eventually, other historical periods such as the Cultural Revolution. The Beijing-based Caochangdi Workstation (Caochangdi

Gongzuozhan) launched the "Minjian jiyi jihua" project in 2009. Combining oral history, theatrical performance, ethnographic fieldwork, and documentary media, the Folk Memory Project collects peasant memories of the famine era by allowing survivors to share with the viewing public their traumatic experiences. As Wu has put it, this is in the spirit of allowing repressed memories to finally surface: "The 'hunger memories' of 50 years ago have long constituted a blank space in official histories, emerging only occasionally in the form of scattered words and phrases sounding like little more than hearsay in the conversations of elderly people who experienced it."[37] The hundreds of oral accounts of the Great Famine collected so far vary in form, content, and presentation method. Exemplary in Wu's "Folk Memory Project" is Zou Xueping's series about Zoujia village (*Starving Village* [*Ji'e de cunzi* 饥饿的村子, 2010], *Satiated Village* [*Chibao de cunzi* 吃饱的村子, 2011], *Children's Village* [*Haizi de cunzi* 孩子的村子, 2012], *Trash Village* [*Laji de cunzi* 垃圾的村子, 2013], and *Fool's Village* [*Shazi de cunzi* 傻子的村子, 2014]), which illustrates the potential of participatory documentary filmmaking.[38] Efforts such as Zou's have given survivors "a way to reconcile the double trauma that they have endured: first suffering through the famine itself, and then being deprived of the right and opportunity to voice their lived experience and to engage a communal, public defense against organized oblivion."[39]

Such memorializing efforts have become a *practice* in which archival research, performance, stylistic aestheticization, and (auto)ethnography, among others, join forces to commemorate and often monumentalize (in the form of the scope and length of the project) the Chinese past and the oral accounts supporting the project. This is not to say that issues of authenticity, performance, accuracy, and validity are no longer relevant, but that the supplemental value accorded to oral evidence has been reconsidered given the paucity of sources and the debunking of written sources as the only reliable source of information within historiographical circles. The creation of "official history" in a country where propagandistic forces alter the past signals the need to rely on oral historical findings to transmit what has never been transmitted before and to reconsider what can function as counter-memories or counter-hegemonic historical discourses.

## Notes

1. In this chapter, I use the expression "'Anti-Rightist' trilogy" to designate the three films that Wang Bing made about the Anti-Rightist Movement and the Great Famine between 2007 and 2018.
2. Frank Dikötter, *Mao's Great Famine: The History of China's Most Devastating Catastrophe, 1958–62* (New York: Vintage, 2010), 344.
3. Wang Bing, "La memoria rimossa della Cina. Conversazione con Wang Bing," in *Wang Bing: Il cinema nella Cina che cambia*, ed. Daniela Persico (Milan: Agenzia X, 2010), 32.
4. Wang, "La memoria rimossa della Cina," 33.

5. For oral and documentary histories of the period, see Ralph A. Jr. Thaxton, *Catastrophe and Contention in Rural China: Mao's Great Leap Forward Famine and the Origins of Righteous Resistance in Da Fo Village* (Cambridge: Cambridge University Press, 2008); Zhao Xu, *Jiabiangou can'an: fangtan lu* (Washington, DC: The Laogai Research Foundation, 2008), https://d18mm95b2k9j1z.cloudfront.net/wp-content/uploads/2019/01/25-夹边沟惨案访谈录.pdf; Zhou Xun, ed., *The Great Famine in China, 1958–1962: A Documentary History* (New Haven, CT: Yale University Press, 2012); Zhou Xun, *Forgotten Voices of Mao's Great Famine, 1958–1962* (New Haven, CT: Yale University Press, 2013); and Wang Ning, *Banished to the Great Northern Wilderness: Political Exile and Re-education in Mao's China* (Vancouver: UBC Press, 2017).
6. Chris Berry and Lisa Rofel, "Alternative Archive: China's Independent Documentary Culture," in *The New Chinese Documentary Film Movement: For the Public Record*, ed. Chris Berry, Lu Xinyu, and Lisa Rofel (Hong Kong: Hong Kong University Press, 2010), 152.
7. Louis Montrose, *The Purpose of Playing: Shakespeare and the Cultural Politics of the Elizabethan Theatre* (Chicago: University of Chicago Press, 1996), 5.
8. Felix Wemheuer, *A Social History of Maoist China: Conflict and Change, 1949–1976* (Cambridge: Cambridge University Press, 2019), 6.
9. Wemheuer, *A Social History of Maoist China*, 14.
10. Klaus Mühlhahn, "The Concentration Camp in Global Historical Perspective," *History Compass* 8, no. 6 (2010): 544.
11. Shenshen Cai, "The Chronicles of Jiabiangou (Jiabiangou jishi): An Analysis of Contemporary Chinese Reportage Literature Using the Theory of Totalitarianism and Power," *Modern China Studies* 23, no. 1 (2016): 131.
12. Wang Bing, "Filming a Land in Flux," *New Left Review* 82 (2013): 126.
13. Wang Bing, *Alors, la Chine. Entretiens avec Emmanuel Burdeau et Eugenio Renzi* (Paris: Les Prairies ordinaires, 2014), 106.
14. Yang Jisheng, *Mubei: 1958–1962 nian Zhongguo da jihuang jishi*, 2 volumes (Hong Kong: Cosmos Books, 2008). Abridged English translation: Yang Jisheng, *Tombstone: The Great Chinese Famine 1958–1962*, trans. Stacy Mosher and Guo Jian (New York: Farrar, Strauss and Giroux, 2012).
15. Philip F. Williams, and Yenna Wu, *The Great Wall of Confinement: The Chinese Prison Camp through Contemporary Fiction and Reportage* (Berkeley: University of California Press, 2004), 6–7.
16. Jean-Luc Domenach, *Chine: l'archipel oublié* (Paris: Fayard, 1992), 71–72.
17. Williams, and Wu, *The Great Wall of Confinement*, 159.
18. Wemheuer, *A Social History of Maoist China*, 113.
19. Wemheuer, *A Social History of Maoist China*, 114.
20. Wemheuer, *A Social History of Maoist China*, 96.
21. Wemheuer, *A Social History of Maoist China*, 97.
22. Wemheuer, *A Social History of Maoist China*, 97.
23. Wemheuer, *A Social History of Maoist China*, 98.
24. Wemheuer, *A Social History of Maoist China*, 98.
25. Kimberley Ens Manning and Felix Wemheuer, "Introduction," in *Eating Bitterness: New Perspectives on China's Great Leap Forward and Famine*, ed. Kimberley Ens Manning and Felix Wemheuer (Vancouver: UBC Press, 2011), 6.
26. Wemheuer, *A Social History of Maoist China*, 121.
27. Wemheuer, *A Social History of Maoist China*, 122.

28. Wemheuer has noted the "political significance" of determining how many died during the Great Leap famine (*A Social History of Maoist China*, 147–52). He cautions to examine the issue with the "serious demographic studies, backed by solid statistical analysis and survey data." The most dramatic element about the Great Famine is that "it could have been avoided" (152).
29. Wemheuer, *A Social History of Maoist China*, 135.
30. Wemheuer, *A Social History of Maoist China*, 141.
31. Wemheuer, *A Social History of Maoist China*, 143.
32. Ens Manning, and Wemheuer, "Introduction," 2.
33. Ens Manning, and Wemheuer, "Introduction," 14.
34. A useful filmography of independent documentaries on the Mao era from 1992 to 2015 can be found in Judith Pernin, "Filmed Testimonies, Archives, and Memoirs of the Mao Era," in *Popular Memories of the Mao Era: From Critical Debate to Reassessing History*, ed. Sebastian Veg (Hong Kong: Hong Kong University Press, 2019), 137–60.
35. Pernin, "Filmed Testimonies, Archives, and Memoirs of the Mao Era," 143.
36. Janet Walker, "Rights and Return: The Perils of Situated Testimony after Katrina," in *Documentary Testimonies: Global Archives of Suffering*, ed. Bhaskar Sarkar and Janet Walker (London / New York: Routledge / AFI Film Readers, 2010), 85.
37. Wu Wenguang, "Opening the Door of Memory with a Camera Lens: The Folk Memory Project and Documentary Production," *China Perspectives* 4 (2014): 37.
38. For analyses of Zou's films, see Paul G. Pickowicz, "A Hundred Years Later: Zou Xueping's Documentaries and the Legacies of China's New Culture Movement," *Journal of Chinese Cinemas* 10, no. 2 (2016): 187–201, and Paul G. Pickowicz, "Zou Xueping's Postsocialist Homecoming," in *Filming the Everyday: Independent Documentaries in Twenty-First-Century China*, ed. Paul G. Pickowicz and Yingjin Zhang (Lanham, MD: Rowman & Littlefield, 2017), 69–83. For an interview with the filmmaker, see Chen Huei-yin, "Interview with Chinese Documentary Filmmaker Zou Xueping," August 10, 2022, https://www.asiancinemablog.com/interviews/interview-with-chinese-documentary-filmmaker-zou-xueping/.
39. Jiayun Zhuang, "Remembering and Reenacting Hunger: Caochangdi Workstation's Minjian Memory Project," *TDR: The Drama Review* 58, no. 1 (2014): 121.

# 2
# *Fengming, a Chinese Memoir*

## The Embodied Archive

*Fengming, a Chinese Memoir* (2007), which is the first film in Wang Bing's "Anti-Rightist" trilogy, lays the foundation for the revisionist approach to documenting and archiving the Anti-Rightist Campaign (1957–1959), the Great Leap Forward (1958–1962), the forced labor camps, and the Great Famine (1958–1962) further explored in *The Ditch* (2010) and *Dead Souls* (2018). The central subject of the film, He Fengming, bears witness to the historical events surrounding the Great Leap Forward, in addition to the Cultural Revolution's reeducation campaign and the rehabilitation of those deemed "rightists" in the Deng Xiaoping era. Through He's words, the spectator is taken on a historical journey covering over 50 years of Chinese history, from the foundation of the republic in 1949 to the early 2000s when Wang Bing recorded the long-form interview in He's small apartment in Lanzhou, Gansu Province.

Commissioned by the KunstenFestivalDesArts in Brussels to create a piece for one of its exhibitions in 2005, Wang decided to make a film about He Fengming, with whom he had previously been in touch. The first version shown at the festival lasted two hours and fifteen minutes. Praised by critics, *Fengming* premiered at the Cannes Film Festival at a Special Screening in 2007 in a longer version (230 minutes) than the official version, which is shorter (185 minutes). The film won the "Robert and Frances Flaherty Prize" at the Yamagata International Documentary Festival. Wang Bing has noted the difficult conditions under which he and his team had to work: "We didn't know until the last minute that we were going to Cannes, so a final cut of *Fengming* had to be done in about ten days."[1] Having been featured at prestigious film festivals such as Yamagata and TIFF, the film would also be exhibited in the form of a video installation at the Galerie Chantal Crousel in Paris in 2009, where it was shown with Wang Bing's *Man with No Name* (*Wumingzhe*, 2009).

This chapter examines the type of audiovisual archive of the Great Leap Forward and famine that Wang Bing constructs with the help of He Fengming. In the absence of open archives in China, what kind of sources can be accessed and shared with the public, and how can one survivor's memories supplement or even replace historical sources, which remain unavailable for the most part? I argue that Wang Bing's subject shares her memories over three hours, and the retelling of He's lived experiences during the Great Leap Forward allows her to become a living, embodied archive of the period possessing an unexpected affective and performative charge.

Moreover, a closer examination of *Fengming* leads to the exploration of various intertextual resonances within Wang Bing's film. The labor of history is reflected in the three modes of archiving found in the following texts: He Fengming's 2001 memoir, *Jingli: wo de 1957 nian* (Experience: My Year 1957); Yang Xianhui's fictionalized oral history account, "Tanwang Wang Jingchao" ("A Visit to Wang Jingchao"), which revisits He Fengming's life via the fictional character of He Sang; and the long-form interview with a single survivor, He Fengming, in Wang's documentary film. By addressing these three genres and media, a different picture of the period emerges that supplements the reception of Wang Bing's *Fengming* and the "Anti-Rightist" trilogy.[2]

Finally, what makes *Fengming* particularly fascinating is how the film challenges the binary opposition between oral testimony and archive within archive theory. Indeed, Wang's documentary film questions received ideas within archive theory that cannot accommodate the singular performance of a subject such as He Fengming and the oral history film in which she appears. The archive that is constituted within the film is an embodied, experiential archive of memories that has had difficulty finding a place within archive theory. It is the construction of what Phay, in her discussion of Rithy Panh's *L'Image manquante* (2013), has called "*archives-oeuvres*"[3] that is at stake in Wang Bing's "Anti-Rightist" trilogy, and what modalities of address such embodied archives use to mediate between the past and the present.

In Wang Bing's film, He Fengming performs the life of He Fengming for the camera. This performative form of retelling is characterized by the absence of hesitations, the seemingly perfect workings of memory, and the clarity and precision of her diction, all of which denote a discourse that seems learned by heart. The fact that He performs her life experiences for the camera does not detract from the veracity of these experiences and their impact. On the contrary, the performative witnessing mode adds a layer of complexity to the film. In addition to the intertextual relations between He's memoir and Yang's fictionalized accounts, this kind of performative delivery sutures the film, and this strategy makes the spectator reflect on the discourse of the tragic victim who is willing to perform so that her experiences reach a greater audience. This is certainly the role a film such as Wang's plays in making He's experiences reach a global audience via the audiovisual modalities of cinema and transcend the limitations of the written word and the published memoir. It is indeed other experiences that Wang's film archives, and the film paves the way for a critical archive theory informed by embodiment, affect, performance, and trauma that answers Derrida's call to "redevelop a concept of the archive"[4] considering the horrors of the Maoist era.

## Introducing *Fengming*

On his way to Paris in 2004, where he had been invited by the Cannes Film Festival Cinéfondation to work on a new project, Wang Bing read Yang Xianhui's collection of nineteen fictionalized accounts, *Jiabiangou shiji* (abridged English translation: *Woman from Shanghai: Tales of Survival from a Chinese Labor Camp*), based on interviews with survivors of the Jiabiangou labor camp.[5] Mindful that his work could be censored by the Chinese authorities, Yang wrote a fictionalized treatment of both his interviews with survivors and the tragic deaths of those who died in the Jiabiangou labor camp. Wang Bing thought of turning some of these short stories into a fiction film based on reenactments in which life in the labor camp would be the central focus. This project would eventually become the second film in the "Anti-Rightist" trilogy, *The Ditch*. After acquiring the rights to Yang's short stories in 2004, Wang expressed the wish to meet some of the survivors, and Yang put the filmmaker in touch with some of them. That is how the filmmaker first crossed paths with He Fengming, who was born in Lanzhou (Gansu Province) in 1932. Wang would eventually postpone his fiction film project to document the life of a single woman, He Fengming, a retired journalist living in Lanzhou, whose husband, Wang Jingchao, died from exhaustion and starvation in the Jiabiangou labor camp in 1961.

In the film, He's account of historical events adopts a chronological approach, from when she dropped out of Lanzhou University (where she was an English student) at the time of the foundation of the republic in 1949, to her time at the *Gansu Daily*, where she and her husband, Wang Jingchao, worked as journalists, to the early 1990s when she and her son visited the Jiabiangou labor camp site to find her husband's grave. Less than ten years after the foundation of the PRC, He Fengming and her husband were deemed "Rightists" by the regime and sent to different labor camps: Jingchao to Jiabiangou and Fengming to Collective Farm #10 in Anxi. In the film, He tells the heartbreaking story of her efforts to find her husband's body and grave at the camp after hearing of his death. He's life story, a "veritable odyssey"[6] according to the filmmaker, offers riveting tales of abuse, corruption, and exploitation that make the viewer further reflect on Mao's Great Leap Forward, the Anti-Rightist Campaign, the Great Famine, the forced labor camps, and their legacy in twenty-first-century China.

He Fengming had previously appeared in fictionalized form in Yang Xianhui's "Tanwang Wang Jingchao" ("A Visit to Wang Jingchao") as the He Sang character, and He herself had published her memoir, *Jingli: wo de 1957 nian* (Experience: My 1957) in 2001. As Wang Bing mentions in an interview, He's memoir was the only publication on the topic of the labor camp to have appeared in mainland China at the time. Unfortunately, the memoir was not widely distributed as it was published by a small Gansu press.[7] The filmmaker points out that at the heart of the memoir lies the desire to hear silenced voices: "In fact, it was a social phenomenon at the time; many people who had lived through that period wanted to write their memoirs and tell their stories. Why? Because our mainstream culture, the dominant ideology, does not offer them an identity through which they could recognize their own lives across the passage of time."[8] He's memoir offers a vivid testimony of the events surrounding the labor camps, the Great Famine, and her husband's tragic death.[9]

*Fengming* functions as an oral history project that goes beyond both Yang Xianhui's "A Visit to Wang Jingchao" (in which a fictionalized version of He Fengming appears) and He's memoir itself in terms of content.[10] There are clear cinematographic, narrative, and mise-en-scène strategies that emerge over the course of *Fengming*. The film is framed using an establishing sequence in which the spectator follows He around the building complex and enters her small apartment where the interview is to be filmed. The filmmaker privileges frontal views of the subject, who sits in an armchair in her dimly lit living room. Regarding framing strategies, Wang uses three different ones: framing the entire living room wall behind He; closing in on his subject and framing the armchair; and using the close-up, which he does only for one emotionally driven, fifteen-minute sequence. Throughout the film, Wang relies on available light until it is no longer possible to do so. On one occasion, he will ask his subject if it is possible to turn on the light. Noteworthy is that Wang does not have recourse to archival images to supplement He's testimony. His camera, perched on a table facing the subject, relentlessly captures the subject for hours on end, as the film tries to reproduce the real-time effect of what took place in He's apartment that afternoon. In that sense, the film does reflect the main tenet of *xianchang* filmmaking, whereby the goal is to capture what happened in front of the camera at a given point in time. The ending sequence shows He receiving a phone call from a survivor based in Kunming, Yunnan Province, indicating that she is part of a network of survivors and that her quest to right the wrongs of the revolutionary past will continue well after Wang has turned off his camera.[11] Wang Bing, as a *minjian* intellectual himself, thus films He Fengming, who also corresponds to the *minjian* intellectual who works outside the academic or judicial system, and who draws on "their specific knowledge rather than on official channels or commercial incentives (many of them disseminate their journals via email and rely on retirement pensions as their only income) to collect and publicize material that challenges the official historical narrative."[12]

Stylistically, *Fengming* signals a great departure from the strategy used in Wang's first film, *West of the Tracks*. While the 2003 epic features the movements of the filmmaker's body in space and the recording of workers' bodies during the last moments of state-owned enterprises and planned production, the film about He Fengming's life story offers a very static experience over three hours. The camera is positioned on a tripod, and the subject occupies the center of the frame. The fixed frame is the result of the film having been first conceived as a commissioned video piece for an art gallery rather than a cinema and the fact that Wang did not have much time to make the piece.[13] According to the filmmaker, most of the finished film footage was shot in one afternoon.[14] Except for the opening and ending sequences, where He is seen walking outside and going from room to room in her apartment, the film documents her life story in a monotonous way. Eschewing the interview format per se and the recourse to archival footage or reconstructions, the filmmaker focuses his efforts on recording He's monologue and affect, the subject sitting in the same chair for over three hours of screen time. This stylistic strategy and minimalist mise-en-scène would highly contrast with Wang's next production, the fictional *The Ditch*, which relied on reenactments shot in the Gobi Desert where the Jiabiangou labor camp was located.

In the film, He Fengming performs the role of the all-knowing historical witness, telling her life story and that of her husband through the tumultuous decades of China's twentieth century without relying on notes. Aside from a few rare emotional moments, especially when discussing the tragic fate of her husband and what would have become of her children had she died in the reeducation camp, He's retelling and delivery are free of gaps or other self-imposed interruptions. Over three hours, the fluid nature of He's account strikes the viewer as simply remarkable under the circumstances. She seems invested with the duty to tell the life stories of those close to her and those who are no longer capable of telling their stories. Both her memoir and Wang Bing's film thus act as a diptych whose memorial function cannot be denied. Against the ravages of history, He and Wang, as *minjian* intellectuals, combat forgetting by rethinking the kind of mise-en-scène that would best lend itself to bearing witness to tragedy. Avoiding the more traditional historical account, Wang has remarked: "As far as I'm concerned, I don't want to do 'History' [*faire de l''Histoire'*], at least not in the film [*Fengming*], but I try to build a rapport between she [He Fengming] and I where we are in the same space and the same time."[15]

It soon dawns on the spectator that Wang Bing's approach to history supports a broader historical purpose. Indeed, reflecting on the dedication that appears at the end of *Fengming*, the spectator is intrigued by the filmmaker's emphasis on the notion of revolution in the concluding moments of a three-hour interview with a single subject. Dedicated to the *"gemingzhe he bei gemingzhe,"* that is, the revolutionaries and the "revolutionized," the credits underscore the diverging subjective positions of those whose aim was to revolutionize Chinese society, and those who faced said revolutionaries and their often life-shattering actions. While the address to the victims is unsurprising, the shared dedication demonstrates a certain level of empathy even for those who caused unnecessary hardships and sufferings as cogs in the communist machine. It is twentieth-century China's "revolutionary ethos" that

Wang Bing seems to contest in dedicating the film to both the revolutionaries and the "revolutionized." By doing so, the filmmaker introduces a progressive critical discourse on witnessing and memory in contemporary China, which also concerns, by extension, how the filmmaker implicitly challenges received ideas about the act of witnessing and its relationship with the archive. As discussed below, what is particularly relevant for the study of Wang Bing's "Anti-Rightist" trilogy is the way in which the films contest received ideas within archive theory and the rigid demarcations between witnessing and the archive. Regarding *Fengming*, the film instructs the spectator to closely examine what remains on the margins of influential theorizations of the archive that fail to account for the type of traumatic experience his cinema addresses and the kind of embodied and performative subject He Fengming is as a witness.

## The Unplaceable Witness

In his monumental work of 2000, *Memory, History, Forgetting*, French philosopher Paul Ricoeur makes thought-provoking reflections on what distinguishes the act of witnessing from the archive. He begins by noting how testimony not only preexists the archive, but that it is also ultimately preferable to the document in the archive: "Yet we must not forget that everything starts, not from the archives, but from testimony, and that, whatever may be our lack of confidence in principle in such testimony, we have nothing better than testimony, in the final analysis, to assure ourselves that something did happen in the past, which someone attests having witnessed in person, and that the principal, and at times our only, recourse, when we lack other types of documentation, remains the confrontation among testimonies."[16] Ricoeur initially postulates and reiterates the Western belief in orality as the unequivocable sign of self-presence. As described by the philosopher, the relationship between witnessing, testimony, and the archive would adopt a teleological trajectory that, we can only assume, is valid for all forms of testimony and for all subjects under the sign of epistemological certainty: "With testimony opens an epistemological process that departs from declared memory, passes through the archive and documents, and finds its fulfillment in documentary proof."[17]

While Ricoeur proposes a general model for understanding the epistemological stakes of testimony and its difference from the archive per se, it is most enlightening to see what remains on the margins of his theorization, namely, the kinds of experience that the written document in the archive and its supposed stability and reliability cannot seem to accommodate. Ricoeur himself seems aware of the difficulties that his standardized account of testimony will face for "extreme experiences," as he calls them, but also for others that do not concern the written document. He writes: "Furthermore, at the very interior of the historical sphere, testimony does not run its course with the constitution of archives; it reappears at the end of the epistemological inquiry at the level of the representation of the past through narrative, rhetorical devices, and images. Moreover, in some contemporary forms of deposition arising from the mass atrocities of the twentieth century, it resists not only explication and representation, but even its being placed into some archival reserve, to the point of maintaining itself at the margins of historiography and of throwing doubt on its intention to be truthful."[18] In passages like the preceding one, Ricoeur does several things at once. First, he acknowledges that the testimony in the archive can take many (non-written) representational forms, and he rightly notes that the testimony of a survivor, for example, struggles to enter the archive because it defies representation and exegesis. While such concessions do not appear to be problematic or novel for that matter, what remains questionable in Ricoeur's account is that experiences such as the "mass atrocities of the twentieth century" tend not to conform to the epistemological model proposed and that the written word seems to implicitly carry more weight than other forms of (non-written) testimony. Ricoeur will not pursue these extreme experiences, preferring instead to settle for the type of testimony that is "sealed by its being placed into an archive and sanctioned by documentary proof."[19] It is unfortunate that Ricoeur seems unwilling to integrate this kind of unplaceable testimony into his argumentation, for it would have allowed his theorization to explore limit cases and the type of resistance they demonstrate. As he admits himself about the Holocaust: "These are testimonies that resist historiographical explanation and representation. And it is entry into an archive that they first of all resist. The problem posed then is that of the meaning of these limit-case testimonies along the trajectory of a historiographical operation that runs into its own limits at each step along the way, up to the most demanding kind of reflection."[20] Just as these important reflections are relegated to an endnote in his study, these "limit-case testimonies" fail to be deemed crucial enough to appear in the philosopher's discussion of testimony and the archive and their potential relationship rather than supposed ontological opposition.[21]

Ricoeur's case is instructive for documentary studies. Firstly, the binary distinction that is established between testimony and archive needs to be challenged as more and more documentary films have blurred the boundary between the two. Secondly, the "limit-case testimonies" that Ricoeur mentions in passing are precisely the ones that can challenge any study of testimony and the archive that neglects gender, race, exploitation, or genocide. If the entry into the archive means sanitizing history of its horrors, then cases such as the Holocaust or the Great Famine will rhyme with self-censorship. Consider the ending of the section on the archive, where Ricoeur's fascination for unexplainable "limit cases" comes back to haunt his argumentation: "There remains the limit case of certain fundamentally oral testimonies, even when written in pain, whose being placed into archives raises a question, to the point of soliciting a veritable crisis concerning testimony. Essentially, it is a question of the testimonies of those who survived the extermination camps of the Shoah, called the Holocaust in English-speaking countries."[22]

It is quite telling that such "limit-case experiences" return on numerous occasions in the sections on testimony and the archive, only to be quickly dismissed because they cannot be accommodated. Ricoeur further notes: "Why does this genre of testimony seem to be an exception to the historiographical process? Because it poses a problem of reception that being placed in an archive does not answer and for which it even seems inappropriate, even provisionally incongruous. This has to do with such literally extraordinary limit experiences—which make for a difficult pathway in encountering the ordinary, limited capacities for reception of auditors educated on the basis of a shared comprehension. This comprehension is built on the basis of a sense of human resemblance at the level of situations, feelings, thoughts, and actions. But the experience to be transmitted is that of an inhumanity with no common measure with the experience of the average person. It is in this sense that it is a question of limit experiences."[23] Issues of representation crop up in these remarks, which concern the impossibility for trauma to be represented, shared, and understood ultimately. But, as numerous documentary films have shown, "limit experiences" do not have to be relegated to the margins of both history and archive theory because they do not correspond to the more readily sharable or understandable. Failing to discuss or integrate such "limit experiences" is no solution, in other words.

In addition to issues of representation and reception, Ricoeur takes issue with the testimony of the survivor, which would lack objectivity and critical distance because of its being imbued with too much affect and horror: "To be received, a testimony must be appropriated, that is, divested as much as possible of the absolute foreignness that horror engenders. This drastic condition is not satisfied in the case of survivors' testimonies. A further reason for the difficulty in communicating has to do with the fact that the witness himself had no distance on the events; he was a 'participant,' without being the agent, the actor; he was their victim."[24] Intent on playing up the objectivity of the witness who is not at the same time a victim, Ricoeur closes the door on the profoundly consequential ramifications of witnessing and testimony located at the intersection of trauma and victimhood. While the philosopher names the "crisis of testimony" that such accounts signal, he fails to address them with as much rigor and verve as he does the less traumatic cases. By limiting his list of limit cases to Holocaust survivors Robert Antelme and Primo Levi, who both published their experiences of the concentration camps, Ricoeur also denies documentary's profound investment in audiovisual instances of limit cases as found in Claude Lanzmann's *Shoah* (1985), a film glaringly absent from his graphocentric discussion of the Nazi atrocities.

Wang Bing's "Anti-Rightist" trilogy contests the kind of rationale used by Ricoeur to demarcate witnessing, testimony, the archive, and the victim to fully confront the hermeneutical challenges associated with the kind of atrocities to which the philosopher alludes, but which he ultimately refuses to consider because it would cause the collapse of the epistemological edifice he erects in his study. Wang's "Anti-Rightist" trilogy serves as a case study for both thinking through "limit-case experiences" when archives are either absent or inaccessible and considering the issues that arise when testimonies take the form of documentary images inflected by affect and performance. Ricoeur provides an intriguing instance of a philosopher haunted by what stands on the margins of his discourse, which is to say what remains to be fully integrated to support a critical archive theory fit for the atrocities of the twentieth century. The final sentence of the section on testimony and the archive is quite telling in that regard: "But there are also witnesses who never encounter an audience capable of listening to them or hearing what they have to say."[25] In a film such as *Fengming*, Wang Bing implicitly argues that it is possible to find an audience capable of negotiating the difficult experiences at the intersection of horror and trauma. He Fengming offers an excellent example of the kind of witness who stands on the margins of Ricoeur's theory and whose testimony found an audience around the world. What is particularly fascinating in the case of Wang's film is how He Fengming's discourse enters into dialogue with other texts, which paint a more comprehensive portrait of her life experiences without making the full understanding of these other sources a requirement to receive her testimony. Retracing how these various sources inform Wang Bing's film is a crucial step toward understanding how it constructs an audiovisual discourse that is embodied by He Fengming herself.

## He Fengming's Memoir: Siting Experience

*Fengming* belongs to a group of oral and documentary histories of the Great Leap Forward and famine that have adopted a revisionist take on this crucial period of Chinese history. Alongside works such as Wu Wenguang's *1966—My Time in the Red Guards* (*1966 nian, wo de hongweibing shidai*, 1993), Zou Xueping's "Zoujia village" series (2010–2014), and Ai Xiaoming's *Jiabiangou Elegy* (*Jiabiangou jishi*, 2017), Wang Bing's film demonstrates how Chinese documentaries can revisit some of the most troubling events of the Mao era and exemplifies the work of *minjian* artists and intellectuals. In the case of *Fengming*, it is a rich audiovisual tapestry that is offered to the spectator, and it is quite instructive to compare other documents such as He's memoir and Yang Xianhui's fictionalized testimonies with Wang Bing's film to better understand what his documentary adds to the portrayal of the Great Famine, and how the film sets the stage for the two other films in the trilogy. Other important questions concern the status of the film as a documentary adaptation of He Fengming's published memoir. Does He's retelling in the film follow the unfolding of events in the memoir? What are the differences and similarities, and where are those located in the film and to what effect? Such questions help to better frame how the printed text and the audiovisual work can potentially interact in the creation of an audiovisual archive.

The relationship between Wang Bing's film and He Fengming's memoir is an intriguing one. After all, it is difficult not to consider He's memoir as an *urtext* with which the film should be compared. That is why it is quite puzzling that scholars writing on *Fengming* have not paid closer attention to He's memoir. Aside from the occasional mention, the memoir has gone completely unexamined in the literature. Still unavailable in translation, *Jingli: wo de 1957 nian* offers in-depth coverage of He's life experiences during this most tumultuous period of Chinese history. Written in the 1990s and published at the beginning of the 2000s, the memoir offers a chronological approach to He's life story and experiences.

The title of the memoir contains only one word, *jingli*, which can refer to both the substantive "experience" (e.g., my experience of 1957) or its phenomenological variant in the form of the verb "to experience" (e.g., how I experienced 1957). The emphasis on the concept of experience in the memoir echoes other survivors' writings, obviously. Williams and Wu have posited that the notion of experience plays a great role in how survivors conceive of their duty to bear witness: "An important motivation for the Chinese ex-inmates to write about their experience has been a sense of moral duty. Aware of how the CCP has attempted to conceal its errors and has urged its citizenry to forget about the recurring suppression of basic civil rights in the PRC's history, the survivor-authors feel the need to publicize the truth and preserve those memoires. In their memoirs, they bear witness to [*jianzheng*] the injustice that has befallen themselves, their families, and various other inmates."[26] Oscillating between the noun and the verb, the memoir's title posits experience as the fundamental category to understand He's life, and this emphasis makes the viewer reflect on how Wang Bing grapples with the notion of experience in his film and on how he comes to terms with archiving traumatic life experiences.

What may have been particularly striking for the rare Western viewers who had read He's memoir before watching Wang Bing's documentary is that the interviewee closely follows the events in the memoir in her retelling for the camera. Equally interesting is the absence of long pauses, false starts, or hesitations on the part of the interviewee over three hours, thus implying that He might have memorized the structure of the memoir to reproduce the chronological account of the text for the camera. Such a viewer may wonder why the filmmaker simply asked He to repeat her major life events as they appear in chronological order in the memoir. Is this a rare kind of documentary film adaptation: the memoir-to-documentary film adaptation? What could justify the need for this kind of audiovisual repetition in other words?

Beyond the necessity for a documentary filmmaker to make films, I believe there is a greater imperative in this case that concerns the lack of archival evidence for the events described in He's memoir and the equally important need for the subject to become the archive, which is to say the opportunity to embody these events through her gestures and voice. The archives become the witness, and, in turn, the witness becomes the archives. Turning the memoir into a script to be adapted would not have had the same impact as the subject herself carefully speaking and repeating words for the camera.

Given that Wang Bing does not interrupt his subject mid-sentence to ask a probing question or challenge He's account of the events based on his own historical knowledge or what is found in the memoir, the film does not function as an investigative report seeking to corroborate the authenticity of the memoir. In fact, He's memoir is not cited per se in the film, nor is it referenced as a meaningful source for the spectator to cross-reference particular events, with the exception of one casual remark. In that sense, the film functions independently of the memoir; it does not need the published text to justify its existence as would be the case for a typical adaptation. The credits sequence does not acknowledge the existence of the memoir either, even as a source of inspiration for the film. While the film succeeds at erasing the traces of He's memoir as a source of inspiration, it fails to do so as a structuring device for the retelling of events, which follows the chronological approach adopted in the memoir.

## Fictionalizing Oral History

Yang Xianhui was born in Gansu Province in 1946. In the 1990s, he started documenting the Great Famine and interviewing survivors of the Jiabiangou reeducation camp (*laojiao*) located in Jiuquan County in Gansu Province. As a thought-provoking example of genre-bending reportage literature about the Anti-Rightist Movement and the Great Famine, Yang's collection, *Jiabiangou jishi* (first published in 2002; second, expanded edition titled *Gaobie Jiabiangou*, 2003, reprinted in 2008 under the original title, *Jiabiangou jishi*), provides a singular account of the inhuman excesses of the Mao regime that took the form of purges and persecutions affecting millions in what is often described as "documentary fiction" (*jishixing xiaoshuo*). Based on the author's field work and interviews with survivors, the fictionalized accounts, first serialized in the journal *Shanghai wenxue* in 2000, focus on Jiabiangou, which was set up in 1954 and converted into a *laojiao* facility in 1958, and what individuals had to do to survive during the Great Famine. Yang's collection reflects the work of a *minjian* intellectual: "It was all based on personal initiative; I had no support. Since this was a 'forbidden area,' if the local government had found out, they might well have kicked me out. There was no chance at all of getting near the archives. The people whom I interviewed were all contacted through unofficial channels and friends, from one to another. For 'Jiabiangou jishi,' I interviewed more than 100 people, of whom about 60 or 70 were survivors, the others relatives."[27] The nineteen stories in the collection depict scenes of extreme human behavior such as cannibalism and the various strategies used for dehumanizing inmates at Jiabiangou. As Veg notes: "Yang Xianhui's clinical descriptions focus on corporeality rather than ideology, suggesting that the deprivation of basic humanity (eating vomit, 'digging' in constipated inmates' bowels) may be the true objective of the *laojiao* system, a policy to break down dignity and reduce humans to self-destruction."[28] A publication such as Yang's participates in a larger social movement whose goal is to rewrite the history of Maoist China from a critical perspective that greatly depends on the work of amateur or unaffiliated researchers working in collaboration with *minjian* intellectuals, witnesses, and survivors. Their collective endeavor seeks to rewrite the historical narrative of the PRC by emphasizing history from below, that is, microhistorical narratives detailing the lives of the marginalized whose experiences and memories had been suppressed by the regime.

Yang Xianhui's "A Visit to Wang Jingchao" occupies a strange place in this story. Clearly based on He Fengming's memoir, Yang's fictionalized oral history account recasts He's life experiences in an intriguing way. The fictionalized account begins with the first-person narrator addressing the reader about Gansu weather and climate.[29] Is the climate a dry one like the narrator seems to believe? He Sang (whose life experiences correspond to those of He Fengming) begs to differ. She remembers the great snowfalls in the winter of 1960, when she received a letter from her father informing her of Wang Jingchao's declining health condition in the Mingshui annex (which was part of the larger Jiabiangou camp). The text retraces He Sang's steps as she journeys from the *laojiao* where she worked to the Mingshui annex to visit her ill husband, named Wang Jingchao in the text (which was the actual name of He Fengming's husband), only to find out upon arrival that he died eight days before.

The narrative strategies used in Yang's fictionalized account greatly depart from those of Wang Bing's film. Indeed, the text uses various rhetorical strategies (such as analepsis) to reimagine He Fengming's experiences through the character of He Sang. Midway through, the narrative is interrupted by an addendum (*fuji*)[30] in which He Sang takes over from the narrator in a more informal style. He Sang will go on to tell her story from September 1961 to the early 1990s, which is also the ending point of Wang's film when Fengming mentions the trip to find her husband's grave. The fictionalized account thus uses different strategies for evoking the workings of memory alongside the microhistorical events in He Sang's life against the background of the *laojiao* in the countryside, the Cultural Revolution, and her rehabilitation in 1978. The text ends with the narrator remarking that "[o]ver the last two years, she [He Sang, i.e., He Fengming] has been writing a book titled 'Jingli: wo de 1957 nian.' She writes day and night."[31] The narrator expresses his admiration for this woman who writes her life story for future generations.

Memory plays an important role in Yang's fictionalized account, as do responsibility and culpability in Wang Jingchao's death. Yang implicitly brings to the fore a notion that has been relatively absent from the literature on Wang Bing, which concerns the representation of gender in his cinema, especially in the "Anti-Rightist" trilogy. After all, one could argue that the trilogy would be unimaginable without the memorable presence, words, and actions of women. In the case of *Fengming*, He Fengming's life is the foundation for the entire film, and He herself the foundation for the character of Gu Xiaoyun in Yang's "Woman from Shanghai" (who appears in *The Ditch*), which is based on He Fengming's memoir. Yang's text offers a fascinating reflection on the challenges and dilemmas that women faced as their rightist husbands were sent to labor camps such as Jiabiangou. Wives such as He Fengming, and the character of He Sang in Yang's fictionalized account, were in an untenable position: they had to choose between being loyal to their husbands or being loyal to the CCP, which demanded of wives that they openly forsake their rightist husbands. As Wemheuer has noted: "Millions faced the burden of being known as the wives, husbands or children of rightists in their work units. The party demanded that they 'draw a line' with bad family members."[32] This is a recurring concern that has been explored in oral histories and memoirs of the period.

## Becoming-Archive: Voicing the Performance of *Suku*

Considering the preceding discussion of Fengming's memoir and Yang's fictionalized account, two recurring questions haunt the analysis of Wang Bing's *Fengming*. First, why did the filmmaker decide to adapt a memoir and ask its author to repeat her life experiences for the camera in stylized, minimalist fashion? Second, given that Wang Bing was familiar with Yang's "A Visit to Wang Jingchao," why did he prefer to follow the chronological approach of He's memoir instead of the more challenging, nonchronological approach of Yang's text in which memory plays a fundamental role and contests traditional storytelling's linearity? I would like to explore two hypotheses to answer these questions. The first concerns the need to materialize the account of the witness, which is to say the process of oralizing He's memoir via the human voice and body. The second refers to the filmmaker's refusal to experiment with more complex narrative strategies than the one afforded by the chronological approach. I posit that both strategies—oralizing the memoir and adopting the chronological approach—reflect the filmmaker's predilection for observational realism, which returns us to the title of He Fengming's memoir—*Jingli* (Experience)—and the need for greater experiential realism in documentary filmmaking.

As previously mentioned, it is a phenomenological, embodied experience that is adapted and archived in Wang Bing's film, and it is translated into an audiovisual experience characterized by a minimalist mise-en-scène, strange repetitions, and performative elements. In fact, *jingli* oscillates between the phenomenological experience of an event, which is to say how an experience moves someone, and the naming of that experience in the form of a historical event. In He's case, on a macrohistorical level, this concerns the Great Leap Forward, the labor camps, and the famine, and, on a microhistorical level, it relates to her husband's tragic death in the labor camp and her experiences trying to come to terms with his death. Therefore, it is the understanding of what He herself experienced from the point of view of phenomenology and the act of naming and voicing that experience that merits greater attention. The film archives He's experiences as she retells them in real time, and it also archives the naming of the historical events that were the Great Leap Forward and the famine. As such, Wang's film embeds the testimonial function via the treatment of He's voice.

It is crucial to bear in mind that He's tragic experiences began with the liberation of the people's voices that was supposed to be the Hundred Flowers Campaign's goal. He and her husband imagined, like so many others, that the CCP's injunction to criticize the party during the Hundred Flowers Campaign was an honest endeavor leading to the betterment of the country. As the party would crack down on those who had criticized it, the airing of grievances turned into struggle sessions in which the voices of the accused were not legitimately heard, and a public confession functioned as the only possible escape for the couple.

*Fengming* thus functions as a film about both the silencing of voices during the Great Leap Forward and the potential liberation of voices that the documentary mise-en-scène enables in the form of the imperative to testify, once again. Regarding the choice to have He Fengming repeat her experiences for the camera, Wang Bing seems to have prioritized oralizing the memoir over rethinking the order of the events in the memoir to avoid a linear retelling. This preference also concerns the possibility for the witness to imbue her experiences with affect and accentuate certain elements of her testimony through her voice and gestures. The order of the events does not seem to have been the main concern, the filmmaker privileging the chronological treatment found in He's memoir in the end.

Wang Bing certainly did not want to draw attention to himself with either the camera movements or his questioning. Wang's role is to record He's fluent speech; he is not an interviewer per se. The filmmaker is present to record the theater of voices in which He has the main role, addressing not only the spectator but also history itself in the form of poignant injunctions to the Chinese authorities in a way that was impossible at the time. The chronological approach to telling her life experiences turns into a polyphonic affair in which various voices appear, disappear, and often reappear in He's direct addresses in the present tense. In this apparently simple chronological retelling, it is an admittedly cathartic form of address that Wang Bing offers his subject with this carefully designed mise-en-scène.[33]

The type of catharsis afforded by the documentary mise-en-scène deserves closer attention in the Chinese context. In his review of *Fengming*, Andrew Chan makes an insightful remark on the type of oral discourse at the heart of the film. He writes: "*Fengming* paves a new path by looking back, evoking traditions that shaped Chinese subjectivity in the last half century. It's tempting to read the film as a persecuted bourgeois intellectual's reclamation of *suku*, the Communist practice that encouraged peasants to exercise political agency by airing their grievances in public."[34] Chan's reference to Chinese history and the practice of *suku* (speaking bitterness) allows for a richer historical contextualization of Wang's film as a form of microhistorical counter-discourse that the oral history film is well known for, but that has not drawn a lot of attention in analyses of Wang Bing's film.

*Fengming* sets the tone for the "Anti-Rightist" trilogy by serving as a counter-discourse to the propagandistic practice of *suku*. However, within Wang's film, the *suku* discourse no longer serves the CCP but supports survivors such as He Fengming and the numerous others who have published their memoirs or fictionalized accounts of their experiences during the Great Leap Forward. He Fengming's practice of *suku* thus serves a counter-historical purpose, as she constructs a subjective position in which victim and performer merge for the camera. The grain of He's voice, the carefully chosen words and controlled diction, and the selective affect displayed all contribute to create a material, embodied archive of the period as important as the macrohistorical events related. Pernin has gone so far as to claim that the modulations in He's voice give the interview "an almost theatrical dimension."[35] This is unsurprising as He's speech is the speech of a perverted *suku* practice whose goal is no longer to buttress the CCP's propaganda with affect-laden tales of past bitterness to praise the present revolutionary moment, as was the case in the 1960s, but whose function is to critically revisit the past so that it be more than the sum of discrete historical events. It is the laborious construction of collective memory and political subjectivity in which documentary participates that the viewer is asked to consider. More than the published memoir ever could, the documentary film's mise-en-scène perverts the historical practice of *suku* to free one survivor's memories of the period and allow their historical, embodied contents to finally emerge.

As the first film in Wang Bing's "Anti-Rightist" trilogy, *Fengming* does not take the place of the loved ones who tragically died of starvation in the labor camps, but it asks the spectator to bear witness to events that are missing from the official archives. To do so, Wang Bing constructs a mise-en-scène for his subject to revisit the past without asking for veracity or proof. As Phay notes: "Archive-oeuvres are not proofs, but *visual forms of thought* that create meaning precisely where an act of destruction has taken place."[36] The truth of the survivor is to be found in the filmic unfolding and affective revelation that the mise-en-scène allows to be created. As a result, a new image of thought has been generated for archive theory. This is the labor of history as documentary film understands it, a practice in which "history leaves the field of representation and visuality to move towards a performed history with the help of orality, gesture, and memory."[37]

## Conclusion

The various sources discussed in this chapter—published memoir, fictionalized accounts based on interviews, and documentary film—indicate how complex He Fengming's story is, considering the efforts of *minjian* intellectuals and artists such as Wang Bing who try to make sense of twentieth-century Chinese history. The complexity of this history reflects the numerous stories used—or that could have been used—to recreate this period of Maoist history in Wang Bing's film. Ricoeur's binary understanding of testimony and the archive shows limitations insofar as one must confront a multiplicity of sources and evidential traces such as He's memoir, Yang's fictionalized accounts, and Wang's documentary film to come to terms with this period of Chinese history. If there is a potential truth to emerge from He's story—that is, this survivor's *experience*—it is at the intersection of these textual and visual sources. It is not so much the comparison of sources that seems to matter as the multilayered nature of several sources, their montage as it were, on the same topic. As Didi-Huberman has argued, the archive "is by no means the pure and simple 'reflection' of the event, nor its pure and simple 'evidence.' For it must always be developed by repeated cross-checkings and by *montage* with other archives."[38] In the end, is it realistic to rely on a single document in a story as complex as He Fengming's? While researchers await the opening of state archives in China, documentaries such as *Fengming* teach a lesson on the overconfidence of the historian or philosopher who puts too much stock in the truth that can be had in the single document in the archive. Far from being readily available or readable, the archival document needs to be reconstructed.

In characteristic binary fashion, Ricoeur defines the archive as "the moment of the entry into writing of the historiographical operation. Testimony is by origin oral. It is listened to, heard. The archive is written. It is read, consulted."[39] As shown in this chapter, Wang Bing's film and its related texts (He's memoir and Yang Xianhui's fictionalized accounts) allow the expansion of such a restrictive definition of the archive to make room for not only the "limit cases" alluded to by Ricoeur, which he chose not to consider, but also other texts that can complicate the accounts given and the entry into the archive, which can also take an embodied form, as is the case with He Fengming's performative "becoming-archive" captured on video, a "force of individuation"[40] that challenges the notion of witness fixed in time and space. Her testimony is listened to, *heard*, as Ricoeur mentions, but her physical presence and performance are most importantly archived in Wang Bing's film for generations of viewers to come. That archived testimony, in all its performative elements, possesses tremendous value for the understanding of this historical period. It is unfortunate that a philosopher such as Ricoeur failed to contemplate the possibility that some of the most insightful archives of our time take alternative forms, and that they possess equal symbolic, political, or emotional value to the traditional document in the archive. The first film in Wang Bing's "Anti-Rightist" trilogy certainly shows that all documents are produced, and that some of the most enlightening testimonies take an embodied form. This begs the question: Why would Wang Bing abandon the kind of complex documentary presentation of Chinese history used in *Fengming* to explore fiction filmmaking in the second film of the trilogy, *The Ditch*?

## Notes

1. Robert Koehler, "Ghost Stories: Wang Bing's Startling New Cinema," *Cinema Scope* 31 (2007), accessed May 27, 2022, https://cinema-scope.com/cinema-scope-magazine/interviews-ghost-stories-wang-bings-startling-new-cinema/.
2. It is quite intriguing that the relations between these three texts have not been examined in the literature on *Fengming*. While Chinese documentary scholars do acknowledge the existence of He's memoir, the contents of said document, or its potential relation with Wang's film, have remained in the dark.
3. Soko Phay, "L'archive-oeuvre à l'épreuve de l'effacement," in *Un art documentaire: enjeux esthétiques, politiques et éthiques*, ed. Aline Caillet and Frédéric Pouillaude (Rennes: Presses universitaires de Rennes, 2017), 278.
4. Jacques Derrida, *Mal d'archive. Une impression freudienne* (Paris: Galilée, 1995), 144.
5. Yang Xianhui, *Jiabiangou shiji* (Guangzhou: Huacheng chubanshe, 2008). Abridged English translation: Yang, Xianhui, *Woman from Shanghai: Tales of Survival from a Chinese Labor Camp*, trans. Wen Huang (New York: Anchor Books, 2010). Only thirteen of the nineteen pieces appearing in the 2008 edition are found in the English translation.
6. Wang Bing, *Alors, la Chine. Entretiens avec Emmanuel Burdeau et Eugenio Renzi* (Paris: Les Prairies ordinaires, 2014), 101.
7. Wang, *Alors, la Chine*, 99.
8. Wang Bing, "Filming a Land in Flux," *New Left Review* 82 (2013): 127.
9. Excerpts from He Fengming's memoir have appeared in French translation. See He Fengming, "Les lettres de Jingchao. Extraits de *Année 1957, Mon vécu*," in *Actualités critiques. Capricci 2012*, ed. Thierry Lounas (Paris: Capricci, 2012), 62–69.
10. Unfortunately, "A Visit to Wang Jingchao" does not appear in the English translation of Yang Xianhui's collection. Yang Xianhui, "Tanwang Wang Jingchao," in *Jiabiangou shiji* (Guangzhou: Huacheng chubanshe, 2008), 224–53.
11. On the last page of her memoir, He shares her address and phone number with the reader so that her "fellow sufferers" (*nanyou*) can get in touch with her and share their experiences. He Fengming, *Jingli: wo de 1957 nian* (Lanzhou: Dunhuang wenyi chubanshe, 2001), 369.
12. Sebastian Veg, *Minjian: The Rise of China's Grassroots Intellectuals* (New York: Columbia University Press, 2019), 90.
13. Wang Bing, "La memoria rimossa della Cina. Conversazione con Wang Bing," in *Wang Bing: Il cinema nella Cina che cambia*, ed. Daniela Persico (Milan: Agenzia X, 2010), 30.
14. Wang, *Alors, la Chine*, 101.
15. Zhang Yaxuan, "Je suis un conservateur. Entretien avec Wang Bing," in *Actualités critiques. Capricci 2012*, edited by Thierry Lounas (Paris: Capricci, 2012), 77.
16. Paul Ricoeur, *Memory, History, Forgetting*, trans. Kathleen Blamey and David Pellauer (Chicago: University of Chicago Press, 2004), 147.
17. Ricoeur, *Memory, History, Forgetting*, 161.

18. Ricoeur, *Memory, History, Forgetting*, 161.
19. Ricoeur, *Memory, History, Forgetting*, 161.
20. Ricoeur, *Memory, History, Forgetting*, 529–30.
21. Étienne Anheim provides an excellent overview of the archival issues at the heart of Ricoeur's influential publication. See Étienne Anheim, "Singulières archives. Le statut des archives dans l'épistémologie historique. Une discussion de *La mémoire, l'histoire, l'oubli* de Paul Ricoeur," *Revue de synthèse* 5 (2004): 153–82.
22. Ricoeur, *Memory, History, Forgetting*, 175.
23. Ricoeur, *Memory, History, Forgetting*, 175.
24. Ricoeur, *Memory, History, Forgetting*, 176.
25. Ricoeur, *Memory, History, Forgetting*, 166.
26. Philip F. Williams and Yenna Wu, *The Great Wall of Confinement: The Chinese Prison Camp through Contemporary Fiction and Reportage* (Berkeley: University of California Press, 2004), 163.
27. Yang Xianhui, "Wenxue, zuowei yizhong zhengyan—Yang Xianhui fangtan lu," *Shanghai wenxue* 12 (2009): 94.
28. Sebastian Veg, "Literary and Documentary Accounts of the Great Famine," in *Popular Memories of the Mao Era: From Critical Debate to Reassessing History*, ed. Sebastian Veg (Hong Kong: Hong Kong University Press, 2019), 123.
29. Yang, "Tanwang Wang Jingchao," 224.
30. Yang, "Tanwang Wang Jingchao," 246.
31. Yang, "Tanwang Wang Jingchao," 253.
32. Felix Wemheuer, *A Social History of Maoist China: Conflict and Change, 1949–1976* (Cambridge: Cambridge University Press, 2019), 116.
33. The need for repetition also concerns the possibility for He's testimony to be heard and seen outside of China, as even there its distribution had been limited.
34. Andrew Chan, "Fengming: A Chinese Memoir," December 3, 2008, accessed March 2, 2022, http://www.reverseshot.org/reviews/entry/571/fengming_chinese_memoir.
35. Judith Pernin, *Pratiques indépendantes du documentaire en Chine: histoire, esthétique et discours visuels (1990–2010)* (Rennes: Presses universitaires de Rennes, 2015), 195.
36. Phay, "L'archive-oeuvre à l'épreuve de l'effacement," 279, emphasis in original.
37. Aline Caillet, *Dispositifs critiques. Le documentaire, du cinéma aux arts visuels* (Rennes: Presses universitaires de Rennes, 2014), 62.
38. Georges Didi-Huberman, *Images in Spite of All: Four Photographs from Auschwitz*, trans. Shane B. Lillis (Chicago: University of Chicago Press, 2008), 99.
39. Ricoeur, *Memory, History, Forgetting*, 166.
40. Emmanuel Housset, "L'objet du témoignage," *Philosophie* 88 (2005): 5, https://hal.archives-ouvertes.fr/hal-01878462/document.

# 3
# *The Ditch*

## Techniques of Creative Repetition

Premiered the same year as *Fengming, a Chinese Memoir*, Wang Bing's fourteen-minute short *Brutality Factory* (2007) was the filmmaker's first foray into fiction filmmaking. Made for the Gulbenkian Foundation's omnibus "O Estado do mundo" (The State of the World) project, Wang's short appeared alongside the work of other filmmakers such as Pedro Costa, Chantal Akerman, and Apichatpong Weerasethakul at Cannes, Directors' Fortnight, in 2007. For many film critics, it was surprising to see Wang Bing turn to fiction after the critical success of both *West of the Tracks* and *Fengming*. What could have piqued the filmmaker's interest in fiction after devoting so much time and energy to honing his skills as a documentary filmmaker?

*Brutality Factory* offers a glimpse into a "struggle session" set in the Cultural Revolution during which a woman, accused of being a counter-revolutionary, is tortured by revolutionary guards and pressured into giving up information about her husband in the basement of a factory. The mise-en-scène, and the stunning choice of having ghosts haunt the torture chamber, supports a shocking tale of repression and persecution that relies on a nightmarish reenactment that few expected from a documentarian such as Wang Bing. *Brutality Factory* could not but evoke *Fengming* given that both films focus on a female subject caught in the web of twentieth-century Chinese history, facing the horrific acts associated with the Great Leap Forward and the Cultural Revolution. The departure from the demands of documentary to explore how fiction and reenactment could frame historical material acted as a trial run of sorts for the filmmaker who would eventually make *The Ditch* (*Jiabiangou*, 2010), which explores the same historical period as *Fengming*.

This chapter examines Wang Bing's turn to fiction filmmaking and reenactments to further explore the Anti-Rightist Campaign and the experiences of inmates using a different kind of mise-en-scène than the one employed in *Fengming*. Wang's decision to forego the documentary approach perfected in *West of the Tracks* and *Fengming* and turn to fiction and reenactment in his third feature film was puzzling to say the least. Regarding the content of *The Ditch*, the filmmaker has stated that he wanted to address a sense of national amnesia about the period from 1949 to 1965, which is to say the period from the foundation of the republic to the events leading up to the beginning of the Cultural Revolution. Ignored by the Chinese themselves, this crucial historical moment, according to the filmmaker, deserves close attention because it led to the formation of contemporary China. In fact, Wang has said that *The Ditch* is "the first film explicitly focusing on the recent political past" in China.[1] With regard to form and style, the *minjian* filmmaker has intimated that one of the main reasons for turning to fiction filmmaking and reenactment was to better understand the relationship between the moving image and history, and how storytelling functions differently in fiction: "I wanted to rethink how to view cinema and history, including how to handle time and narrative. I didn't try to present the story in its totality; what I included in the film is only a tiny part of the larger historical event."[2]

A few essential questions remain unanswered: What is it about the potential of fiction and reenactment to tell the story of the Great Famine differently that attracted Wang Bing? Why was the use of semiprofessional and nonprofessional actors a crucial element to tell this story? What was it about the filmed oral account of a survivor such as He Fengming that was deemed unsatisfying or incomplete? Veg has argued that "Wang Bing's engagement with the labour camp theme gives rise to two films [*Fengming* and *The Ditch*] that probe the question of the ethics of representation across the boundary between fiction and documentary."[3] In this chapter, I build on Veg's insight and reframe the debate over representation and visual ethics to highlight the *techniques of creative repetition* at the heart of *The Ditch*. I use the concept of creative repetition to reconsider the multifaceted implications of having recourse to fiction and reenactment to retell the life experiences of inmates and Great Leap Forward famine survivors.

There are two main techniques of creative repetition within *The Ditch*: adaptation and reenactment. Regarding the former, it is important to bear in mind that Wang Bing has used two sources to lay the foundation for his film: Yang Xianhui's fictionalized account titled "Shanghai nüren" ("Woman from Shanghai"), which appears in the collection discussed in the previous chapter on *Fengming*, and rare archival photographs of the camps. The second technique of creative repetition concerns reenactment. Drawing on the work of scholars such as Bill Nichols, Ivone Margulies, and Aline Caillet, I further inquire into and reframe the practice of reenactment as a creative act. Departing from the single testimony of *Fengming* and the demands of the oral history film, I argue that *The Ditch* capitalizes on the affordances of reenactment to rethink the process of constructing Chinese history. Inspired by Gilles Deleuze's reflections on repetition, it is as a singular form of "creative repetition," that is, the creative treatment of Chinese history in this case, that I address the notion of reenactment in Wang Bing's third feature. Using both adaptation and reenactment, the filmmaker engages in a critique of documentary representation in

*The Ditch*, which is predicated on techniques of creative repetition that have received little attention.

## *The Ditch*: A Cinema of Repetition

Premiered at the Venice Film Festival in 2010, *The Ditch* is Wang Bing's only venture into feature-length fiction filmmaking to date. As was the case with *Fengming*, Wang Bing's fictional treatment of the Jiabiangou camp adapts certain episodes in Yang Xianhui's collection of fictionalized accounts of labor camp life, *Jiabiangou shiji*, which is listed in the opening credits. In that sense, the 2010 film and *Fengming* could be said to be a diptych drawing on the same collection of fictionalized accounts of labor camp life. Whereas *Fengming* drew on only one fictionalized testimony in Yang's collection, "Tanwang Wang Jingchao" ("A Visit to Wang Jingchao"), the 2010 fiction film draws on several accounts in Yang's collection to paint a horrific portrait of the struggles of a group of prisoners who must survive under inhumane conditions. *The Ditch* appropriates the transfer of inmates from the Jiabiangou camp to the more remote Mingshui annex in 1960 (an episode also referenced in *Dead Souls*, the third film in the "Anti-Rightist" trilogy) from Yang's "Gaobie Jiabiangou" ("Farewell to Jiabiangou," which closes the original collection).[4] The focus of *The Ditch* clearly is on the Mingshui annex where the most inhuman acts of violence were perpetrated. Another narrative thread, based on "Yihao bingfang" ("Dispensary #1"), features the man put in charge of the dispensary who listens to the inmates' reflections on their conditions in the camp. "Taowang" ("Escape") serves as the foundation for the final sequence in the film featuring the escape of a young man and an elderly prisoner, who is finally left to die in the desert. Finally, the second part of the film featuring Dong Jianyi's wife, Gu Xiaoyun,[5] is indebted to the account of a woman who makes the trip from Shanghai to Gansu only to find her husband dead and then insists on giving him a proper burial. This fictionalized account, "Shanghai nüren" ("Woman from Shanghai"), bears striking similarities to He Fengming's own journey to Gansu as reported in her memoir, *Jingli: wo de 1957 nian*, and in Wang Bing's *Fengming*.

Wang Bing's *Fengming* and *The Ditch* both engage creative repetition at the level of adaptation practice. What deserve closer attention than has been the case so far in the literature is the techniques of repetition used, and the fact that both films offer repetitions within repetitions, which correspond to a fascinating case of documentary *mise-en-abyme*. Indeed, both films draw on Yang Xianhui's collection of accounts, *Jiabiangou jishi*. These accounts, we must remember, are not fictional narratives; they are based on interviews with survivors, and they themselves must be seen through the prism of creative reinterpretation. Wang Bing has used these accounts to make *Fengming* (based on Yang's "A Visit to Wang Jingchao") and *The Ditch* (mainly based on "Woman from Shanghai"). In the case of the latter, Yang's account is based on conversations with Li Wenhan, a former rightist sent to

Jiabiangou in 1957. The account of the woman from Shanghai, Gu Xiaoyun, is based on the story of a man Yang had befriended: "He [Li Wenhan] and I shared a room near a goat pen for three years. Over that period, we got to know and trust each other. In the long winter nights, he entertained me with many Jiabiangou stories. Li's stories stayed with me."[6] There thus appear to be two main creative acts of repetition: Yang Xianhui's refashioning of the tale of the woman from Shanghai as told by Li Wenhan and the transformation of this tale by Wang Bing in the script for *The Ditch*.

Thinking that more than Yang Xianhui's fictionalized accounts would be needed to address the complexity of this historical period and the horrors of labor-camp life, Wang used various documents (interviews, photographs, and memoirs) to fill in the gaps and provide a fuller picture of the Jiabiangou and Mingshui camps (one survivor, Ti Zhongzheng, is mentioned in the opening credits). Researching the topic, the filmmaker learned about over one hundred survivors of the Anti-Rightist Campaign who had been detained in the Jiabiangou and Mingshui camps, and he decided to interview many of them.[7] Some of these survivors and the material shot in preparation for *The Ditch* would appear in *Dead Souls*. As was the case for *Fengming*, the 2010 film features an ambiguous dedication that blurs the boundary between victims and perpetrators: "*Cipian xiangei naxie baojing kunan, yijing daoxia he jixu qianxing de renmen* / This film is dedicated to all those who suffered, to those who fell and to those who survived." The filmmaker seems to suggest that the fate of these individuals, both victims and agents of the communist machine, was as much a product of contingency as a product of agency.

In *The Ditch*, Wang Bing lays bare the ethical stakes of creative repetition.[8] The act of recreating the inhuman conditions in which inmates lived in the Mingshui camp cannot but raise the question of the ethical and moral standards of the filmmaker. Deprived of dignity, the inmates had recourse to the most atrocious acts of survival during the Great Famine. Showing such acts makes great demands on both the actors, who were amateur or semiprofessional, and the director, who, we assume, wishes to avoid sensationalism in the recreation of these moments based on a combination of fictional and documentary elements. Veg has noted that "[r]ather than seeing an ethically loaded opposition between a documentary based on testimony and a fictional reconstruction that relies on a form of trivialization, Wang Bing shows that both genres run the risk of a problematic dramatization: the director's work is to address this risk through specific cinematographic techniques."[9] He goes on to argue that "[f]ictional representation does not, in the final analysis, raise ethical issues that are different from those raised by a non-representational documentary; however, in both cases, what is important are the inseparably aesthetic and ethical choices made by the director."[10] The main ethical strategy that Wang Bing uses in *The Ditch* is to adopt the same visual style used in his previous documentaries and to maintain a critical distance between his actors, even when the scene takes place underground in a confined space. Using a wide-angle lens, the filmmaker is able show the entire space and the actors within it, whether they be moving in and out of frame, or lying in bed famished and exhausted. Rarely relying on the close-up for dramatic effect, *The Ditch* maintains the same kind of distanced approach used in *West of the Tracks* and *Fengming*. As is typical of the filmmaker, Wang follows the actors from a distance when walking outside in the desert (where the wind is omnipresent in the soundtrack).

The technique of repetition also extends to location shooting. In addition to its multilayered nature, the film reenacts labor camp life at the Mingshui camp, which was located about 200 kilometers from the original camp site in the Gobi Desert between Gansu and Mongolia. Veg has implicitly noted how repetition, location, and history are intimately connected in *The Ditch*: "By filming on a location close to by the original site of the camp, Wang Bing is able to create this effect of a nightmarish return of the repressed past in the form of ghostly rightists emerging from hidden burrows in the midst of what may at first appear as a documentary representation of the fascinating landscape of today's Gobi desert."[11] Wang shot seventy-five days in extremely difficult conditions in the desert between October 2008 and January 2009.[12] The shoot, totalizing over 130 hours of footage, went undisturbed by the Chinese officials as it took place in a remote area, which Pollacchi has described as "a desert site where caves could be dug underground and where the wintery climate would be as unbearable as in the real camp. After a visit to the remnants of the real camp, the filmmaker decided not to use it as a location. This site would have been too sensitive for all those who had witnessed the Anti-Rightist movement, above all, the survivors and the relatives of the victims."[13] The expression "clandestine production" thus befits *The Ditch*, the remote location making it unlikely that the Chinese authorities would shut down production.

The 2010 film adopts a straightforward narrative structure with an opening sequence, a two-act middle section, and a conclusion. The opening sequence locates the action in "Mingshui, annex of Jiabiangou camp, Gobi Desert, October 1960." Mingshui annex, which was part of the larger Jiabiangou complex and the main reference of the original Chinese title, refers to the camp where prisoners were transferred in October 1960. The spectator is then introduced to the difficult working and living conditions of the inmates who are tasked with digging a ditch. There are two distinct spaces in the film. As Wang points out, there is an above-ground section and an underground section, which were not shot the same way: "The underground is lived in, that's where we most often see the characters. Above ground, however, there's no one. Humanity doesn't exist, only nature exists, absolutely empty."[14] The above-ground sequences feature harsh desert conditions, and they make the viewer think about how unlikely it would have been for prisoners to survive in the desert if they escaped. The first part focuses on the deteriorating living conditions at the camp when the famine hit. Famished and weakened, the prisoners can no longer work and act as quasi-lifeless figures underground. Throughout the film, men who die of hunger are buried outside in the desert in shallow, unmarked graves.[15] The prisoners begin to commit unthinkable acts to survive such as eating rats or vomit, in addition to practicing necrophagy.[16] The second part of the film is inspired by Yang Xianhui's account "Woman from Shanghai," in which the wife of a prisoner travels from Shanghai to Gansu to find her husband, Dong Jianyi, only to be told upon arrival that he died eight days before. The second half of the film focuses on Gu Xiaoyun's quest to find her husband's body and the location of his burial site in the desert—an unmarked grave. The film ends with the escape of two prisoners (drawn from Yang Xianhui's "Escape") and the political decision to free the remaining inmates. These events cannot but recall He Fengming's own retelling in both her memoir and in Wang Bing's *Fengming*. The intertextual references connecting the first two films in the "Anti-Rightist" trilogy, and the great role Yang Xianhui's fictionalized accounts play in the making of the film, cannot be overstated as the foundation for Wang's acts of creative repetition.

## Proof of the Real: From Reportage to Photography

In a short piece titled "The Image as Proof of the Real," which was published in French with translations of letters written by prisoners held at Jiabiangou, Wang Bing tells the story of how he came into possession of two photographs taken in a labor camp. The filmmaker writes that until he started shooting *The Ditch*, he had believed that photographic documentation of the camps did not exist: "I hadn't found any document, any image of the camps, and yet I had interviewed several people."[17] Having been in touch with a man who had worked in one of the camps, Wang visited him, and, to his great surprise, the man gave him photographs showing the camp where he worked in 1957.[18] The man in question was Zhu Zhaonan, who worked as a guard overseeing logistics and accounting at Jiabiangou.[19] Were it not for having been put in touch with Zhu, Wang Bing would not have come into possession of these rare pictures of the camp.[20] Zhu's death is mentioned in *Dead Souls*, and it is accompanied by one of the photographs given by the former camp guard appearing in Wang Bing's piece.

One photograph, in portrait orientation, shows prisoners sitting down with mountains in the background. It is a desert scene showing Zhu Zhaonan riding a bicycle in the foreground, on the right-hand side, facing the photographer. Wang makes two observations on this image. First, the filmmaker carefully describes the type of lodging, blankets, ragged clothes, and everyday objects in the image. Second, the image is clearly torn, and the filmmaker speculates that it is in such a state because someone back in the 1950s did not want the viewer to see someone or something in the image (Wang mentions that the undesirable person in the picture could have been the camp director). Strangely, Wang does not describe the second photograph in his text. The photograph shows a camp guard riding a camel, who is framed in the center of the image and clearly aware that his portrait is being taken, looking directly at the photographer. Wang Bing remarks that *The Ditch* is based on hours spent closely observing the landscape and the men in the photos, paying special attention to how they dressed. In addition to serving as the visual foundation for the "look" of the film, the filmmaker notes that another purpose of the photographs is to help those who did not experience the camps "to visualize [*se figurer*] what happened," and he adds that the most important thing is to be able "to see these men."[21] Pollacchi has echoed Wang Bing's focus on observation and perception: "The plot of the film is purposely fragmentary so that its main concern becomes the observation of a group of men sent to a labour camp in the desert, where they contend with physical exhaustion, cold, and starvation."[22] The filmmaker notes that, after taking possession of these two photos, "it was very important for me to film this story."[23]

In the absence of visual archives to testify to the existence of the labor camps and to serve as the foundation for a fiction film on the topic, we can imagine Wang Bing's euphoria upon seeing these photographs. Wang goes on to describe the content of the images and makes claims about the indexical validity of the pictures and their status as proof of the real. The filmmaker notes that we must talk about what happened in the labor camps, but those discussions will remain limited if there is no indexical proof: "Discussing the camps without proof has no purpose, no value. If these photographs exist, then it's not the same thing. No one can deny the facts."[24] Wang makes the case for the role of these photographs to prove the existence of the camps and to support the potential claims of survivors and potential visitors: "Those who visited the site can recognize the place: mountains can't change! All of it can't change."[25] One can appreciate how, as the foundation for an act of creative repetition, the photos are enmeshed in discourses of originality, indexicality, deniability, veracity, and adaptation. The act of visual adaptation that supports *The Ditch* points to a web of rhetorical figures whose purpose is to convince the audience of the historical existence of the camps—their undeniability—which would result from the very existence of these photographs and their contents. Just like no one could deny the fact of their existence, Wang Bing writes, no one could deny the fact that the visual document tells the truth about the past.

It is not Wang Bing's often naïve claims about indexicality, the real, and immediacy that deserve close attention in his cinema in my opinion. Such claims about representation have been debunked within documentary studies for decades. What matters is the fact that as so-called proofs of the real, these photographs served as the visual foundation for the recreation of the camp in Wang's film and add another layer of complexity to the techniques of creative repetition that the filmmaker has used. The photographs and the film thus enter yet another relationship predicated upon creative repetition that must give us pause. What kind of critical discourse on adaptation could be put forward to discuss this intriguing case involving photographs of labor camp life?

In his polemical interpretation of four photographs from Auschwitz, Didi-Huberman discusses the stakes of images that function as proof of the real. The art historian notes that we turn to either of two positions when it comes to interpretation: either we ask too much, or we ask too little of the image. Asking too much, we run the risk of being disappointed if we ask "the whole truth" of the image: "images are merely stolen shreds, bits of film. They are therefore inadequate."[26] Images are inadequate because what the Chinese documentarian can see in the photograph—a group of men sitting and talking, a guard riding his bicycle—does not even compare to what we know about the labor camps: the number of prisoners who died there, the horrible acts committed, or the struggles to survive reported in memoirs. The other danger is asking too little of the image, which can take the form of reducing the image to the status of simulacrum or, quite interestingly for our purposes, to the status of document. In this case, images would be detached "from their phenomenology, from their specificity, and from their very substance."[27] According to Didi-Huberman, one consequence of misapprehending images is "subjecting them to hypertrophy, in wanting to see everything in them. In short, it consists in wanting to make them *icons* of horror."[28] The other potential danger consists in "reducing, desiccating the image; in seeing in it no more than a *document* of horror."[29] In both cases, the image is prevented from serving a historical purpose: historical events can never be truly represented, or there is no truth to be found in images of the sort in the first place.

Eschewing this untenable position, Didi-Huberman proposes to describe how the image "is made *of all*: by this I refer to its nature as an amalgam, an impurity, visible things mixed with confused things, illusive things mixed with revealing things, visual forms mixed with a certain thought in action."[30] Combined with another concept, the "tear-image" (*image-déchirure*)[31]—which corresponds to the actual material status of one of the photographs that Wang Bing received—the primordial task is to observe the "dialectical plasticity" of images, which ultimately describes the built-in ambivalence of images and "the *dual system* of their working: visible and visual, detail and 'patch,' resemblance and difference, anthropomorphism and abstraction, form and formlessness, comeliness and cruelty, and so on."[32] The art historian concludes that what is at stake is the "dual system of images, the flux and reflux of truth in them. When their surface of *misrecognition* is disturbed by turbulence, by a wave of *cognition*, we cross the difficult but fecund moment of a *test of truth*."[33] What Didi-Huberman describes in these terms is a proposal for a theory of adaptation that, in the case of Wang Bing, tests the limits of adaptation itself. The intriguing status of the film, based on both the adaptation of a fictionalized account and a set of photographs, also tests the notion of historicity indexed as it is to reenactment as a potential carrier of truthful moments.

To fully understand filmmaking as a case of creative repetition, *The Ditch* must be reimbued with ambiguity regarding its combination of fictional and documentary elements. At best, one could speak of the need for proof of the real as the need to experience "proof" to render the experiential and speculative content of the filmic image available again instead of simply accepting the indexical content of any image as guarantee of historical veracity. The notion of reenactment raises important issues about the role of repetition within documentary film and offers a different critique of representation from the one offered within documentary studies.

## Reenactment: The Creative Treatment of History

By having recourse to reenactment in his third feature, *The Ditch*, what was Wang Bing implicitly saying about *West of the Tracks* and *Fengming*? What kind of visible evidence did reenactment help to create? Furthermore, with the benefit of hindsight, what should viewers think of the return to the long-form interview in the third film of the "Anti-Rightist" trilogy, *Dead Souls*, eight years later? What is it about fiction that could have been deemed unsatisfactory to prompt Wang Bing to return to the mise-en-scène and visual approach he had used in *Fengming* in his next film? First, let us examine what reenactment affords the documentary filmmaker as a form of creative repetition in *The Ditch*.

Appearing in several recent award-winning productions, reenactments have played a crucial role in films such as Rithy Panh's *S21: The Khmer Rouge Killing Machine* (2003) and Joshua Oppenheimer's *The Act of Killing* (2012) in which perpetrators are asked to participate in the recreation of past genocidal activities in the absence of archival images. Reenactments have been used in documentary productions when situations are otherwise unfilmable, or "to supplement historical methods that viewers have grown to see as more authentically documentary: interviews, archival or observational footage, and expository narration."[34] A documentarian's recourse to reenactment raises challenging questions about representation, cultural and collective memory, appearance and verisimilitude, narrative construction, testimony, performance, and the ethical stakes of recreating past events in which a person is asked to perform past events.

As a case of creative repetition, reenactment is entangled in issues of indexicality and credibility. Reflecting on reenactment, Nichols writes: "Viewers must recognize a reenactment as a reenactment even if this recognition also dooms the reenactment to its status as a fictionalized repetition of something that has already occurred. Unlike the contemporaneous representation of an event—the classic documentary image, where an indexical link between image and historical occurrence exists—the reenactment forfeits its indexical bond to the original event."[35] The notion of repetition evoked by Nichols is fundamental, as it dovetails with the previous chapter's discussion of He Fengming's performative repetition of her memoir and the arc of Wang Bing's "Anti-Rightist" trilogy, which positions creative repetition as one of the key tropes to make sense of twentieth-century Chinese history. One of the main issues with reenactment, which is singled out by Nichols, pertains to immediacy and situatedness: "The very syntax of reenactments affirms the having-been-thereness of what can never, quite, be here again. Facts remain facts, their verification possible, but the iterative effort of going through the motions of reenacting them imbues such facts with the lived stuff of immediate and situated experience."[36] Reenactments would thus raise questions about the indexical nature of the original event, the illusion of immediacy, and the localized nature of historical experience. As Nichols implicitly frames it, reenactment is always already enmeshed in issues of repetition and doubling (indexicality, mediation, and reiteration) that amount to a radical critique of (documentary) representation.

Gilles Deleuze explored these issues in pioneering fashion in *Difference and Repetition*, in which he orchestrates a wide-ranging critique of representation whose ramifications for artistic practices may not have been fully grasped to this day. Arguing that thought needs the kind of revolution that painting underwent at the beginning of the twentieth century with abstraction, Deleuze posits that the concepts of difference and repetition hold unrecognized potential to accomplish this revolution and generate a new "image of thought." Regarding repetition, which concerns the very essence of reenactment, the French philosopher notes that it "cannot be explained by the form of identity in concepts or representations; in what sense it demands a superior 'positive' principle."[37] Deleuze's goal is to revalorize repetition in the context of the overreliance on identity, representation, and the model-copy dialectic that has been favored in the West since Plato. It is not repetition's identity that is at stake, but finding its singular being: "Repetition must be understood in the pronominal; we must find the Self of repetition, the singularity within that which repeats."[38] For the philosopher, repetition has nothing to do with a mere copy or double: "In every respect, repetition is a transgression. It puts law into question, it denounces its nominal or general character in favour of a more profound and more artistic reality."[39] The reader may ask: what form does this more profound, artistic reality take? Addressing Kierkegaard and Nietzsche as two exemplary philosophers who made repetition a cornerstone of their thinking, Deleuze explains that repetition, as a form of artistic reality, produces unforeseen affects, which is to say, pre-individual movements affecting thought and body: "It is not enough, therefore, for them to propose a new representation of movement; representation is already mediation. Rather, it is a question of producing within the work a movement capable of affecting the mind outside of all representation; it is a question of making movement itself a work, without interposition; of substituting direct signs for mediate representations; of inventing vibrations, rotations, whirlings, gravitations, dances or leaps which directly touch the mind."[40]

Deleuze's wide-ranging reflections on repetition put in perspective both the concept of reenactment as examined within documentary studies and the secondary literature on *The Ditch*, especially regarding the controversial performance of the actors. The new "image of cinematic thought" offered in a film like *The Ditch*, which is predicated on two main techniques of creative repetition—adaptation and reenactment—stages a confrontation between representation, performance, and repetition to the point of excess. This is reflected in what scholars have identified as the theatrical and melodramatic performance of the lead actress, Xu Cenzi, who plays Dong Jianyi's wife. Veg has noted the uneasy relationship between reenactment and performance in the film: "However, where on-location re-enactment traditionally serves to heighten the dramatization of documentary, Wang Bing's performance techniques on the contrary distantiate his fictional representation."[41] He goes on to remark how performance and repetition come together to create a strange historical effect whereby a twenty-first-century film revives dramatic codes from 1950s Chinese cinema, which would result in inauthentic performances: "the acting (mostly by amateurs or semi-amateur cultural workers Wang Bing hired locally in Gansu) seems to 'quote' the propaganda films of the 1950s (inspired by Stanislavsky's 'method'): cadres and prisoners speak in the same ponderous tones, use the same highly theatrical gestures and voice effects."[42] Veg concludes that *The Ditch*, suffering from "excessive authenticity,"[43] is "not so much a re-enactment of 'reality' as a self-reflexive re-actualization of the discursive and visual codes of the Mao era."[44] Pollacchi raises similar issues concerning performance and critically notes that "[e]ven when the viewers have been prompted to accept the assumption of a historical re-enactment, the excessively stylized performances, and the clashing of this with the starkness of the location continue to expose the fictional apparatus so that the process of film-making becomes the real focus of the viewing experience."[45] She concludes that the actors' "exaggerated manners of representation often make them look unskilled: either over-expressing their roles or being detached from their characters so as to increase the perception of displacement and absurdity that imbues the picture."[46]

It is important to put in perspective Veg's and Pollacchi's critical views of *The Ditch*. Given that the criticisms seem to boil down to theatrical and performance issues, it is instructive to address the film's supposed shortcomings from the point of view of the differences that Deleuze identified between the "theatre of representation" and the "theatre of repetition." Deleuze notes that "[t]he theatre of repetition is opposed to the theatre of representation, just as movement is opposed to the concept and to representation which refers it back to the concept. In the theatre of repetition, we experience pure forces, dynamic lines in space which act without intermediary upon the spirit, and link it directly with nature and history, with a language which speaks before words, with gestures which develop before organised bodies, with masks before faces, with spectres and phantoms before characters— the whole apparatus of repetition as a 'terrible power.'"[47]

Combined with Deleuze's reflections on repetition as forms of displacement and disguise, Nichols' insight into artistic interpretation leads to the conclusion that reenactment proposes a singular case of repetition that bears the mark of creative agency first and foremost. In addition to the typological distinctions that Nichols makes between fantasmatic types of reenactment, what may be his most important insight concerns what reenactments truly offer the spectator and what they fail to deliver: "They [reenactments] do not provide evidentiary images of situations and events in the historical world . . . It is, in fact, not historical evidence but an artistic interpretation, always offered from a distinct perspective and carrying, embedded within it, further evidence of the voice of the filmmaker."[48] A film such as *The Ditch* provides a "cinema of repetition" in which reenactment plays a rhetorical, performative role in acting as an agent of historical and critical persuasion by appealing to perception, emotion, affect, and rationality. As put to work in *The Ditch*, reenactment corresponds to how Deleuze describes the work of repetition and what it entails: "The powers of repetition include displacement and disguise."[49]

Margulies echoes some of the preceding points on reenactment as a technique of creative repetition imbued with powers to displace and disguise in her study of reenactment in postwar and contemporary cinema. Margulies addresses the notion of repetition and unpacks the temporal aspect of reenactment by zeroing in on embodiment, belatedness, and the kind of archive that is constituted through repetition: "Reenactment is an explicitly after-the-fact practice that obviates the conventions ruling the adjustments between the different temporalities of the cinematic apparatus, narrative, and reality . . . The films push us to ask how the gap between past and present is configured within the work, what the force of citation is in the political present, and how reenactment contributes, through embodied experience, to a future archive."[50] The issue of temporality, especially belatedness, is compounded by the problem of mediation in the case of reenactment, as Margulies points out when discussing "the impossibility to match reenactment's chronological indeterminacy (a person standing for herself twenty years earlier) and the indexical precision of direct record evident in archival footage."[51] Margulies goes on to tease out the temporal, historical, and ethical implications of reenactment, noting its "split agency and elastic temporality."[52]

As a technique of creative repetition, reenactment illustrates the philosophical stakes at the heart of the concept of repetition within documentary studies. The preceding discussion of reenactment as a case of creative repetition helps to rethink the achievements of a film such as *The Ditch*. As Nichols and Margulies imply, reenactment is a singular form of creative repetition whose indexical and temporal ramifications deserve closer attention. Functioning as a technique of creative repetition, reenactment raises ontological questions about the status of the document by calling into question its relationship to the historical event represented; it creates the illusion of an immediate access to the past, the event, and the people involved; it can only provide one perspective on a past event, that of the filmmaker, whose voice should not be confused with the actual, irretrievable past; it is more about the creative license of the filmmaker than historical accuracy; and, finally, either as an emotional appeal or a rational plea, the efficacy of reenactment rests on an affective charge that cannot go unmentioned, which denotes an embodied experience of repetition. The archive that is constituted through reenactment reflects the creative treatment of history in other words. As Caillet has argued, reenactment is not about representing or reproducing a past event. Rather, it mobilizes the resources of the present to propose an "interrogation of the process of history writing"[53] in audiovisual form. That is its singularity as an ambiguous form of representation that challenges representation itself.

That is how reenactment reveals the undeniable, although often overlooked, creative side of repetition when it moves away from a logic of representation to support a logic of repetition that troubles the relationship between original and copy. The fact that this troubled mimetic relationship is indexed to performance signals the performative dimension of reenactment and, therefore, an unexplored aspect of repetition. The ambiguous regime of truth that reenactment proposes evades a logic of representation predicated on the original and the copy to privilege a critique of representation in which actions and performances take center stage. Reenactment is the source of a performative archive in *The Ditch* in which the process of history writing is subverted, only to be contained by the fictional elements. I concur with Caillet when she claims that reenactment is a "critical mode of representation" that has generated "a praxis-based regime of knowledge."[54] Reenactment would not so much signify the revelation of historical truths as offer the opportunity "to rethink the past to better evaluate and criticize it."[55] As shown in Wang Bing's *The Ditch*, the performative dimension of reenactment forces the documentary rewriting of Maoist history and the constitution of an audiovisual archive combining elements of fiction and documentary that has yet to find a name.

## Conclusion

Wang Bing's *The Ditch* laid the foundation for what *Dead Souls* would offer eight years later. With its close observation of the degradation and humiliation that characterized the lives of those who lived in the camp, the film provides a stimulating addition to the "Anti-Rightist" trilogy given that *Fengming* had failed to *visualize* the camp site itself in the Gobi Desert. *Dead Souls* would combine visual and rhetorical strategies derived from both *Fengming* and *The Ditch*, and the 2018 film would show the actual camp sites and remains of inmates in the desert without relying on voyeuristic tendencies. In *Dead Souls*, the spectator can appreciate how Wang Bing, as a *minjian* intellectual and artist, builds a complex audiovisual monument to the victims and survivors of Maoist politics and its ravages as revealed by the landscape itself. It is difficult to imagine that Wang Bing would have arrived at the masterful mise-en-scène and exploration of *Dead Souls* had he not gone through the experiences of making *Fengming* and *The Ditch*, the two films that tested Wang Bing's ability to tell the stories of Jiabiangou, and had he not used the techniques of creative repetition (adaptation and reenactment) discussed in this chapter.

One could argue that it is with *The Ditch* that Wang Bing became increasingly interested in the role that the landscape of the camp could play to reconstruct Chinese history in a way that would complement the oral history film (*Fengming*) and the fiction film (*The Ditch*). It is the initial foray into a critical topography of the Gobi Desert that is offered in *The Ditch*, one that will occupy more screen time in *Dead Souls* in which testimonies will share the screen with landscape sequences that Wang Bing had first explored in his short, *Traces* (*Yizhi* 遗址, 2014). In the end, it is not so much making the decision between documentary and fiction that seemed to matter for the filmmaker as the intention to test two techniques of creative repetition having to do with the adaptation of reportage literature and the reenactment of historical moments on location. In *Dead Souls*, the filmmaker would turn to the dialectical potential of documenting both human and nonhuman survivors.

## Notes

1. Wang Bing, "La memoria rimossa della Cina. Conversazione con Wang Bing," in *Wang Bing: Il cinema nella Cina che cambia*, ed. Daniela Persico (Milan: Agenzia X, 2010), 15.
2. Wang Bing, *Alors, la Chine. Entretiens avec Emmanuel Burdeau et Eugenio Renzi* (Paris: Les Prairies ordinaires, 2014), 128.
3. Sebastian Veg, "The Limits of Representation: Wang Bing's Labour Camp Films," *Journal of Chinese Cinemas* 6, no. 2 (2014): 184.
4. This account does not appear in the abridged English translation of Yang Xianhui's *Jiabiangou jishi*.
5. In Yang Xianhui's "Woman from Shanghai," Gu's first name is given ("I'm from Shanghai. My name is Gu Xiaoyun" (*Woman from Shanghai: Tales of Survival from a Chinese Labor Camp*, trans. Wen Huang [New York: Anchor Books, 2010], 40), while in Wang Bing's film, it is not. I will refer to her as Gu Xiaoyun in this chapter.
6. Yang, *Woman from Shanghai*, 28.
7. Wang, "La memoria rimossa della Cina," 15–16.
8. The ethical scenario is even more complicated if one considers that Yang Xianhui's fictionalized accounts, on which the script draws, themselves contain extreme moral dilemmas concerning matters of survival and inhumanity.
9. Veg, "The Limits of Representation," 183.
10. Veg, "The Limits of Representation," 183.
11. Veg, "The Limits of Representation," 180.
12. Wang, "La memoria rimossa della Cina," 18. Wang tells of the hardships he faced during the shoot, including directing the actress playing the "woman from Shanghai" and working in the desert. Reflecting on his struggles directing his only feature-length fiction film to date, Wang has few good memories to share (Wang, *Alors, la Chine*, 122–27). Wang has also confessed that he did not ask for his subjects' consent and told them he was making a fiction film, fearing

that they would not have collaborated had he said he was shooting a documentary about Jiabiangou (Wang, *Alors, la Chine*, 109–10).
13. Elena Pollacchi, *Wang Bing's Filmmaking of the China Dream: Narratives, Witnesses and Marginal Spaces* (Amsterdam: Amsterdam University Press, 2021), 134.
14. Wang, *Alors, la Chine*, 117.
15. Williams and Wu report that there existed a significant gap between theory and practice when the time came to dispose of bodies, which is reflected in the struggles of Dong Jianyi's wife, Gu Xiaoyun, to recover her husband's corpse: "According to a laogai manual for cadres and guards, a dead prisoner's ash urn or corpse is supposed to be held for the deceased's relatives to pick up within a prescribed period of time. If nobody comes to pick up the inmate's remains within that time, then they are supposed to be buried in a marked grave. In actual practice, however, countless deceased inmates have been buried in unmarked graves." Philip F. Williams and Yenna Wu, *The Great Wall of Confinement: The Chinese Prison Camp through Contemporary Fiction and Reportage* (Berkeley: University of California Press, 2004), 143–44.
16. In the literature on *The Ditch*, scholars write of cannibalistic acts having been performed in the camp, when in fact what took place was necrophagy.
17. Wang Bing, "L'image comme preuve du réel. À propos d'images des camps," in *Wang Bing. Un cinéaste en Chine aujourd'hui*, ed. Caroline Renard, Isabelle Anselme and François Amy de la Bretèque (Aix-en-Provence: Presses Universitaires de Provence, 2014), 147.
18. Two photographs frame Wang Bing's "L'image comme preuve du réel. À propos d'images des camps." They appear on pages 146 and 150, respectively.
19. It is the only time in the "Anti-Rightist" trilogy that a perpetrator is allowed to share his memories of the camp on screen. This is a rare occasion for the viewer to see Wang Bing the interviewer in action, asking questions of the subject without adopting an inquisitive or reproachful tone. What is crucial to underline, in a way that connects *The Ditch* and *Dead Souls*, is that it is because of the gift of a perpetrator, Zhu Zhaonan, that Wang could show a photograph of the Jiabiangou camp in *Dead Souls*. Given that the guards were in their forties or fifties at the time, most of them have passed, and that explains the presence of only one guard in the film, according to the documentarian.
20. In Wang, *Alors, la Chine*, 115, the filmmaker mentions that Zhu Zhaonan gave him *three* photographs, while only two appear in Wang's article, "L'image comme preuve du réel." In the same interview, Wang Bing points out that the first photograph was the portrait of another guard, and it is this picture that is not reproduced in the article. This unidentified guard in the image is the same man who rides a camel in one of the two photographs framing Wang's article on p. 150.
21. Wang, "L'image comme preuve du réel," 148.
22. Pollacchi, *Wang Bing's Filmmaking of the China Dream*, 136.
23. Wang, "L'image comme preuve du réel," 148.
24. Wang, "L'image comme preuve du réel," 148.
25. Wang, "L'image comme preuve du réel," 148.
26. Georges Didi-Huberman, *Images in Spite of All: Four Photographs from Auschwitz*, trans. Shane B. Lillis (Chicago: University of Chicago Press, 2008), 33.
27. Didi-Huberman, *Images in Spite of All*, 33.
28. Didi-Huberman, *Images in Spite of All*, 34, emphasis in original.
29. Didi-Huberman, *Images in Spite of All*, 34, emphasis in original.
30. Didi-Huberman, *Images in Spite of All*, 65, emphasis in original.
31. Didi-Huberman, *Images in Spite of All*, 79.

32. Didi-Huberman, *Images in Spite of All*, 79, emphasis in original.
33. Didi-Huberman, *Images in Spite of All*, 83, emphases in original.
34. Jonathan Kahana, "Introduction: What Now? Presenting Reenactment," *Framework: Journal of Cinema and Media* 50, no. 1–2 (2009): 48.
35. Bill Nichols, *Speaking Truths with Film: Evidence, Ethics, Politics in Documentary* (Berkeley: University of California Press, 2016), 35.
36. Nichols, *Speaking Truths with Film*, 41.
37. Gilles Deleuze, *Difference and Repetition*, trans. Paul Patton (New York: Columbia University Press, 1995), 19.
38. Deleuze, *Difference and Repetition*, 23.
39. Deleuze, *Difference and Repetition*, 3.
40. Deleuze, *Difference and Repetition*, 8.
41. Veg, "The Limits of Representation," 180.
42. Veg, "The Limits of Representation," 179.
43. Veg, "The Limits of Representation," 180.
44. Veg, "The Limits of Representation," 183.
45. Pollacchi, *Wang Bing's Filmmaking of the China Dream*, 136.
46. Pollacchi, *Wang Bing's Filmmaking of the China Dream*, 144.
47. Deleuze, *Difference and Repetition*, 10.
48. Nichols, *Speaking Truths with Film*, 49.
49. Deleuze, *Difference and Repetition*, 288.
50. Ivone Margulies, *In Person: Reenactment in Postwar and Contemporary Cinema* (Oxford: Oxford University Press, 2019), 5.
51. Margulies, *In Person*, 13.
52. Margulies, *In Person*, 13.
53. Aline Caillet, *Dispositifs critiques. Le documentaire, du cinéma aux arts visuels* (Rennes: Presses Universitaires de Rennes, 2014), 97.
54. Caillet, *Dispositifs critiques*, 106.
55. Caillet, *Dispositifs critiques*, 106.

# 4
# *Dead Souls*

## Documenting Human and Nonhuman Survivors

Described as a Chinese *Shoah* (1985) by film critics, Wang Bing's *Dead Souls* (*Si linghun*, 2018) is an eight-hour-long cinematic tour de force documenting survivors' life-shattering experiences of the Jiabiangou and Mingshui reeducation camps located in Gansu Province, as well as the camp sites themselves. The *film-fleuve* belongs to a select group of recent documentaries such as Patricio Guzmán's *Nostalgia for the Light* (2010) and Almudena Carracedo and Robert Bahar's *The Silence of Others* (2018) that have captured the imagination of spectators because of their stunning ability to evoke traumatic historical experiences, including Ai Xiaoming's thematically related *Jiabiangou Elegy* (2016) and Wu Wenguang's "Folk Memory Project" (2010–). In his 2018 film, Wang erects a visual monument to the survivors and pays homage to the souls of those who starved to death in the labor camps. Distilled from one hundred and twenty testimonies and over six hundred hours of rushes, the film offers extended interviews with survivors—most of whom were in their eighties at the time—that provide a unique immersive viewing experience. The memorable encounter with the survivors' bodies and voices complements the published oral histories of the historical period by singling out the act of witnessing as an embodied, affective process to be experienced over several hours.

Premiered at the 2018 Cannes Film Festival, *Dead Souls* is a film of exceptional length, but it is not the first of its kind in Wang Bing's body of work. Indeed, in addition to the fourteen-hour *Crude Oil* (2014) meant for the gallery space, the filmmaker came to prominence in 2003 with his breakthrough documentary film, the nine-hour-long *West of the Tracks*. As the final work in Wang Bing's "Anti-Rightist" trilogy, *Dead Souls* serves as the culminating point of the journey that began in 2007 with the release of *Fengming*. What kind of relationship is established between the audiovisual strategies used in *Fengming* and *The Ditch*, which include documenting the Anti-Rightist Campaign and the Great Famine by turning the female body into an embodied archive and drawing on techniques of creative repetition (namely, adaptation and reenactment) and *Dead Souls*? As this chapter argues, the 2018 film provides a thoughtful reflection on the stakes of documenting both human and non-human survivors.

*Dead Souls* adopts a more challenging approach to the survivor interview than *Fengming*, whether it be in terms of content or recording technique, and the 2018 film offers a more diverse viewing experience combining interviews and landscape sequences that allow the filmmaker to distance himself from the typical testimonial setting and the mise-en-scène of the oral film (still amply used in the film). Where the work greatly departs from the previous efforts in the trilogy is in its nonchronological approach to testimony and its inclusion of three thought-provoking landscape sequences. In this chapter, I pay particular attention to how, as a *minjian* filmmaker, Wang Bing documents human survivors by playing with the chronology of the interviews in the film and how he documents the historically charged landscapes of the Mingshui annex and the nonhuman material traces that serve as evidence of intergenerational and historical trauma. After discussing how the landscape sequences shot for *The Ditch* differ from those of *Dead Souls*, I turn to how the filmmaker, in the final work of the trilogy, is not only interested in human survivors, but also captivated by the nonhuman remnants that have equally survived the passage of time in the Chinese landscape. The chapter closes with some considerations on landscape as both a view and a site calling for its own ontology, epistemology, and practice.

## The Time of the Human Survivor

At the preproduction stage, *Dead Souls* bore a different title ("Past in the Present"), for which Wang Bing wrote a treatment in 2012. In addition to the synopsis, the treatment offers background historical information on the Anti-Rightist Campaign, data on the number of prisoners held at Jiabiangou, descriptions of the conditions in which the prisoners lived, and mention of the pardons that the Chinese government issued between 1978 and 1981. The filmmaker notes that he met and interviewed over one hundred survivors of the Jiabiangou labor camp at the preproduction stage and that "their stories and recollections have been crucial in helping me to understand the three decades that followed the establishment of the People's Republic of China in 1949. Their words and their lives are a window to our shared history. Over the course of many years and many exchanges, I have come to know and perhaps even understand these elderly survivors of the gulag. Now in their seventies, eighties or nineties, they are considered by some to be eccentric, even odd. Many are in poor or failing health, living in poverty, estranged from their families or socially isolated, distrustful of strangers and psychologically scarred. They escaped the gulag only to return to a life of hardship, and spent decades living as social and political pariahs before they were finally rehabilitated and cleared of outstanding charges."[1] As previously mentioned, it is in the name of historical rectification, and as an educational initiative, that Wang Bing has made the "Anti-Rightist" trilogy. He adds:

"For anyone who hasn't lived through it, it is difficult to comprehend the suffering they experienced, perhaps because people today seem to pay such scant attention to history. This lacuna of historical awareness was my motivation for embarking on a long documentary project about the present-day lives of the Jiabiangou survivors."[2] The filmmaker further notes that the disconnect between past and present reflects the choice of not making a traditional oral history film: "If we were to focus only on narrating past events, the survivors would become nothing more than talking heads, alienating the audience from the events being described onscreen. Because we exist in a different time frame, we cannot rely solely upon our imaginations to return us to the past, or to bridge the gap between past and present truths. In addition, this is a period in Chinese history that will be unfamiliar to many Chinese and most overseas audiences. For the survivors themselves, the Anti-Rightist Campaign is not just history but part of their lives, an experience they lived through. For those who haven't lived it, it is a tale from the distant past, an experience far removed from our present reality."[3] The filmmaker makes two crucial distinctions in the preceding quote. First, Wang's wish not to make an oral history film such as *Fengming* is quite revealing, as it indicates the implicit disposition not to reuse the mise-en-scène of the 2007 film and its focus on only one survivor. Second, the documentarian elaborates on the potential disjunction between the Chinese past and present and on what implications it might suggest for spectatorship, history, and temporality.

*Dead Souls* was shot over several years across China, and the camp sites referenced in the film are Jiabiangou, Mingshui, and Xintiandun. As previously mentioned, Jiabiangou refers to the larger group of camps with the central unit named after it; Xintiandun was located seven kilometers from the Jiabiangou central unit; and the Mingshui camp, located eighty kilometers from Jiabiangou, opened in the fall of 1960 and gives its name to the 2018 film's tripartite structure: Mingshui I, Mingshui II, and Mingshui III. Each part begins with the same intertitle providing background historical information on the Anti-Rightist Campaign. Each part ends with the same intertitle indicating the number of survivors and when they were rehabilitated by the regime. The intertitle directly addresses the survivors interviewed in the film and acknowledges that their "pain has woken the sleeping souls of the deceased so that all the hardships endured be known to as many people as possible."

There are only twenty-four sequences in this eight-hour-long documentary, seventeen of which are devoted to oral testimonies. The film adopts a simple structure: the first segment presents six interviews totaling two hours and twenty minutes of screen time. The interviews present the historical background and the various relationships between the survivors. A recurring theme in many of the interviews is the notion of culpability, and the survivors asking what it is that they were guilty of, many of whom having had the best interests of the CCP at heart when they first criticized it following the recommendation of Chairman Mao. The film generally alternates between a series of oral testimonies and in-situ documentation of the camp. Compared to the other works in the trilogy, the film makes a crucial departure by including landscape sequences and an interview with a former guard in which he appears in the frame with the filmmaker asking direct questions of the subject, which represents a first in Wang Bing's cinema. This is the last witness to be interviewed in the film. Another stunning interview features Fan Peilin, the wife of a deceased prisoner, and visible evidence of the camp in the form of letters and photos shown on screen. The monumental film ends with the filmmaker's camera exploring the landscape, searching for remains that it can visually collect.

Each interviewee's name and age appear the same way on screen, as do the location and date when the interview was recorded. The camera is most often set on a tripod facing the interviewee and offering a frontal view. Beds, sofas, and chairs fill the frame, and doorways and windows provide natural light. The interviewee is either alone or shares the space with a spouse or family members. With just a few exceptions, interviewees are almost all men; the few women remain silent for the most part (though the last interviewee is a widow, Fan Peilin, whose testimony is particularly heartbreaking). Like He Fengming, the interviewees share their memories of the period, express their incomprehension, and retell traumatic experiences in the camps. However, the interviewees in the 2018 film do not share He Fengming's fluid speech and apparently flawless memory as they often labor to finish their sentences. The interviews are lengthy, each survivor having between 20 and 40 minutes of uninterrupted screen time. The interviews took place over two periods of time: in 2005–2006, that is, at the preproduction stage of *The Ditch*, with additional interviews shot in 2016–2017, when Wang Bing returned to add new material and reinterview certain subjects.

Reminiscent of *Fengming*, oral history sits at the methodological center of *Dead Souls*, and the film acts as a vivid counterpart to the published oral histories of the period, such as Zhou Xun's *Forgotten Voices of Mao's Great Famine, 1958–1962*, which features the voices of survivors and their tales of horror, including acts of necrophagy, and the first documentary history of the Great Famine drawing on previously unknown documents such as official correspondence, letters, confessions, and interviews;[4] Frank Dikötter's historical study *Mao's Great Famine: The History of China's Most Devastating Catastrophe*;[5] and Yang Jisheng's *Tombstone: The Great Chinese Famine 1958–1962*, originally published in Hong Kong in 2008 and banned in China.[6]

The extreme length of both Yang Jisheng's *Tombstone* and Wang Bing's *Dead Souls* makes us pause and reflect on the apparent need for extreme durational experiences to bear witness to the Anti-Rightist Campaign and the Great Famine. As a monumental documentary, *Dead Souls* faces similar challenges to those of other extremely long documentary films such as *The Sorrow and the Pity* (1969), *The Battle of Chile* (1975–1979), *Shoah* (1985), and Wang Bing's own breakthrough epic, the nine-hour-long *West of the Tracks*. All these films have their longueurs, but the value of such extreme visual experiences lies in how they structure the work of collective memory and testimony as a series of moments to be shared over a long period of time. As such, they embed a sustained reflection on temporality that deserves closer attention. Indeed, Wang's film is an additive and affective experience of duration, which functions as a gigantic vehicle for experiencing the evils of the Communist regime and sharing the survivors' lived time as they engage in testimonial interview sessions. What is particularly fascinating is how the survivors' re-experienced lived time intersects with an extremely long process of revelation.

*Dead Souls* makes extreme demands on human perception over several hours. The documentary is, from an epistemological point of view, also about time passing, historically speaking, and the ravages of time on collective memory. Restoring a sense of time and experience in their durational aspects, whereby the documented unfolding of history comes to dominate, is key in Wang's film. The phenomenology of cinematic duration, and its related affects, is predicated on a nonchronological treatment of historical temporality in the film, which is manifested in how the interviews are sequenced. Indeed, the nonchronological approach challenges the typical linear treatment found in published oral histories of the Anti-Rightist Campaign and the Great Famine because of the cyclical temporality—or loop quality—that plays with the past and the present. What is particularly interesting is that *Dead Souls*, as opposed to traditional interview-based historical documentaries, uses a web of cross-references that challenges the chronologically linear witnessing process and, therefore, better renders the nonchronological functioning of individual memory.

Most crucially, *Dead Souls* plays with time by alternating the two key periods of shooting: 2005–2006 and 2016–2017. Consider Zhou Huinan's interview, shot in 2005, which opens the documentary. He is framed sitting on the couch, and his wife, Gao Guifang, 86, is sitting next to him. This first interview, lasting thirty-five minutes, provides broad historical contextualization for the rest of the film by focusing on the subject's retelling of the events that led to the historical debacle of the late 1950s. This first interview lasts thirty-five minutes. After having shown a five-minute interview with Zhou Huinan's brother, Zhou Zhinan, and his funeral and burial (eighteen-minute sequence), we unexpectedly return to Zhou Huinan's wife, Gao Guifang, but this time the year is 2016, and she is now ninety-seven and poignantly expresses her wish to die. The eleven-year gap between the 2005 interview with her husband, now deceased, and the 2016 interview creates an uncanny temporal loop for the viewer that is used on numerous occasions in the film to challenge both the idea of chronological time in the case of survivors and their family members and the viewers' own understanding of historical time and memory.

Wang's approach to chronology makes his documentary a complex, multi-layered affair in terms of temporality. A different temporal strategy is found in the first part of the film, "Mingshui I," where we are introduced to two survivors, Cao Zonghua and Chen Zonghai, who were interviewed in August and October 2016, respectively. At the beginning of "Mingshui II," Wang's handheld camera follows an unidentified man walking in the desert. It turns out the man is Chen Zonghai. What is particularly fascinating is that we have gone back in time at the beginning of Mingshui II: the year is 2005, and thus Chen is eleven years younger. We have gone from the 2016 interview with Chen (who was eighty-five in Mingshui I) to the beginning of Mingshui II where he is seventy-four. A similar temporal loop also occurs for Cao Zonghua at the beginning of Mingshui II. The filmmaker's ingenious strategy is to play historical time against chronological time in this sequence, as both survivors revisit the camp site after more than forty years. Bearing in mind the filmmaker's comments in the treatment for "The Past in the Present," the nonchronological approach to Chinese history adopted in such sequences demonstrates a concern for the temporality of the survivor's memory as it negotiates spaces of past trauma and present-day realities that often reveal the disjointed nature of the mnemonic process. I return to this sequence featuring both Chen Zonghai and Cao Zonghua below to tease out the importance of landscape in the film and how it is indexed to the nonhuman.

## Landscape Matters: From *The Ditch* to *Dead Souls*

Wang Bing's innovative approach to chronology and storytelling in *Dead Souls* makes the spectator think about the "Anti-Rightist" trilogy as a whole and how the order in which some sequences have been shot does not follow the actual release dates of the films themselves. Indeed, some documentary material shot at the pre-production stage for *The Ditch* ended up in *Dead Souls*. *The Ditch*, which came out in 2010, features sequences shot in the six years prior to its release. Premiered in 2018, *Dead Souls* contains interviews and landscape sequences shot in 2005 and 2006, which correspond to the period when the filmmaker was hard at work on *The Ditch*. The spectator watching *Dead Souls* may not realize that the landscape sequences in Mingshui I and Mingshui II were actually shot as preparatory work for *The Ditch* in 2005 and may think that, because *Dead Souls* was released in 2018, its material postdates *The Ditch* when in fact it is not the case. For example, the first two landscape sequences in *Dead Souls* were shot in 2005, whereas the final landscape sequence was shot in 2012, that is, after the release of *The Ditch* in 2010. These facts indicate how complex *Dead Souls* is in terms of chronology as both the production schedule and, as previously discussed, the sequencing of the interviews and landscape segments emphasize that chronology is an issue affecting both the production of the film and the way its historical material is structured and processed. Comparing the landscape sequences in *The Ditch* to those of *Dead Souls* helps to better understand the transition from recording reenactments in the desert to documenting human and nonhuman survivors on site in *Dead Souls*.

The original Chinese title of *The Ditch*, *Jiabiangou*, denotes the importance of naming and locating the forced labor camp compared to translations that put the emphasis on the admittedly less impactful "ditch." On the one hand, such transformations signal the fear that Western audiences will not know to what Jiabiangou refers geographically, politically, and symbolically in the Chinese mind. On the other hand, changing *Jiabiangou* to *The Ditch* has ethical implications for both the significance of the camp in Chinese history and the sufferings of those who died there, including the family members who grieved their passing. It is the name of the camp itself, rather than the ditch (which, for all intents and purposes, does not play an important role in the film), that orients a particular understanding of place, space, and landscape. This last point relates to the importance of shooting on location and the otherworldly effect that the desert lends the film considering the horrors that happened there.

In *The Ditch*, place, space, and performance join forces to create a unique affective audiovisual experience in which gender and landscape reveal another side of the Anti-Rightist Campaign and the forced labor camps that concerns the unsuspected role of landscape in the film. While scholars have discussed the affected performance of actress Xu Cenzi, who plays Dong Jianyi's wife, Gu Xiaoyun, and its indebtedness to tropes of melodrama, they have not discussed how the actress's performance is intimately linked to the representation of landscape in the 2010 film.[7] Wang's first film shot in HD, *The Ditch* departed from the aesthetics of *West of the Tracks* and *Fengming* and not only captured Xu's performance as Gu Xiaoyun, whose journey to find her dead husband's grave occupies the second half of the film, but it also recorded pristine images of the desert and memorable scenes of nighttime videography. What deserves closer attention is how the performance of the actress is indexed to the representation of the desert.

In *The Ditch*, there are three sequences featuring Gu Xiaoyun and the landscape. The first is when she leaves the dormitory and walks aimlessly in the desert in search of her husband's grave. The second is the five-minute sequence in which Gu examines unmarked graves, trying to find the name of her husband on one of them. Finally, there is the moving scene when Gu does find Dong Jianyi's body, which is followed by the burning of his body in the desert before she returns to Shanghai. These three scenes exemplify the role of reenactment as creative repetition combining the fictionalized account in Yang Xianhui's "Shanghai nüren" (Woman from Shanghai), which is itself based on He Fengming's account of her quest to find her husband's unmarked grave, the performance of Xu Cenzi, and the arid landscape. These scenes in *The Ditch* thus function as a second repetition—after Yang Xianhui's version—of a wife coming to terms with finding her husband's abandoned body in the desert.

The fourteen-minute sequence combining Gu Xiaoyun and the landscape itself is a masterful instance of a filmmaker erecting an audiovisual monument to one woman's sufferings. In the early morning hours, Gu is seen exiting the underground cave where she was invited to stay the night. Having learned of her husband's death, she decides to go outside and search for his unmarked grave. The authorities do not know where Dong Jianyi was buried, which makes Gu's search a difficult one because there are hundreds of unmarked graves in the desert. In what direction should she go? What strikes the viewer is the overbearing presence of the wind in the soundtrack, as the camera follows Gu's exploration of the desert. The windswept landscape greatly complements the images of Gu's journey in the desert where we empathize with a woman who wishes to find her husband's grave, but who receives little help from the prisoners. She will spend an entire day looking for the body, fighting the elements and digging graves with her bare hands. The following morning, Gu turns to Xiao Li and tells him that she needs a shovel to continue her search. Making a run for it, Li wants to reach Dong's body before Gu does because he knows his body has been desecrated. Upon reaching the body, Gu emits a heartbreaking wail and cries uncontrollably; she collapses over her husband's body, and then she resists the men who want to take her away. The end of the sequence shows the cremation of Dong's body, which is placed on a big pile of firewood. Finally, Gu collects her husband's ashes and bones and takes them back to Shanghai. It is her last appearance in the film.

Yang Xianhui's "Woman from Shanghai" provides the blueprint for this scene. What the medium of film contributes to Yang's depiction is twofold. First, the audiovisual elements greatly add to the literary depiction. As captured in the film, the Gobi Desert offers an unforgettable background to Gu's sufferings. The loud wind gusts in the soundtrack, the blinding dust, and the unwelcoming expanse of arid land frame the actions of a woman whose quest to find her husband in such conditions appears hopeless. Second, Xu Cenzi's performance as the helpless wife commands the attention of spectators when ceaselessly looking for her dead husband's body in the desert. Her unsteady movements, cries for help, and despair; her relentless desire to find her husband facing uncooperative men; her inability to contain her sorrows upon finding the body; and her wailing combining pain, grief, and anger[8] are all affect-laden elements that evoke the pain that countless women must have felt upon learning of their husbands passing in the camps and facing the inability to pay them their last respects.

## The Landscape of the Nonhuman and the "Wind of History"

There are three landscape sequences in *Dead Souls* in which Wang Bing departs from the mise-en-scène previously adopted to record the testimonies of survivors. These landscape sequences cannot but call to mind *The Ditch* and the various scenes in which the Gu Xiaoyun character appears in the desert looking for her husband's unmarked grave. To make sense of the differences in approaches from *The Ditch* to

*Dead Souls*, I am inspired by what Margulies has said of the limitations of reenactment and the impeding return to the original site serving as evidential proof: "The performative efficacy of reenactment films dealing with mass atrocity depends on the actual return of original victims or perpetrators to former sites of physical or psychological trauma so their testimonials may serve parajuridical, evidentiary roles as well as a posttraumatic gauge of the presence of the past now."[9]

It is plausible that Wang's experiences of shooting the landscape sequences for *The Ditch* sparked greater interest in landscape itself, and the nonhuman remains on site, and prompted him to return to the landscape material shot in 2005 and integrate it into *Dead Souls*. The 2018 film would thus use landscape to supplement both the sit-down interview mode of the 2007 oral history film, *Fengming*, and the reenactment-based retelling of *The Ditch*. That is not to say that the first two films in the trilogy are either incomplete or unsuccessful. Rather, in *Dead Souls*, Wang Bing seems to have wanted to not only document aging survivors' labor camp experiences in long-form interviews, but he was also interested in further exploring an aspect of the Anti-Rightist Campaign that he had not fully documented before that concerned the actual landscape of nonhuman material traces that is still visible in the Gansu Desert. Pollacchi captures what motivated Wang Bing to explore the landscape of the Mingshui annex and depart from the reenactment-based approach of *The Ditch*: "For approximately 40 minutes, the camera keeps exploring the original site of the Mingshui camp, allowing the viewers to mentally insert the witnesses' narratives in their actual space. What in *The Ditch* was a cinematic re-enactment, here has turned into an abstract re-enactment that takes place in the viewers' minds with the help of documentary evidence. The space of the camp is not re-built or verbally described by a voice-over commentator, but somehow visually experienced by means of different textures. These include the texture of the soil that the camera captures, the texture of the bones in the hands of the filmmaker, and those found by some of the people Wang talks to in that area, as confirmed in the interviews with the farmers who settled later in that same site."[10] With the photos of the camps in his possession and the experience of shooting landscape sequences for *The Ditch*, Wang Bing would embark on the final work of the trilogy and make of landscape a cornerstone of the 2018 film to better support the testimonies of survivors by showing where the events took place and what kind of nonhuman evidential field still exists in the Gansu Desert.

The three landscape sequences in *Dead Souls* were shot on the Mingshui annex site. The images shot at Mingshui in fact recall the exploratory nature of the twenty-five-minute single-channel video installation *Traces*, whose footage Wang captured on 35 mm black-and-white film stock in 2005, as Wang's wandering camera offered a critical topography of the site and recorded the human remains, bones, and skulls that have populated the landscape for over sixty years. In *Dead Souls*, the filmmaker captures the landscape and includes on-location interviews. As Fiant has insightfully remarked, it is the "complementarity between oral testimonies and material traces—the latter confirming the former—that is at stake in *Dead Souls*."[11] In other words, it is the relationship between oral testimonies, material traces, and landscape that deserves closer attention, especially how the actual location of the Mingshui annex is put to work in the last installment of the trilogy. W. J. T. Mitchell has argued that "[l]andscape exerts a subtle power over people, eliciting a broad range of emotions and meanings that be may difficult to specify. This indeterminacy of affect seems, in fact, to be a crucial feature of whatever force landscape can have."[12] In the case of a film such as *Dead Souls*, the goal is to better understand the "indeterminacy of affect" that landscape elicits in both the survivors and the spectators observing it, and how the nonhuman traces in the landscape affect our understanding of this period in Chinese history. The landscape sequences in *Dead Souls* capture such traces of unrepresentable experience and affect, as human remains function as material traces that silently testify to the dead souls still haunting the otherwise deserted landscape.

The first landscape sequence concludes the first part of the film, Mingshui I, and it is divided into two parts. The first part, lasting about five minutes, begins with the filmmaker handholding the camera and walking aimlessly on the historically charged site where prisoners were detained and hundreds died. The camera abruptly turns downward to examine what lies on the ground. The filmmaker's pace is fast, almost erratic, as he surveys the ground for material artefacts that could testify to what happened there. What immediately catches the attention of the viewer are the shallow graves, scattered bones, skulls, and other human remains on the ground, the filmmaker making no apparent effort to carefully frame these remains. It is difficult to believe that those would still be visible in the landscape after many decades.

Surviving the sun, wind, rain, and various changes of seasons, these material artefacts provide a different kind of testimony from the ones given by the human survivors in the film. As nonhuman witnesses, they act as an ambiguous, haunting presence within the frame, and they remind us of those who lost their lives, whose remains refuse to leave the site. Their silent presence speaks a muted language that the filmmaker tries to decipher with the help of his camera as he explores mounds of dirt, zeroing in on the bones and skulls themselves, which fail to speak with a human voice, as the survivors do for most of the duration of the film, but whose undeniable contribution lies in their nonhuman gravitas. Their silence contrasts with the windswept soundscape and Wang Bing's own footsteps that give the soundtrack an uncanny rhythm playing the silence of the nonhuman against the noises of the human.

After five minutes, the second part of the landscape sequence begins and sets the tone for a different kind of land exploration. Zooming in on a lonely walking figure in the distance, Wang starts walking toward it. The figure in the landscape is Fu Haisheng, who has lived on the land for decades and is more than willing to answer the filmmaker's questions about the site and serve as guide. Focusing on how much the landscape has changed over the past fifty years, Wang Bing asks Fu, who moved there in 1987, what discoveries he made back then when he started working the land. In addition to the bones already documented in the first part of the sequence, Fu mentions finding shallow graves, caves, a well, and, quite strikingly, handcuffed wrists. An unnamed man eventually joins Fu and Wang Bing. The locals remark that they did not displace the earth if there were human remains such as bones and skulls, as they did not wish to alter the burial sites. Wang Bing asks Fu how the site was when he moved in 1987, and the man notes that the landscape has changed a lot because of the irrigation strategies and agricultural planning of the government. Wang then asks if there were many skulls when they started working the land, to which Fu replies that when they leveled the area for cultivation purposes, they moved countless bones and skulls. Fu notes that the government filled up ravines, ditches, and caves at the time when they leveled the terrain. During the conversation, Fu casually offers to show the filmmaker the well that was used on the camp site in the 1960s. On their way, they meet two young children playing outside, moving in and out of frame, a timely reminder that the historical baggage of the area does not weigh equally on the minds of the locals. The first landscape sequence ends with the filmmaker finding the well.

Wang Bing has made a crucial revelation when comparing the work of testimony to that of walking on location. Asked about the personal nature of testimony, the filmmaker confides that at the beginning of the project, in preproduction, he never felt as close to the truth as when he walked on the site of the old camps, in the middle of these deserted areas where the bones of the prisoners could still be found, abandoned for decades and at the mercy of the elements. It is this sensation that he wanted to recover with the testimonies of survivors, but had failed to do so, according to him. It is not farfetched to imagine that the three landscape sequences in the film try to recapture that lost moment of proximity and truth mentioned by the filmmaker.

The second part of *Dead Souls*, Mingshui II, opens with a twenty-three-minute landscape sequence, the longest in the film, which differs markedly from the previous one. Indeed, at the beginning of Mingshui II, Wang Bing has recourse to a visual trope of his, which is following individuals without exactly knowing where they will lead him. The filmmaker will make his presence less felt in the second part of the sequence, as he does not question the survivors and locals (at least on camera) and seems content to document what happened on site that day. The sequence begins with the filmmaker's handheld camera following an unidentified man walking in the desert. We soon learn his identity: he is Chen Zonghai, whom we met in "Mingshui I" where he gave a sit-down interview in 2016. As previously discussed, we have gone back in time at the beginning of Mingshui II: Chen now is eleven years younger, and the year is 2005. Cao Zonghua also appears in this sequence; he is the survivor featured in "Mingshui I" when he was eleven years younger. In addition to the intriguing treatment of temporality, the sequence documents the activities of several survivors exploring the site as a group and sharing their experiences and memories. They are seen turning over stones, picking up bones and skulls, and closely examining rocks and other artefacts. A key moment in the first part of the sequence is when Chen shows a rock with red paint on it. It soon dawns on the group that there is a name and a two-character first name inscribed in the rock that are still visible after all these years. At this crucial moment, the group collectively bears witness to a fellow inmate whose fate in the camp tragically differed from theirs. Wang Bing will go on to document an onsite ritual performed by the survivors and visitors, including burning money for the deceased.

The second part of this sequence features a local man named Li Jianguo. Wang films the discussion between Chen Zonghai and Li, who proceeds to show the survivor the remaining ditches and caves in the area. As a piece of oral history, the second part of the sequence featuring Chen and Li is quite instructive. Li serves a history lesson, noting how the area and the landscape have changed over decades, echoing the words of Fu Haisheng in the Mingshui I landscape sequence. What is equally striking in this part is how Wang pauses on Chen's face on numerous occasions, the survivor clearly trying to find his bearings and remember where the camp site was located vis-à-vis the information provided by Li. Chen's bewildered facial expressions make the viewer reflect on the disconnection between the survivor's memories and the actuality and presence of the site in the twenty-first century. While it is plausible that both locals and government would have proceeded to change the area over decades, the clear wish to remember on the part of the survivor despite these changes to the land is what captures the spectator's imagination. The second landscape sequence concludes with the filmmaker further documenting caves and ditches where prisoners lived and died, and, as opposed to Mingshui I, the landscape sequence serves as an introduction to the testimonies of survivors in the remainder of Mingshui II.

The accumulation of oral testimonies over a period of eight hours can leave the spectator in a state of visual fatigue. Is another way of bearing witness possible in a documentary relying so much on the frailty of human voices? Wang Bing was profoundly aware of this issue, and he designed an alternative to the oral testimony that is used on three occasions in the film to make the spectator perceive the horrors of the regime differently. The most compelling way that Wang uses to complement the oral testimonies is to explore these deserted landscapes themselves where the camps were located and to document material traces as further evidence of the veracity of the survivors' retellings. Pointing his camera toward the ground, he comes across the scattered bones and skulls of numerous men who died of starvation in reeducation camps sixty years ago—a truly lifeless landscape whose haunting images will stay with the viewer for a very long time. Human remains and material traces thus come to supplement the original treatment of historical time previously discussed and the testimonies of the survivors. It is as if the filmmaker needed the support of nonhuman, material artefacts and traces to complete the portrait painted by the survivors themselves after hours of interviews. The complementary nature of human and nonhuman subjects seemed to have been the key to portraying the horrors of Jiabiangou and Mingshui in all their complexity. In that sense, Wang Bing's filmmaking could be said to contribute to a revisionist understanding of phenomenology whereby the privilege accorded to the human observer is questioned in order to pay greater attention to the so-called background (that is, landscape) and how it works to destabilize and reintegrate the human in unexpected fashion. The Chinese filmmaker thus is embedded in the landscape, rather than towering over it, to self-assuredly ground his presence. On that revisionist account, one could return to the fundamental tenets of *shanshui* in Chinese thought and how it breaks down the Western binary between subject and object: "China's interest in landscape/*shanshui* lies not so much in landshape as in essence, in the energy that animates the land, the same energy that runs through us all."[13]

The eleven-minute landscape sequence that closes the last part of the film, "Mingshui III," not only signals the end of *Dead Souls* but it also serves as a thought-provoking coda to the "Anti-Rightist" trilogy. After numerous hours of testimonies, the spectator accompanies Wang Bing one last time. The third landscape sequence is dated January 2012, which corresponds to almost seven years after the other two landscape sequences were recorded. At the beginning of the third sequence, Wang is once again by himself, as he was at the beginning of the first landscape sequence (Mingshui I). The filmmaker seems to value the material traces of the camps so much that he felt the need to return to the site and end both the 2018 film and the trilogy with images of himself exploring the landscape with no other apparent purpose than to find new material remains of the past. It is as if the filmmaker himself were haunted by the landscapes he had documented in 2005, and an irresistible urge to return to the site overtook him. After all, what do these images at the end of *Dead Souls* add to the film that the spectator has not already seen in the other two landscape sequences? Had the few years that had passed dramatically changed the landscape, thus justifying a third sequence that would shed new light on the site and that period of Maoist China?

As was the case with the first sequence, the spectator can hear Wang Bing's footsteps and the wind in the soundtrack, both providing a sonic accompaniment to a haunted space whose testimony takes the form of bones, skulls, and jaws dispersed on the ground. In an interview with Antoine de Baecque, Wang Bing notes that, in *Dead Souls*, he wanted "to show what resists the passage of time: the words of the last survivors . . . and the desert that, today, produces [*rend*] the bones of the thousands of dead left there."[14] Therefore, it is not only the documentation of what is still visible after all these years that fascinated the filmmaker, but also the nonhuman forces that make the hitherto invisible visible in the landscape. In the same interview, the filmmaker mentions that the desert is attacked on all fronts: vegetable crops and trees have been planted and now encroach on this singular space, yet "the place resists, and the wind is a particularly efficient agent of resistance; the wind that erases, of course, but which also reveals the bones, the wind of history."[15]

Where the documentary style diverges from that of the other sequences in the film concerns how the remains themselves are framed and the duration of the shots. Indeed, whereas in Mingshui I Wang Bing's camera gave the impression that it was reacting in real-time to the findings on the ground with no apparent compositional design, at the end of the trilogy the filmmaker uses a more deliberate compositional style and pacing: the bones, skulls, and femurs are carefully placed within the frame, creating arresting visual tension between the objects, lines, and patterns found on site. Equally important is the duration of these shots. Whereas the previous sequences had habituated the spectator to somewhat hyperactive, shaky camera movements that seemed eager to find the next grouping of bones and skulls, at the end of the film Wang pauses for what seems an inordinate amount of time on each ensemble. An interesting example is the carefully framed femurs on the ground, an assemblage of bones that is on screen for over one minute. Another key shot features two skulls almost facing each other in the frame, an inaudible dialogue of the dead. Such memento mori moments give the impression that Wang's is an investigative camera that decidedly knows what to find, where to find it, and how to frame it at the end of the film. I do not believe that such shots were staged considering the filmmaker's ethical predisposition, but that, having shot the landscape sequences for Mingshui I and Mingshui II, Wang Bing had developed greater spatiotemporal awareness for capturing such moments. Holding these shots for longer than expected, the filmmaker draws attention to these bones in a way that avoids the more voyeuristic perspective that could be said to have characterized the Mingshui I landscape sequence. The camera will eventually turn upward, then revealing a shaky horizon line and contributing a final perspective on what happened on this site—an abrupt ending that denies closure after eight hours.

## Conclusion: Landscape as Ontology, Epistemology, and Practice

Wang Bing's monumental reconstruction of an admittedly forgotten chapter in twentieth-century Chinese history offers a pathbreaking interpretation of the Anti-Rightist Campaign, the reeducation camps, and the Great Famine. In addition to how the film juxtaposes chronological and historical time to bridge the gap between the voices of survivors and the silence of dead souls to tell a story of trauma and collective amnesia, the weight of material evidence comes to bear in the final sequence and lends credence to the horrors of the Maoist years as retold by survivors. Perhaps most importantly, documenting the landscapes allows not so much to make the viewer forget about the survivors at this point in the documentary, as to establish the connection with present-day China and show how sites endure regardless of the unfolding historical forces. This critical perspective on the trilogy raises questions about how place, space, and landscape matter in political, historical, and aesthetic terms. Thus conceived, landscape becomes an iconic, dynamic space where collective identity and memory enter in relation with site-specific concerns and material artefacts.

In this concluding section, it is important to further reflect on the "Anti-Rightist" trilogy considering the distinctions that Mitchell has made on the topic of landscape in the preface to the second edition of his landmark collection, *Landscape and Power*. Mitchell posits that one should establish meaningful differences between three words that often get confused: place, space, and landscape. He writes: "One might think, then, of space, place, and landscape as a dialectical triad, a conceptual structure that may be activated from several different angles. If a place is a specific location, a space is a 'practiced place,' a site activated by movements, actions, narratives, and signs, and a landscape is that site encountered as image or 'sight.'"[16] Mitchell's conceptual triad puts in perspective Wang Bing's trilogy as it negotiates the Jiabiangou and Mingshui camp sites (place), the activities of actors reenacting past events and survivors exploring camp sites (space), and Wang Bing's trilogy itself, whose landscapes are visually consumed as documentary images (landscape).

An equally relevant strategy would be to map Mitchell's triad onto the philosophically charged triad of *ontology* (the being of place), *epistemology* (the knowledge of space), and *practice* (filmmaking activities resulting in the documentation of landscape). I believe that Wang Bing's "Anti-Rightist" trilogy does exactly that: it offers a thought-provoking visual inquiry into the being of the camps as places in the Gansu Desert; through oral testimonies and reenactments, it provides a sustained look at how the camps, as spaces where prisoners, guards, and cadres lived, were characterized by horrific actions, and it forces the spectator to rethink the historical narratives of political revolution that have supported efforts to produce knowledge about the Chinese past. Finally, the trilogy makes a sustained practice of documenting otherwise inaccessible landscapes over several years, sites to be repeatedly explored and then shared as indelible images.

I believe it is crucial to understand that the conceptual triad introduced by Mitchell needs to be supplemented by a greater concern for temporality, and that is why this chapter began by turning to the temporal aspect of *Dead Souls*, showing how the film plays with chronology to creatively repeat the time of testimony, memory, and trauma. As Helsinger has pointed out: "In many respects it would make better sense to think of landscape as necessarily a spatio-temporal concept. Even landscapes as material forms, one might argue, presume temporal extension."[17] I have explored Wang Bing's concern for expressing the workings of time in the non-chronological approach to the presentation of the interviews and in the filmmaker's emphasis on the nonhuman traces in the landscape in the three sequences previously discussed. This is not to deny the resourceful nature of Mitchell's triad—or my own remapping in the form of ontology, epistemology, and practice—but to suggest how time is embedded within places, spaces, and landscapes, and how it works to destabilize any understanding of Maoist history in this case.

In fact, a closer look at landscape demonstrates how it works against the grain of history to negate the triumph of (historical) time and make of its own persistence an object of historical inquiry: "Landscape *outlives* history; it surpasses it. Over time—and almost as a function of its earth, its soil—landscape absorbs the events played out on its surface; it inters the marks of past practices as much as it also bears its traces."[18] The landscapes of Jiabiangou and Mingshui reveal the hitherto invisible spaces and landscapes of Maoist history, which would correspond to what Mitchell has called an "apperception of space."[19] Wang Bing's practice allows spectators to finally apprehend these landscapes, whose inhabitants are the dead souls to whom the film is dedicated.

In a recent interview, Wang Bing took many by surprise when he claimed that his eight-hour-long documentary, *Dead Souls*, is part one of a larger project: "As regards *Dead Souls*, for the moment I have only directed one part of it. There are still two parts that have not yet been edited. It is a project in three parts: the first part thus consists of 8 hours and 15 minutes; the second part will be a little longer. Anyway, the project will be one in which each of the sections is about eight or nine hours long."[20] Wang's words raise the question of what it is that he has yet to document and share on the topic, and which strategies he intends to employ to reveal yet another face of the Anti-Rightist Campaign.

Having explored the multifaceted ways in which Wang Bing has documented the labor of history in the figure of the survivor, Part Two turns to the second obsession at the heart of the *minjian* filmmaker's cinema: the figure of the worker and the transformation of Chinese labor in twenty-first-century China.

## Notes

1. Wang Bing, "Past in the Present. Director's Statement," 2012, https://www.sabzian.be/article/past-in-the-present.
2. Wang, "Past in the Present. Director's Statement."
3. Wang, "Past in the Present. Director's Statement."
4. Zhou Xun, *Forgotten Voices of Mao's Great Famine, 1958–1962* (New Haven, CT: Yale University Press, 2013).
5. Frank Dikötter, *Mao's Great Famine: The History of China's Most Devastating Catastrophe, 1958–62* (New York: Vintage, 2010).
6. Yang Jisheng, *Mubei: 1958–1962 nian Zhongguo da jihuang jishi*, 2 vols. (Hong Kong: Cosmos Books, 2008). Abridged English translation: Yang Jisheng, *Tombstone: The Great Chinese Famine 1958–1962*, trans. Stacy Mosher and Guo Jian (New York: Farrar, Strauss and Giroux,

2012). The original Chinese edition totaled more than 800,000 characters and was published in two volumes with a length of over 1,200 pages. The original Chinese edition collects over twenty years of research and acts as a profound indictment of China's authoritarian regime under Mao.
7. See Sebastian Veg, "The Limits of Representation: Wang Bing's Labour Camp Films," *Journal of Chinese Cinemas* 6, no. 2 (2014): 173–87, and Elena Pollacchi, *Wang Bing's Filmmaking of the China Dream: Narratives, Witnesses and Marginal Spaces* (Amsterdam: Amsterdam University Press, 2021), 144.
8. A similar scene is found in Yang's "Woman from Shanghai": "She [Gu] started to cry. Her wailing came from deep inside her chest. A great sob shook her frame. She covered her face and hunched over her bag. Tears streamed down her hands." (Yang Xianhui, *Woman from Shanghai: Tales of Survival from a Chinese Labor Camp*, trans. Wen Huang [New York: Anchor Books, 2010], 41–42.).
9. Ivone Margulies, *In Person: Reenactment in Postwar and Contemporary Cinema* (Oxford: Oxford University Press, 2019), 16.
10. Pollacchi, *Wang Bing's Filmmaking of the China Dream*, 163–64.
11. Antony Fiant, *Wang Bing: un geste documentaire de notre temps* (Laval: Warm, 2019), 204.
12. W. J. T. Mitchell, "Preface to the Second Edition of *Landscape and Power*: Space, Place, and Landscape," in *Landscape and Power*, second edition, ed. W. J. T. Mitchell (Chicago: University of Chicago Press, 2002), vii.
13. Jerome Silberberg, "Landscape Theory from a Chinese Space-Time Continuum," in *Landscape Theory*, ed. Rachael Ziady DeLue and James Elkins (New York: Routledge, 2008), 281.
14. Antoine de Baecque, "Wang Bing, *Les Ames mortes*," *Transfuge* 123 (2018): 44.
15. de Baecque, "Wang Bing, *Les Ames mortes*," 45.
16. Mitchell, "Preface to the Second Edition," x.
17. Elizabeth Helsinger, "Blindness and Insights," in *Landscape Theory*, ed. Rachael Ziady DeLue and James Elkins (New York: Routledge, 2008), 326.
18. Jessica Dubow, "The Art Seminar," in *Landscape Theory*, ed. Rachael Ziady DeLue and James Elkins (New York: Routledge, 2008), 100.
19. Mitchell, "Preface to the Second Edition," viii.
20. Wang Bing, Dominique Chateau, and José Moure, "Documentary as Contemporary Art—A Dialogue," in *Post-cinema: Cinema in the Post-art Era*, ed. Dominique Chateau and José Moure (Amsterdam: Amsterdam University Press, 2020), 363.

# Part Two

# The History of Labor

# 5
# Observing the Workers

## Chinese Governmentality and Critical Realism

When Wang Bing was a photography student at the Lu Xun Academy of Fine Arts in Shenyang, Liaoning Province, in the early 1990s, he lived near a gigantic industrial district, Tiexi, that would become the subject of his first documentary film, *West of the Tracks* (2003). After working for more than three years as a cameraman in the film industry in Beijing, Wang decided to develop a personal film project that would take him back to a city where he spent a lot of time as a student. The filmmaker adds: "When I was a college student in Shenyang, I often went there to photograph at weekends. Its factories, its workers, and residents—I became very familiar with the place."[1] *West of the Tracks* expresses Wang Bing's fascination with Tiexi, and it adopts a critical perspective on the state of industry and labor in the context of the end of state-owned enterprises in an industrial district located in the capital of Liaoning. But it is not so much the changing industrial landscape that prompted Wang to document the place as "a feeling of desolation that reminded me of Tiexi District—the sense that a history which used to be important was now slowly declining, dissolving in front of our eyes."[2] Committing to memory a significant period of Chinese industrial life thus functioned as the main impetus for the film that would launch Wang's career on the international stage.

With *Coal Money* (*Tongdao*, 2008) and *Bitter Money* (*Ku qian*, 2016), Wang would pursue his obsession with Chinese labor and the fate of workers sustaining China's economic boom, a variation on the theme first explored in *West of the Tracks*. A journey from Tianjin and Tanggu to the southern ports of Guangzhou, Shenzhen, and Zhejiang Province, *Coal Money* concerns natural resource extraction, the transportation of coal, and its status as a negotiable commodity in the Chinese Anthropocene. While *West of the Tracks* deals with the final years of heavy industry in Tiexi and documents a community of workers and where they live, *Bitter Money* zeroes in on the plight of migrant workers in the textile workshops and offers a close look at the employment and living conditions of migrant workers in Zhejiang Province. Wang Bing explains the changing nature of work within China now that the government no longer maintains the social safety net associated with the *danwei* system: "Factories of the past still had a collective spirit. Workers' lives were related to the factories. For instance, if you were a formal worker here, you would be considered part of the ownership of the workplace. Likewise, people's daily life was closely related to their work relation at the factory. That is no longer the case for production units today—now there is a contract-labour system everywhere."[3] Noting the precarious status of temporary workers, Wang associates the rise of the Chinese precariat with loss of community and dependence on the state, which was a hallmark of the socialist production system for decades. For Wang, the goal was "to talk about the Chinese economy, to see what it is: from the small businessman to the big enterprises, all at the same time."[4] He adds: "What's important today is to see what people are doing to China. If we don't see this, we see nothing. When we look at China, we see only the economy, but without seeing what lies behind it, what people are really doing."[5] *West of the Tracks*, *Coal Money*, and *Bitter Money* function as a tripartite endeavor to show what labor has become in China since the economic reforms.

This chapter introduces the socioeconomic and governmental issues at the heart of Part Two of this study, as well as the description of the critical visual approach that Wang Bing uses to make sense of the development of labor practices within China. First, I contextualize Wang's history of Chinese labor in the twenty-first century by addressing the transition from Maoist state planning to Chinese governmentality, which is to say the transition from state socialism to a technology of government inspired by Western governmentality but adapted to the Chinese context. Second, I describe the observational method that Wang Bing has developed to document the evolution of Chinese labor and workers drawing on Allan Sekula's concept of "critical realism." I argue that these two elements—Chinese governmentality and critical realism—lay the foundation for a more comprehensive understanding of a documentary practice taking Chinese labor and the fate of workers in the twenty-first century as its main object of study. While the three films at the heart of Part Two do not constitute a trilogy per se, they certainly reflect some of the most dramatic changes in the history of Chinese labor, ranging from the dismantling of state-run industry in the late 1990s to the emergence of coastal factories and the unprotected migrant worker. In more ways than one, Wang Bing's labor films echo Lukács' famous claim in *History and Class Consciousness* that "the fate of the worker becomes the fate of society as a whole."[6]

## From Maoist State Planning to Chinese Governmentality

The history of the working class in China under CCP rule offers fascinating insights into how the regime has dealt with the development of worker subjectivity and labor struggles. After all, for decades the regime had insisted that its workers were the masters of the workplace and owned the means of production. The fact of the matter is that Chinese workers did not enjoy much control over their working lives and did not participate in the decision-making process. This became abundantly clear in the 1990s when came the time to dismantle state-owned enterprises. Sheehan writes: "Unrest among Chinese workers, including strikes and attempts to organize independent unions, has continued since 1989, and among state workers levels of unrest have risen sharply towards the end of the 1990s. The plans outlined at the Fifteenth Party Congress in September 1997 to allow most SOEs [state-owned enterprises] to be sold off, merge, or go bankrupt, will only increase unrest."[7] What Sheehan had predicted is very well captured in Wang Bing's *West of the Tracks*, in which the soon-to-be-laid-off workers were the last to learn about forthcoming factory closures, and their collective surprise at the very thought of being "unemployed permanent workers" in the socialist mode of production revealed their status as mere cogs in the machine rather than agents of their professional destiny. Contrary to what one might think about the socialist labor environment, the relations between the CCP and the workers have always been fraught, as historians of Chinese labor have shown. With China's transition to the market economy, pressures on both leaders and workers exacerbated contradictions to the extreme.

Twenty years after the liquidation of SOEs, China has become the workshop of the world, and few would remember the struggles of laid-off workers were it not for a documentary such as Wang Bing's *West of the Tracks*. Hurst reports that between 1993 and 2006, more than 60 million jobs were lost in SOEs and collective sector enterprises alone, which "represented a net downsizing of more than 40 percent of formal sector urban jobs over less than 15 years."[8] What is the meaning of the socialist model of production and worker protection under these circumstances? Was it realistic to expect that the great majority of these workers would gain employment in the private sector thereafter? Clearly, the *danwei* system that provided housing, food, education, and health care to state workers—often referred to as the "iron rice bowl" employment system that was the hallmark of Chinese labor practices—was a thing of the past, and the role of workers would have to be redefined as they transitioned from the urban social life they were used to under the socialist regime to being private-sector employees in the newly arisen factories where precarity and the absence of benefits are the norm.

Wang Bing's *West of the Tracks* documents the deterioration of working-class identity in the largest industrial district in Shenyang. The downfall of large heavy industrial firms under the supervision of the state actually led to the redefinition of working-class identity in China. Hurst notes: "Working class society is a three-dimensional concept encompassing class identity (i.e., workers' views of themselves as members of a working class), the structure of workers' social ties, and popular perceptions of the Maoist past."[9] Based on the decision to transform SOEs into profit-seeking firms, laying off workers became a priority to ease the transition, no matter the human cost. Self-employment and entrepreneurship would come to occupy center stage in the CCP's post-socialist dream. That is not to say that the transition has been an easy one: "As the Communist Party withdrew from its old role of working-class vanguard, SOE workers were abandoned by their political champion and revolutionary master. Not only did the working class become less able to act meaningfully in its own interest; it also lost the puppeteer that had so successfully pulled its strings on the political stage for nearly eight decades."[10] It is this long-cherished identity that the Chinese government would target as it developed new forms of societal organization under the sign of governmentality.

Introduced by Michel Foucault in the late 1970s, the notion of "governmentality" refers to the radical reconceptualization of both power and government as previously imagined within social and political science circles. Foucault defined governmentality as "[t]he ensemble formed by the institutions, procedures, analyses and reflections, the calculations and tactics that allow the exercise of this very specific albeit complex form of power, which has as its target population, as its principal form of knowledge political economy, and as its essential technical means apparatuses of security."[11] Often characterized as the shift from "government" to "governance" in the form of the "conduct of conduct," governmentality departs from the traditional application and maintenance of the state's power and the preservation of control to accentuate "the diversity of forces and knowledges involved in efforts to regulate the lives of individuals, and the conditions within national territories, in pursuit of various goals. In doing so, it suggests that government is neither operationalized nor exercised strictly through prohibitions and controls."[12] Governmentality embodies an apparently decentered, flexible approach to how populations should be managed within neoliberal societies because of the gradual decline of the welfare state and socialism in the West.

The changing conception of governance associated with Foucault's notion of governmentality echoes recent theorizations of citizenship that have become intertwined with issues or problems relating to population, the body, and life itself, which reflect the concerns of "biopower" and "biopolitics," that is, the cultivation and preservation of the various aspects of biological life such as population, fertility rates, birth planning, public health, disease, life expectancy, and sexuality as the central end of government. In Western democracies, the management of life in all its forms (biological, social, public, economic, and political) has become the focus of governmental efforts, and the COVID-19 pandemic can only be said to have exacerbated this situation. Citizens are now seen as consumers whose life choices, desires, and skills form the locus of governmentality and biopolitics. They are "entrepreneurs of the self" whose task it is to find solutions to socioeconomic problems such as unemployment that the state itself often creates because of shortsighted, profit-driven agendas. One of the advantages of turning to Foucault's understanding of governmentality is to have forced a long-overdue reconsideration of the categories that have governed political science, such as the state, the subject, the public, and the private, among others, to better explain how power and control are exercised in neoliberal democracies.

Writing in the late 1970s and early 1980s, Foucault's analysis of governmentality targeted Western Europe first and foremost, with the occasional glance at the United States. Numerous scholars have discussed how Foucault's framework could be extended to non-Western or non-democratic forms of governance. It has been argued that alternative spheres of political influence and control such as China could be said to function as Foucault's blind spot in his admittedly Eurocentric perspective, a point Greenhalgh and Winckler emphasize when stating that "Foucault's analysis is Eurocentric and needs to be amended to include alternative modes of biopolitical differentiation and 'improvement.'"[13] A country such as China poses a great challenge to the Foucauldian understanding of governmentality, being an authoritarian regime that does not place an exorbitant value on individual choices and freedom the way liberal democracies do and that has put equal emphasis on the biopolitical management of the quantity and quality of its population. As Jeffreys and Sigley note: "the focus on advanced liberal democracies overlooks the possibility of non-liberal forms of governmentality, in this instance a socialist arts of government or Chinese governmentality, which governs not through familiar tactics of 'freedom and liberty', but rather through a distinct planning and administrative rationality, and which is nonetheless a product of the same processes that Foucault partly outlines in the governmentality lecture."[14]

Dutton and Hindess have described how governmentality functions within the Chinese context: "governmentality in China can be seen as the outcome of a history that is radically different from the one that Foucault traced in the western context. Governmentality, with Chinese characteristics, belongs to the legacy of Maoism. It is part of what remains after Mao's grand projects were abandoned and the CCP directed its attention towards the economy... Maoism, in being centrally concerned with the transformation of everyday life, that is, with the wives and children, households, and (former) 'slaves' of the now 'liberated' China, made the government of these domains central to its mode of rule."[15] It is no wonder that *minjian* Chinese filmmakers, starting in the early 1990s, decided to make of the everyday their central focus as they went about reinventing how documentary filmmaking could relate to activism, witnessing, and invisibility in a changing China.

As a result of China's societal reforms and entry into the world market economy, scholars have observed that, as a non-Western country, China presents a fascinating case study for those interested in how a Western concept such as governmentality can be applied to a political regime that has undergone seismic changes since the late 1970s. Dutton and Hindess explain: "Unlike Maoism, market-based modernization programmes run through, between and sometimes away from the state, rather than being generated out of it. As market forces took hold, the dictatorial, total and repressive Marxist state apparatus splintered into questions of investment economy, profit and the law. It was because of these sorts of concrete changes in China that a number of western scholars of China found a useful toolbox in Michel Foucault's work on mentalities of government."[16] The notion of governmentality supplements the notion of "postsocialism" that has been used in Chinese documentary studies to describe post-Reform China and frame the socioeconomic and cultural context in which a cinematic practice such as Wang Bing's could emerge, and governmentality provides a more comprehensive understanding of the Chinese society in which *minjian* filmmakers create. Indeed, a stronger qualification than "postsocialism" is needed to make sense of the governmental regime facing Chinese documentary filmmakers today. There is no doubt that opening the market to competition and phasing out the socially planned economy have entailed a drastic revision of the notions of subject, community, governance, and the management of everyday life in China, which are all aspects of life related to governmentality, Chinese labor, and the fate of workers under the CCP.

It is crucial to underline the unprecedented hybrid nature of twenty-first-century China's mode of governance. On the one hand, the governance strategy used by the CCP draws on the foundation laid by Maoism in the two decades preceding the reforms and its enduring legacy: "Government in Mao-era China (1949–1976) operated almost entirely through official channels and agencies in a hierarchical and highly regulated system of formal authority. This system administered and mobilized the population through state-run urban work units (*danwei* 单位) and rural collectives to participate in the governing of everyday life. In the post-1978 era of market-based economic reform, the old 'mass-line' mode of government has been progressively replaced, but not entirely supplanted, by more complex and diffuse forms of governance."[17] On the other hand, slowly phasing out the Maoist centralized planned economy to open the door to foreign investors and profit-driven initiatives, the hybrid model of governance that the CCP has adopted merges social engineering and socialist planning with neoliberal strategies. Combining socialism and market economy rationality, the Chinese case shows how Foucault's work can be expanded to consider a type of governmentality that is both non-Western and non-democratic.

Deng Xiaoping's famous expression, "socialism with Chinese characteristics" (*Zhongguo tese de shehuizhuyi*), perhaps best summarizes what Chinese governmentality embodies in the Reform era in which the socialist market economy (*shehuizhuyi shichang jingji*) has become the unquestioned reference. Chinese governmentality adopts novel ways of observing, shaping, and controlling the lives of the Chinese subject. As a reflection of the type of governmentality developed under Mao, the management of life in contemporary China has adopted more interventionist and coercive forms than in the West, and it has shown a more robust interest in both the preservation of the party and the development of the hybrid, socialist model unique to the country. Launching social engineering (*shehui gongcheng*) and civilizational betterment programs seeking to build a harmonious society (*hexie shehui*) and control the "quality" (*suzhi*) of individual subjects, the CCP has developed a wide-ranging governmental agenda that seeks to intervene in all spheres of the Chinese subject's life: education, reproduction, health, and employment, among others. In other words, the planning imperative at the heart of Chinese political life persists, albeit in modified form in the twenty-first century, and the concern for the scientific management of human and nonhuman resources remains at the forefront for political leaders such as Xi Jinping. Jeffreys and Sigley aptly note: "these new calculations and strategies have become an integral part of the new technoscientific-administrative Party-state—a mixture of conventional Chinese socialist technologies of government such as 'the mass line' and seemingly neoliberal strategies designed to govern through the desires of individuals conceived of as consumers, property-owners, job seekers, and citizens (not as workers for the revolution)."[18] As is the case in the West, China's new model of governance has increasingly relied on the agency of individuals in terms of lifestyle and self-expression. Yet, as numerous scholars have shown, the PRC uses a modified approach to control: "In the place of the crude and occasional intervention of the state, China's people now face a much more subtle yet insidious form of power that is continuous and dispersed throughout the institutions of modern society and within their own selves, and masked by the language of truth and power."[19]

This overview of Chinese governmentality shows that the CCP is not so much interested in grandiose revolutions anymore as in the slow, methodical everyday management of socioeconomic life in all its forms. Perhaps China's greatest surprise on the world stage is to have proposed a type of governmentality that integrates both Western and non-Western dimensions in the form of a socialist-capitalist model that no one had predicted would be as successful. Socialism with Chinese characteristics could also be said to be capitalism with Chinese characteristics. As a response to the critiques of the Mao era, the governmental reforms have prepared the PRC to face the management of widescale social change in the form of challenges such as the massive waves of rural-to-urban migrants (also known as the *nongmingong* or, more pejoratively, the "floating population") moving to coastal cities and seeking employment opportunities in construction and factories. As the most important divide today in China is still between the rural and the urban,[20] time will tell if China's socialist market economy, as a unique proposition in the history of the world, was the appropriate answer to the disavowal of Maoist revolutionary politics and social planning. Alongside other *minjian* filmmakers, Wang Bing has already provided his answer: Xi Jinping's dream of a new China is in fact a nightmare for countless Chinese citizens.

## From Socialist Realism to Critical Realism

How does one document the Chinese governmental regime and its impact on labor and workers in the late twentieth- and early twenty-first century? From the dismantling of state-owned enterprises in the late 1990s to the emergence of textile factories on the east coast in the 2000s, Wang Bing has documented the plight of workers and their everyday lives in the aftermath of the neoliberal policies that have affected both the former state worker and the new segment of the work force associated with rural migration. As films such as *West of the Tracks*, *Coal Money*, and *Bitter Money* demonstrate, Chinese governmentality, and its redefinition of worker identity, has also reinvented the very notion of social life within contemporary China, as workers can no longer expect the regime to provide the social safety net and benefits that state employees enjoyed for decades.

Part Two shows that Wang Bing has designed a singular documentary approach to documenting changes in Chinese labor and workers' lives over the past twenty years. I argue that the notion of "critical realism" as a *documentary method*, rather than a visual style, can help to rethink the notion of observation within a documentary practice focusing on labor and workers.[21] The notion of critical realism has been revived lately to discuss the work of American photographer, filmmaker, and art historian Allan Sekula (1951–2013). For over three decades, Sekula's documentary projects dealt with issues of labor and materialism in a way that can only be said to have been untimely in the post-conceptual and postmodernist era. Sekula's prioritization of the worker, and the Marxist orientation of his analysis of labor and production, may have struck critics as dated when in fact what Sekula offered was a groundbreaking understanding of emerging globalization flows and their impact in the face of widespread postmodern cynicism. Countering the emphasis on postmodern simulacra, Sekula proposed to retrieve the subject of labor whose function would partly be to rehabilitate the notion of realism within art historical and critical circles. In the introduction to *Photography Against the Grain*, Sekula writes: "I wanted to construct works from *within* concrete life situations, situations within which there was either a covert or active clash of interests and representations. Any interest I had in artifice and constructed dialogue was part of a search for a certain 'realism,' a realism not of appearances or social facts but of everyday experience in and against the grip of advanced capitalism."[22]

Over the years, this marked interest in realism, the everyday, and the concrete impacts of capitalism would translate into Sekula's predilection for the representation of the sea, shipping containers, and the globalized spatial processes in which workers evolve, as documented in the *Fish Story* (1995) photobook[23] and the film *The Forgotten Space* (2010, co-directed with Noel Burch). It is the lived experiences of workers under advanced capitalism that Sekula documented in his visual inquiries into modes of production and transportation, and the circulation and accumulation systems that sustain capitalism, which is to say the old question of the relationship between reality, politics, and representation. In sum, it is what Shabtay, in her insightful analysis of *The Forgotten Space*, has called "a visual method of assembling a critical materialist history"[24] of labor. I claim that Wang Bing has been hard at work creating a similar critical materialist history of Chinese labor over the past twenty years, as evidenced in the three films discussed in the second part of this book.

There is no doubt that labor history and the daily challenges of workers have taken a backseat to racial and gender politics within the contemporary art world, and that intersectional approaches have failed to integrate labor as one of the key aspects to examine in the quest for a renewed leftist thought. It is not farfetched to claim that the representation of workers is seen as a thing of the past in the visual arts, as is the materialist reading of history characteristic of the Marxist tradition. In his postface to Sekula's *Fish Story*, Buchloh describes how Sekula's work counters this critical perspective to offer a "model of 'critical realism.'"[25] For Sekula, critical realism is intimately tied to how the notion of labor is defined, and how the laboring body itself is represented. He notes that "[b]oth Socialist Realism and liberal capitalist social documentary share in offering us images of labor in its *positivity*. They are necessarily ignorant of any notion of labor's *contingency*. Labor is always shadowed by the absence of labor, by labor in the negative, by the nightmare of unemployment on one side, and by the utopian dream of genuine freedom from work on the other ... The compulsion to work can be subtracted as easily as it can be added to the body, even if it continues to operate residually in the body of the unemployed. There is no essence within the body that organically gives rise to honorific testimonials to labor as a positive ontological condition."[26] Sekula thus concludes: "So I've always tried to approach labor from this 'negative' or dialectical perspective: work shadowed by non-work."[27] Socialist realism's efforts to monumentalize the working body and the labor process is not what should be revived according to Sekula; it is the dialectical understanding of the employee condition under neoliberalism, oscillating between work and non-work, contingency and uncertainty, that matters. A critical realist approach to documentary pays close attention to such situations and attentively observes the fate of workers caught in a web of forces, both political and subjective.[28]

What makes Sekula's reflections on labor intriguing is that they are both timely and untimely. The concept of critical realism is timely because of the repercussions of globalization around the world and the pervasiveness of precarious labor. The critical realist approach is also untimely because the representation of labor and workers is not what the art world privileges in the twenty-first century and because realism remains tied to the propagandistic campaigns of twentieth-century socialist regimes. As Ruchel-Stockmans explains: "The main difficulty of the contemporary images of the working class lies in the looking risk of falling into one or the other stereotyped representational style. The photographic tradition of sentimentalized and aestheticized labor ... is often transported to a journalistic black-and-white style of photography. On the other hand, there is still a vivid visual memory of socialist realist grandiose representation of workers, which reminds one of the risks of false pretences and propagandistic misuse."[29] It is indeed the aesthetic ideal and the propagandistic intentions of socialist realism that need to be decried. What Sekula sought to discover with the notion of critical realism, however, was what can be salvaged from the realist art of the past to speak to contemporary labor causes.[30]

In sum, Sekula's work has sought to revive the categories of labor and worker and elevate them to the position of prime mover. His critical realist practice focuses on how labor and worker unfold within history, and what had hitherto been invisible can be made visible. As Mitchell notes: "'Social realism' of the sort practiced by Allan Sekula, tends to fuse Lukacs' 'critical realism' with an emphasis on conditions of labor and an interest in exposing the photographic view a world that is overlooked or generally hidden away from public view."[31] Making the invisible visible has translated into labor being radically reconsidered because it is not the realistic representation of workers that should matter now, but the very lack at the heart of the workers' condition. Sekula explains: "For my part, I begin not with a pure positivity of labor ... but with the understanding that work exists in a fundamental condition of negativity, haunted objectively and psychologically by unemployment and by the extraction of surplus value. It's a problem even of language: we are encouraged to believe that we live in a 'postindustrial society,' when in fact the industrial function has been globalized."[32] Sekula thus posits that the representation of labor should equally document unemployment, idleness, and precarity, which goes against the grain of the social realist depiction of the heroic worker building the next utopia. Sekula will go on to remark in the same interview that "[t]he problem of critical realism is this: how do we find the interval within which the idea of freedom resides? By careful attention to time, realizing that the camera too often kills and obscures lived time."[33] Van Gelder has defined such intervals as "multi-layered moments of meaning, abstract overturning moments when information seeps through and prompts reflection. It is therefore both the problem and the duty of the critical realist artistic research to create these empty visual moments."[34]

What emerges from the preceding reflections on critical realism is that the notion concerns a certain methodological perspective on the self. As Mitchell has noted: "Realism has to be earned; it has to be struggled for. It is a historical, contextual, and critical account of a state of affairs. The real is of course the target of this process, but every reality remains a construction, it is the tapestry we weave out of the information we gather during this research. Realism is a project in relation to that process and critical realism would be some critical relation to some constructed reality."[35] Realism thus becomes an embodied practice—a documentary method—whose sine qua non condition is engagement and dedication to process. Wang Bing echoes this perspective when he states that "I need to be immersed in the place before initiating the act of filming. For example, for *West of the Tracks*, I arrived on location in 1992, but I only started filming in 1999. In most cases, when I was filming, I was already familiar with the location and the people, and the time I spent there gave me more freedom of choice. In this case, I am in a state of optimal concentration. It's as though nothing bothers me, nothing interferes with my act of filming."[36] In this process, realism makes personal demands of the Chinese filmmaker who struggles to find the right means to express criticality in image-making.

Part Two of this study adopts the concept of critical realism to account for both the observational behavior of the filmmaker and the documentary records of Chinese labor and workers' bodies in *West of the Tracks*, *Coal Money*, and *Bitter Money*. As an embodied and intuitionist approach, critical realism seeks to explain how observation and criticality join forces to make sense of Chinese labor in the work of Wang Bing. Twentieth-century Chinese literature, visual arts, and cinema were steeped in realism, and Wang Bing's documentaries could be said to be the latest installment in the country's obsession with realistic representation, with the caveat that critical realism actually reacts against socialist realism. This makes of critical realism a central category in the history of Chinese representational practices, as it challenges the tenets of revolutionary realism.

Building on the notion of critical realism as a means for understanding Chinese governmentality, labor, and the working body, the analyses in Part Two address *West of the Tracks*, *Coal Money*, and *Bitter Money*, three films that exemplify how Wang Bing has documented the development of Chinese labor practices in various sociocultural and economic contexts since the early 2000s.

## Notes

1. Wang Bing, "Filming a Land in Flux," *New Left Review* 82 (2013): 123.
2. Wang, "Filming a Land in Flux," 123.
3. Wang, "Filming a Land in Flux," 124.
4. Wang Bing, "Deuxième dialogue avec le cinéaste. Entretien avec Wang Bing réalisé par Isabelle Anselme," in *Wang Bing. Un cinéaste en Chine aujourd'hui*, ed. Caroline Renard, Isabelle Anselme and François Amy de la Bretèque (Aix-en-Provence: Presses universitaires de Provence, 2014), 134.
5. Wang, "Deuxième dialogue avec le cinéaste," 135.
6. Georg Lukacs, *History and Class Consciousness* (Cambridge: MIT Press, 1971), 91.
7. Jackie Sheehan, *Chinese Workers: A New History* (New York: Routledge: 2002), 225.
8. William Hurst, *The Chinese Worker after Socialism* (Cambridge: Cambridge University Press, 2009), 1–2.
9. Hurst, *The Chinese Worker after Socialism*, 27.
10. Hurst, *The Chinese Worker after Socialism*, 139.
11. Michel Foucault, "Governmentality," in *The Foucault Effect: Studies in Governmentality*, ed. Graham Burchell, Colin Gordon, and Peter Miller (Chicago: University of Chicago Press, 1991), 102.

12. David Bray and Elaine Jeffreys, "New Mentalities of Government in China: An Introduction," in *New Mentalities of Government in China*, ed. David Bray and Elaine Jeffreys (New York: Routledge, 2016), 2.
13. Susan Greenhalgh and Edwin A. Winckler, *Governing China's Population: From Leninist to Neoliberal Biopolitics* (Stanford: Stanford University Press, 2005), 324.
14. Elaine Jeffreys and Gary Sigley, "Governmentality, Governance and China," in *China's Governmentalities: Governing Change, Changing Government*, ed. Elaine Jeffreys (New York: Routledge, 2009), 5.
15. Michael Dutton and Barry Hindess, "Governmentality Studies and China: Towards a 'Chinese' Governmentality," in *New Mentalities of Government in China*, ed. David Bray and Elaine Jeffreys (New York: Routledge, 2016), 25.
16. Dutton and Hindess, "Governmentality Studies and China," 18.
17. Bray and Jeffreys, "New Mentalities of Government in China," 3.
18. Jeffreys and Sigley, "Governmentality, Governance and China," 7–8.
19. Greenhalgh and Winckler, *Governing China's Population*, 326.
20. Piketty, Li, and Zucman have shown that "Adult urban population rose from 100 million in 1978 to almost 600 million by 2015, while adult rural population remained roughly stable. The income gap between urban and rural China has always been large, and it has grown over time: urban households earned on average twice as much income as rural households in 1978; they now earn 3.5 times as much. As a result, while the urban share in adult population has grown from 20 percent in 1978 to 55 percent in 2015, the urban share in income has increased from 30 percent to 80 percent." Thomas Piketty, Li Yang, and Gabriel Zucman, "Capital Accumulation, Private Property, and Rising Inequality in China, 1978–2015," *American Economic Review* 109, no. 7 (2019): 2485–86.
21. First coined by Georg Lukács in his theory of the European novel in *The Meaning of Contemporary Realism* (1963), the concept of critical realism stands in opposition to socialist realism, the latter denoting the stylistic form characteristic of Stalinist Russia and its politically charged artistic production. Imbued with propagandistic messages destined to the masses of workers, socialist realism was said to have entered a decadent period, according to Lukacs, and the critical realism he advocated was a progressive gesture in literary works that rejected the reactionary methods of the Soviet era. See Georg Lukács, "Critical Realism and Socialist Realism," in *The Meaning of Contemporary Realism* (Monmouth, Wales: Merlin Press, 2006), 93–135.
22. Allan Sekula, *Photography Against the Grain: Essays and Photo Works 1973–1983*, second edition (London: Mack, 2016), xii, emphasis in original.
23. Allan Sekula, *Fish Story* (Düsseldorf: Richter Verlag, 1995).
24. Talia Shabtay, "The Art and the Politics of 'The Forgotten Space,'" *Oxford Art Journal* 38, no. 2 (2015): 269.
25. Benjamin H. D. Buchloh, "Allan Sekula: Photography between Discourse and Document," in Allan Sekula, *Fish Story* (Düsseldorf: Richter Verlag, 1995), 191.
26. Allan Sekula and Benjamin H. D. Buchloh, "Conversation between Allan Sekula and Benjamin H. D. Buchloh," in *Allan Sekula: Performance under Working Conditions*, ed. Sabine Breitwieser (Vienna: Generali Foundation, 2003), 48, emphases in original.
27. Sekula and Buchloh, "Conversation," 48.
28. Sekula has reflected on the origins of critical realism and what a Marxist philosopher such as Lukács wanted to accomplish with this concept: "Lukacs invented the term 'critical realism' as a counter to the socialist realism or Zhdanovism that became the official aesthetic of the

Soviet Union with the 1934 Writers' Congress. Critical realism maintained contact with the deep currents of history and resisted the sentimental clichés of an official Stalinist aesthetic that Lukacs, late in his life, described as 'establishment naturalism'. For Lukacs, the high road of critical realism was taken by Thomas Mann, by Maxim Gorky, and within the later Soviet period, by Alexander Solzhenitsyn. According to Lukacs, these later realists achieve a grasp of the social totality similar to that achieved in the 19th century by Balzac, before realism degenerated into the descriptive naturalism of Zola." Hilde Van Gelder and Jan Baetens, "A Debate on Critical Realism Today," in *Critical Realism in Contemporary Art: Around Allan Sekula's Photography*, ed. Jan Baetens and Hilde Van Gelder (Leuven: Leuven University Press, 2010), 122.
29. Katarzyna Ruchel-Stockmans, "Loops of History: Allan Sekula and Representations of Labor," in *Critical Realism in Contemporary Art: Around Allan Sekula's Photography*, ed. Jan Baetens and Hilde Van Gelder (Leuven: Leuven University Press, 2010), 34.
30. Facing criticism for reviving the notion of social realist art after the collapse of socialist regimes around the world, Sekula notes that "there is a straw-man realism that is being pummeled in the art world because in fact what the art world requires is an antirealist compact; realism is needed as a kind of bad object." Jack (John Kuo Wei) Tchen, "Interview with Allan Sekula," *International Labor and Working-Class History* 66 (2004): 166.
31. W. J. T. Mitchell, "Realism and the Digital Image," in *Critical Realism in Contemporary Art: Around Allan Sekula's Photography*, ed. Jan Baetens and Hilde Van Gelder (Leuven: Leuven University Press, 2010), 24.
32. Pascal Beausse, "The Critical Realism of Allan Sekula," *Art Press* 240 (1998): 22.
33. Beausse, "The Critical Realism of Allan Sekula," 26.
34. Hilde Van Gelder, "'Social Realism' Then and Now: Constantin Meunier and Allan Sekula," in *Constantin Meunier. A Dialogue with Allan Sekula*, ed. Hilde Van Gelder (Leuven: Leuven University Press, 2005), 84–85.
35. Van Gelder and Baetens, "A Debate on Critical Realism Today," 121.
36. Wang Bing, Dominique Chateau, and José Moure, "Documentary as Contemporary Art—A Dialogue," in *Post-cinema: Cinema in the Post-art Era*, ed. Dominique Chateau and José Moure (Amsterdam: Amsterdam University Press, 2020), 359.

# 6
# *West of the Tracks*

## Embracing a Lost Social Totality

*West of the Tracks* (*Tiexi qu*, 2003) was Wang Bing's breakthrough film, a monumental, nine-hour-long epic shot in the northeastern rustbelt.[1] Hailed as one of "the most extraordinary achievements of world cinema in the new century,"[2] the film captured the imagination of both viewers and film critics alike, and it is the most commented-upon film in Wang Bing's oeuvre. The 2003 documentary addresses the transition that state-owned enterprises (SOEs) underwent at the end of the 1990s, from the socialist mode of production to the uncertainties associated with neoliberalism and the market economy. Described as a "pure work of observation and perception"[3] by the filmmaker, the film focuses on Tiexi, the largest and oldest working-class district in the industrial city of Shenyang, often referred to as the "Ruhr of the East," in Liaoning Province, which shares a border with North Korea. In the 2000s, the Tiexi complex was still in operation, but several factories had gone bankrupt. What happened to this social behemoth that used to be the backbone of industrial China?

In numerous interviews, Wang Bing has reflected on the end of SOEs and its impact on Tiexi. Wang's critical comments address the socioeconomic foundation that the Tiexi complex provided in Shenyang: "In China, the economy was initially based on the Soviet model. All factory workers spent their lives in the workplace. It was the basis for a social system with a planned economy in which a plant couldn't freely sell its production. In *West of the Tracks*, we can see that this planned economy is finished and that a new economy begins to emerge. We perceive in the film how things transform and modify themselves."[4] It is the fate of the workers that particularly interested Wang Bing in this film, the filmmaker adding that it is "the workers themselves who are the leading force behind the documentary."[5] The fate of Tiexi workers is particularly captivating, considering how their lives had radically changed since the glorious days of socialism: "The workers in *Tiexi* were the first in China to move into purpose-built workers' villages. People in other districts particularly admired their lives in multi-storey dwelling houses with telephones and electric lights—the highest urban living standard—from as early as in 1952."[6]

*West of the Tracks* uses a tripartite structure to construct a journey through time and space. The first part, titled "Gongchang" (Factory) (English: "Rust"), documents life within the cable factories, copper and iron smelting works, and plating plants, and the gradual process during which bankrupt factories were shut down and dismantled. The spectator has unprecedented access to the workers, how they pass time on break, including game playing, bickering, and showering. "Gongchang" ends in the hospital where laid-off workers are treated for zinc and lead poisoning. The second part of the film, titled "Yanfen jie" (Yanfen Street) (English: "Remnants"), documents workers' lives outside the factory in one neighborhood where Tiexi workers lived. The economic crisis hitting the neighborhood is quite severe as most are now unemployed. Moreover, they learn that the neighborhood will soon be demolished and that they have only one month to relocate. Some decide not to move out, while others take it upon themselves to destroy their own home and sell whatever parts they can. The third section, titled "Tielu" (Railway) (English: "Rails"), returns to the tracks and the train cars shown in the first part of the film. As the locomotive explores the complex in memorable nighttime scenes, the spectator realizes that what was a vibrant community and industry under the socialist planned economy has turned into a ghost town. The third part limits the scope of its microhistorical inquiry to settle on Du Xiyun and his teenage son, Du Yang, and the challenges of a father-son relationship under such difficult living conditions.

The film's tripartite structure shows the vast industrial complex at the heart of Shenyang.[7] The desire for totalization, for telling the complete story of a decaying industrial complex and its impact on workers and their families, reflects the desire to exhaust a topic and show it as a social totality over nine hours. As Wang himself has noted: "The industrial zone no longer exists, but when we see the film, the area clearly reveals itself in its totality."[8] Taking Wang Bing at his word, I argue that *West of the Tracks* engages in a complex process of documenting a social totality that is slowly disintegrating, which refers to what the filmmaker has described as a "past ideal" (*guoqu de lixiang*).[9] I believe that one cannot analyze this film without addressing its three parts as interrelated components in one long narrative, that is, how the three parts function together as a complex portrait of a disintegrating social totality. While the first part is the most spectacular visually and the one that has attracted the most critical attention, the second and third parts are equally crucial for making sense of how Wang Bing depicts the social life of Tiexi circa 2000. Noteworthy is that Wang Bing's film differs from Jia Zhangke's *24 City* (*Ershisi chengji* 二十四城记, 2008), Lixin Fan's *Last Train Home* (*Guitu lieche* 归途列车, 2009), and Wen Hai's *We the Workers* (*Xiongnian zhi pan* 凶年之畔, 2017) because of its totalizing tendencies and comprehensive macrohistorical and microhistorical representation of the SOEs and social and family life, as well as the impact of Chinese governmentality on the population of Tiexi at the turn of the millennium.

## Chinese Labor in Transition: The Emergence of the Urban Poor

At the Fifteenth Party Congress in September 1997, the representatives of the CCP assembled to reflect on the future of SOEs and *danwei* (work units), and they confirmed the unthinkable: the CCP would authorize the sale of state assets, which would both ensure the financing of much-needed modernizing efforts and avoid the bankruptcy of debt-ridden SOEs. Premier Zhu Rongji promoted increasing market competition, profit-seeking ventures, and "efficiency-enhancing reforms, even at the cost of a painful, medium term spike in unemployment."[10] The CCP's epoch-making decision meant that SOE administrations would engage in the transformation of state capital into joint-stock companies: SOEs could merge in this new financial landscape, and debt could be converted into shares.[11] This was the first step in the privatization process and the opening-up to foreign investors that would mark this unprecedented stage in Chinese economic history. The *danwei* work unit would be the major casualty of the SOE reform program. These decisions reflected the "grasping the large, letting go of the small" (*zhuada fangxiao*) policy, that is, fully embracing the market economy and promoting privatization of small- and medium-sized SOEs that could no longer be competitive. A new type of governmentality predicated on neoliberal principles was thus implemented in China, which would have dramatic social consequences for a city such as Shenyang.

There is no doubt that this monumental change forced SOEs to optimize the use of their workers and maximize efficiency. The goal was to avoid deficits and bring down operating costs, which was an unprecedented managerial perspective in the Chinese industry sector. Equally important in this transformation was the social impact on the socialist employment system, which guaranteed employment for life and a strong social security net with benefits such as housing, childcare, health care, and pensions. It is unsurprising that, in the late 1990s, numerous SOEs started laying off workers in their attempt to cut costs and increase profits. Figures indicate that 23 to 31 million workers were laid off in 1998 and 1999 in China,[12] and, "[b]y the end of the 1990s, 90% of enterprises in Tiexi district either had totally or partially stopped their operations with assets valued at more than 50 billion yuan staying idle. At the same time, 232 medium to large state-owned enterprises did not have the money to pay salaries to their workers."[13] The Chinese working class was utterly transformed as a result, as was the notion of public sector employment.

Wang Bing has said that "*West of the Tracks* can be seen as a slice of Chinese history. The [Tiexi] complex was created by the Japanese in 1934, expanded by the Soviets in the 1950s, and reached its maximum capacity in the 1980s when it employed over one million workers."[14] In their study of industrial heritage in Shenyang's Tiexi district, Fan and Dai add to the filmmaker's description of Tiexi's importance in China's industrial history: "Tiexi is an administrative district in Shenyang City, founded in 1938. The first mint, first arsenal, first truck, first use of mechanical porcelain production in China all occurred in Tiexi during 1900–1929. After the founding of the People's Republic of China, Shenyang became known as the 'Department of Industrial Equipment of China', which was a heavy industry base developed in the first and second Five-Year Plans. Tiexi is called 'the hometown of machine tools', and the birthplace of the metallurgical industry, and the nation's largest foundry enterprise was also located there."[15] The contextual information provided at the beginning of *West of the Tracks* echoes the preceding statement and reveals the socioeconomic environment in which the filmmaker found himself when he started working there in the late 1990s. The region of Shenyang in which the Tiexi neighborhood is located was particularly impacted by Chinese SOEs' entry into the market economy. Kernen and Rocca have argued that Liaoning Province was the most impacted by the turn to neoliberal practices within SOEs, claiming that the workers were "the direct victims of the calling into question of the role of the socialist state in economic development."[16] They add that "[i]n the region of Shenyang, about 70% of the town's workers were employed in SOEs . . . At the end of 1997, nearly 13.7% of the Chinese *xiagang* who had not yet obtained a new job were living in Liaoning."[17]

The term *xiagang* refers to employees who no longer work, but who still receive a portion of their wages. They differ from employees who were forced to take an early retirement (*tiqian tiuxiu*), or those who are on a "permanent vacation" (*fangjia*). However, the *xiagang* designation hides a harsher reality: "Provided that workers are classified as *xiagang*, rather than unemployed, there is no obligation on the government to find them new jobs because they are still *officially* in employment."[18] These various titles and designations describe those who no longer enjoy fulltime, salaried employment within a SOE and the kind of social protection they received for decades because of the profit-seeking efforts of the managerial team. The number of *xiagang* for the city of Shenyang alone is estimated to have been 350,000 at the end of 1997.[19] Responsible for the pension payments of retired workers, SOEs halted pension payments to 306,000 people in Liaoning,[20] and "[i]n Shenyang, by 1998, 27 percent of the city's SOEs simply stopped making pension payments."[21] Smyth and Zhai have posited that "[t]he poor financial position of SOEs in Liaoning reflects the fact that the 'iron rice bowl' mindset persisted longer in Liaoning than in most other provinces and thus Liaoning was much slower to grasp reform."[22] This view is supported by the fact that the share of public sector employment in Shenyang was "96.4 percent in 1990 and 70.4 percent as late as 2004,"[23] which corresponds to several years after the reforms had been implemented. Lee concludes that "[s]ince the 1990s, Liaoning has been plagued by the most severe unemployment problem in the nation. By some estimates, as many as 30 to 60 percent of workers in the state sector were without jobs or pay by the late 1990s, a stark contrast with the province's preeminence in the days of the planned economy."[24]

Based on this historical background and employment data, one can appreciate what Wang Bing meant when he said that "[t]he biggest issue addressed in the film [*West of the Tracks*] is the economy."[25] While many critics have reported the filmmaker's comment that the real "hero" of the film is the factory itself,[26] they seem to have missed the importance of the economic background to the tragedies unfolding within SOEs. After all, the factory is the symptom of what took place in Shenyang at the end of the 1990s; the economic root causes still need to be explained. As outlined above, the root causes of China's neoliberal turn and the staggering unemployment numbers indicate the creation of a new class: the urban poor. The transition from the stability of the socialist salaried system and its generous social safety net to the precarity that ensued from the liquidation of state assets created a new type of worker subjectivity. Kernen and Rocca explain: "Outside certain periods (notably the Great Leap Forward), poverty has always been limited to a fringe group of the population, seen as 'enemies of the regime' and to a minority which had no access to the system of public employment."[27] Poverty was thus relegated to the margins of society, which mainly included rural areas and the peasantry. In the meantime, the new Chinese governmentality made the unemployed "entrepreneurs of the self" whose chief priority was finding "self-supporting employment" (*zimou zhiye*). The goal of this governmental measure was to make workers more "autonomous and self-sufficient. Everyone must create an activity that will support themselves."[28] Chinese workers could not have been farther from the socialist regime that sustained them. The future of the Chinese working class was at stake, and the second and third parts of Wang Bing's film demonstrate what social and urban transformations occurred once the socialist employment system was replaced.

## A Chinese Social Totality

The comprehensive nature of the three parts composing *West of the Tracks* indicates that Wang Bing wanted to treat Tiexi as a socio-industrial totality. I borrow the concept of totality from the work of Georg Lukács, whose pioneering reflections on the subject frame the various elements making up a social totality, how they interact or fail to, and what transformations social life undergoes in the process: "With 'totality' Lukács refers to a whole set of elements that are meaningfully interrelated in such a way that the essence of each element can only be understood in its relation to the others . . . Both individual and social life is in principle capable of forming an integrated totality. However, this is only the case if the essential properties of its elements are intelligible in terms of their relations to other particulars of life. Only in this case, life can have a meaningful form which is not a mere restriction."[29] The three parts of *West of the Tracks* offer insights into a complex of SOEs, the end of the socialist employment system, Chinese labor relations, social life in Tiexi district, forced relocation, and, on a microhistorical level, the precarious living conditions of a family unit. From the macrohistorical to the microhistorical, Wang Bing's epic deconstructs these various parts and reconstructs them for the viewer in a meaningful set of audiovisual relationships. The disintegration of the SOE system mirrors the disintegration of the family units in Tiexi, which relates to how social and individual life confronts the challenges brought about by the loss of totality and social cohesion that the socialist system guaranteed for decades.

The term "social totality" may strike the reader as a dated concept to account for twenty-first-century socioeconomic phenomena such as the end of SOEs and its impact on Chinese workers and families. However, regarding contemporary visual artists, there seems to be a marked interest in reproducing totality in all its complexity. As Day has argued, "[e]ven if most artists still prefer to avoid any talk of 'totality', the efforts of many practitioners today can be said to aspire to 'portray' contemporary social totality."[30] Referring to both Lukács and Sekula, one should point out that the modern totality differs from that of classical idealism, which possessed utopian and teleological tendencies. In the case of the post-Reform era, it is the disintegrating, fragmentary, and contradictory nature of totality that captured the imagination of a filmmaker such as Wang Bing, especially in his 2003 film. Day has shown that the analysis of a social totality requires to "consider the interrelations and interactions between different phenomena, that we relate the parts to the whole—and that we conceive these parts—the whole and all their relations—as mutable, as both materially constraining and subject to human actions."[31] The point is not that a social totality can be visually embraced by the filmmaker. Rather, the main issue lies in how to visually construct a disintegrating whole and give a narrative structure to what remains impossible to grasp from an epistemological viewpoint. The ideal to represent a social totality is just that: a utopian desire on the part of the filmmaker to grasp the entirety of the real. But in the process of searching for the real of a given social totality, encounters are made, and life experiences are shared and documented for the world to contemplate. The critical realist attitude is a subjective ambition to capture totality that the documentarian knows may remain unfulfilled. As Aitken has noted of Lukács and realism, "the role of the aesthetic 'intensive totality' is not to attempt to represent *der Mensch Ganz* in generality but, rather, to portray the crucial factors that figure in any one historical here and now."[32]

This chapter seeks to provide answers to the following questions: How does the *minjian* filmmaker engage the destruction of a social totality that had endured for decades, and what aspects did Wang Bing privilege in the process? How does documentary film record the contradictions at the heart of the capitalist mode of production once China entered the process of transforming its economy? What is documentary's role in registering the loss of totality from a critical realist perspective? Does documentary impose an artificial totality on a situation that should now be considered under the sign of postsocialism, thereby recreating a meaningful totality for those nostalgic for the reassurances of the past? Or does it lay bare the inadequacies of totalizing forces and the unraveling of Chinese labor history in the context of twenty-first-century Chinese governmentality? How does documentary film construct an image of the struggling Chinese proletariat, and how does Wang Bing negotiate the troubled waters of documenting Chinese lives as a product of social mediations in Tiexi district? Finally, how does a nine-hour documentary epic function as an *artistic* totality itself? Does it reflexively confront its status as a necessarily incomplete visual production of knowledge?

The challenges facing Wang Bing as a filmmaker reflect those faced by the documentary scholars who have examined *West of the Tracks*. Indeed, there seems to exist a certain level of uneasiness with the task of accounting for all three parts of *West of the Tracks* and showing how they interrelate. Just like Wang Bing needed to construct a narrative for the three parts of the film at the editing stage, having shot over three hundred hours of footage, scholars have been at pains to explain how the three parts function as a whole, that is, as a cinematic totality. There is no doubt that the first part of the trilogy, focusing on the factories themselves, has been the most privileged in the literature. In fact, some have only examined the first part of *West of the Tracks*, neglecting the second and third parts altogether.[33] In this chapter, I argue that the three parts of the film are equally important to understand Wang Bing's representation of the lost social totality of Tiexi, and I pay close attention to how each part constructs a particular social problem related to the end of SOEs: the end of permanent employment ("Gongchang"), the consequences of unemployment on neighborhood life and forced relocation ("Yanfen jie"), and disenfranchisement and its impact on family ties, especially the father-son relationship ("Tielu"). The three parts of *West of the Tracks* play variations on the set of social problems described in this chapter, which concerns the multifaceted impacts of unemployment once a social totality collapses. Each part alters the perspective on the disintegrating social totality of Tiexi and identifies a set of relations that may not be apparent to the casual observer. This is how Wang Bing's film contributed a pathbreaking audiovisual chapter to the history of Chinese labor at the turn of the twenty-first century.

## Three Variations on a Social Problem

### "Gongchang"

As Wang Bing has admitted, when he started work on his first film, he had no documentary experience.[34] In fact, he had seen only two documentary films before making his 2003 epic: Michelangelo Antonioni's documentary about China, *Chung Kuo, Cina* (1972), and Godfrey Reggio's *Koyaanisqatsi* (1982).[35] One can only surmise what kind of impact these profoundly different filmic experiences had on the aspiring filmmaker whose main problem was finding a narrative structure for his first film. *West of the Tracks* went through several iterations before finding its final form. As Wang reports: "The problem was finding a good rhythm, a balance between storytelling [*racconto*] and fragmentation [*frammentazione*]. I didn't want it to be a film that would be too narrative-based, but I didn't want it to totally lack a narrative thread either."[36] It turns out the literal and metaphorical use of the locomotive entering and leaving the factories would help Wang Bing understand how it could serve as a guiding thread for the first part of the film. Trains and tracks played a central role in the operations of Tiexi district for decades, and the filmmaker could not but notice their imposing presence when he visited the district as a student. As Fan and Dai note: "Tiexi is surrounded by railways and intersected with high density roads and railways. There are 8 railway lines, length 19,553 m, 70 railway crossings and 5 railway overpass bridges distributed throughout this area. They constitute a unique city and space image of Tiexi."[37] It is no wonder that "Gongchang" would begin with footage recorded on a locomotive traversing industrial spaces and residential areas, entering and leaving factories, crossing checkpoints and intersections where gates go up and down. Wang has mentioned that "[t]he most complicated problem was indeed the train, having access to it, because the train controls all the city, enters all the factories. The train was both an instrument of control and, for me, an instrument of freedom, because once on board, I could enter everywhere."[38] One could argue that mounted on the front of a locomotive like it was, Wang's camera provided an original vantage point, echoing the "point of view of totality" that Lukács mentions in *History and Class Consciousness*, albeit a nonhuman one.

Constructing a sense of place and scale was crucial for Wang Bing, and access to the trains was tied to the goal of representing the social totality, which implied striking up conversations with employees and explaining why an art school student wanted to ride such trains in the first place and document his trips. Obviously, the nonhuman assemblage of camera and train supported the filmmaker's objective to construct Tiexi as a visual totality to be appreciated on a large scale. Opening the nine-hour journey with a floating camera going in and out of factories reveals a layer of visual information that could not have been reproduced had Wang Bing simply walked alongside the buildings. The traveling shots from the locomotive give the impression that this machinic assemblage is a living and breathing entity whose exploration of factory spaces is mediated by the camera lens and the snow-covered locomotive window, thus distancing the spectator from immediate access to the Tiexi landscape in movement. Two technological machines—the train and the DV camera—join forces to create a unique gliding experience that does not reproduce the train footage of past efforts celebrating modernity, or capturing the conversations of workers on board, but the end of an era.

As spectators watch the death of the socialist mode of production, they also contemplate the birth of a new form of digital documentary. Having worked with the first Panasonic mini-DV camera at the time when he was with the state studios, Wang soon realized that it was this type of small camera body that was needed to document the kind of subject he had in mind. He eventually borrowed a small camera with the intention of returning it a few months later. He bought fifty tapes and started working on the film.[39] Production started in the fall of 1999, with Wang eventually shooting for a year and a half. Documenting the factory complex and its workers' quotidian movements became an obsession, beginning with the documentation of the tracks themselves.[40] Wang shot about three hundred hours of footage, and the editing process would last a full year. Wang worked alone on this project, and he used the Panasonic NV-MD10000 mini-DV camcorder and the on-camera microphone.[41]

Attached to Wang Bing's DV camera is a wide-angle lens. This lens is not extremely wide; it is the typical 14–24 mm focal length. What characterizes the field of view of a wide-angle lens is its superhuman or nonhuman capacity. While a 50 mm lens reproduces the human field of view, the wide-angle lens provides a dramatically wider context for what has been captured. In the case of a handheld camera such as Wang's DV cam, the movements of his body accentuate the movements of the wide frame and gives the viewer a broad, albeit shaky, perspective on the environment and, in the case of workers, their surroundings. There are metaphysical implications to the use of a wide lens, just like there are in the case of a telephoto lens. Use of the wide lens signals the wish to provide a viewing experience that does not exclude the context or environment. The filmmaker bears witness to not only the subject in front of the camera, but also the space that enfolds the subject. The wide-angle lens thus demands that the spectator appreciate the entire field of view and its contextual elements rather than zero in on whatever detail, object, or face is in the frame. Wang Bing's wide-angle lens, which is the kind of lens he has used in all his films, sometimes to great dramatic effect in enclosed spaces in the case of the bedridden Fang Xiuying (*Mrs. Fang*, 2017), goes hand in hand with the goal of capturing a social totality, at least from a visual perspective. The wide-angle lens thus aspires to create a totalizing field of view.

Wang Bing first turned his DV camera and wide-angle lens to the decaying structures, spaces, and objects within abandoned rooms in the factories. Such sequences in the film remind us of what is referred to as "ruin photography," namely, the work of numerous documentarians that has focused on ghost towns and discarded objects in places that are no longer occupied, such as Chernobyl. Inspired by the images of Westerners whose culture of ruin images was based in the pictorial tradition, Chinese artists developed a predilection for ruin imagery all their own. Wu Hung explains: "What became influential and finally developed into a broad visual culture in twentieth-century China was a different kind of ruin and ruin image. Instead of inspiring melancholy and poetic lamentation, they evoke pain and terror."[42] Whether it be images of war scenes or late twentieth-century urban demolition, ruin images record "destruction that left a person, city, or nation with a wounded body and psyche."[43] As refracted records of events, such images have come to stand in for what Wu has described as a "suspended temporality"[44] that oscillates between the past, present, and future.

Wu's notion of "suspended temporality" does not only apply to images of decaying structures and ruins, which one does find in *West of the Tracks*, but it also speaks to the subjectivity of workers who were torn between the socialist system and its reassurances (past), the probability of losing their job (present), and the uncertainties of the future in Tiexi. What is visually stunning in "Gongchang" is the way in which Wang Bing captures life within concrete situations, that is, the shape that everyday life and experience took once the perspective of becoming unemployed became a reality. As the filmmaker negotiates these complex temporal layers, he makes the conversations among the employees a cornerstone of the first part of the film, thus providing a critical materialist perspective on the situation in crumbling SOEs.

Images of labor and the working body often emphasized nation-building and the generally positive aspects of socialist realism. As explained by Sekula, a critical realist perspective moves away from the "positivity" of labor to reorient the gaze on labor's contingency, which refers to the potential absence of labor and the challenges of unemployment. "Gongchang" is replete with sequences that highlight the contingent and negative aspects of labor in SOEs at the end of the 1990s. These moments correspond to the "intervals"[45] that Sekula mentioned in which a process of emancipation can be glimpsed without a promise of fulfillment. They also remind us of the "empty visual moments"[46] that Van Gelder described in reference to critical realism.

Throughout the first part of *West of the Tracks*, the spectator listens in on the conversations between workers who are profoundly unsatisfied with their conditions and the uncertainty surrounding the fate of their factory. On numerous occasions, workers complain about back wages; they reflect on being unemployed and what it will mean for their family. One worker mentions the fate of unemployed women, a worker's wife having to sell vegetables on the streets of Tiexi to make ends meet. Kernen has reported that 60 percent of the unemployed in Liaoning were women in the late 1990s,[47] which has led many to argue that women have been the most affected in the creation of the urban poor. It is said that 70 percent of the urban poor are former state employees, retired workers, or employees on permanent leave.[48]

A striking example of the critical realist perspective on labor that has not been commented upon is the restaurant scene midway through "Gongchang." Seated at a round table, the employees discuss their uncertain future while others sing karaoke songs. What is particularly fascinating is one woman's discourse on the future of factories and what should be done to ensure a prosperous future in Tiexi. She proceeds to advocate for both privatizing the factory and supporting cost-cutting efforts that will allow the factory to become "financially independent," an expression that would have been anathema just a few years before. This sequence serves an intervallic function contrasting the woman's reflections with the other sequences, which tend to take place within the factories, except for the train sequences shot outdoors. Such reflections on the salvaging power of the market economy would not have been voiced by the average worker; they are the product of a sustained reflection on what it means for a SOE to be indebted and the likely possibility of not receiving pension payments. Wang Bing uses title cards in the second half of "Gongchang" to reveal what most spectators would have expected: factory after factory is closing, and workers are let go. This information brings back to mind the woman in the restaurant whose prophetic words did not find an echo.

The first part of *West of the Tracks* ends with a sequence featuring workers going to the hospital where they will be screened for zinc and lead poisoning. An enigmatic death happens on site, where a man seems to have drowned in a pond. What happened exactly? Did a former employee commit suicide? The restaurant woman and the deceased worker make us pause, considering Lü Xinyu's comment that "'Rust' [that is, "Gongchang"] does not, on the whole, individuate the workers it follows . . . they compose a collective humanity whose destiny forms another polyphonic structure within the film, contrasting and echoing the fate of the factories themselves."[49] While the woman in the restaurant and the drowned man remain nameless, their joint presence in the first part of the film does contribute to individualize the experience from two diverging points of view: the worker who approved the neoliberal changes made to SOEs and Tiexi, and the worker who could not face life in a post-SOE China.

## "Yanfen jie"

The second part of *West of the Tracks*, titled "Yanfen jie," focuses on the multiple existences found within one working-class neighborhood of Tiexi, where numerous individuals used to be employed by SOEs. What emerges over close to three hours is the despair and helplessness of both the young and the old on screen. "Yanfen jie" thus explores an even greater number of intervals where life seems suspended. After a considerable amount of time spent documenting the daily lives and courtship rituals of teenagers in the neighborhood, Wang Bing turns his camera on the citizens facing forced relocation because of the planned destruction of their neighborhood. As the second part of the film unfolds, the spectator has the impression that the few individuals who refuse to be relocated will have to move out one way or another. After the water and electricity have been cut off, their living conditions deteriorate rapidly, culminating in an inconclusive final sequence in which Wang Bing follows Bobo on the street, a seventeen-year-old whose life prospects are rather dim in this environment.

"Yanfen jie" begins with a somewhat intriguing lottery campaign held at a fair where the people in attendance are asked to support the Chinese nation by purchasing tickets. The crowd, we conjecture, is partly composed of men and women who were let go by the very same government that now requests their financial help. It is quite ironic that the man interviewed on stage is now unemployed himself, and, when asked where he got the money to purchase a lottery ticket, he points out that he had to borrow it. Wang Bing's decision to open the second part of the film with this sequence is quite intriguing and unlike anything else in the film because of its caustic tone.

The second sequence establishes the relationship between the filmmaker and the teenagers whom he will follow intermittently throughout "Yanfen jie." The spectator is introduced to Bobo and his friends, all of whom being notably well-dressed for teenagers living in a derelict neighborhood of Tiexi. In addition to discussing love and Valentine's Day gifts, the teenagers reflect on their current activities and how they make money. These teenagers usually gather in a convenience store named "Hongxiang" where they buy cigarettes and hang out. Once Wang Bing has spent about an hour of screen time on these teenagers, he will turn to what is the core of "Yanfen jie": the demolition of the neighborhood and the relocation challenges faced by many.

A significant portion of the dialogue in the second part of the film concerns forced relocation and the struggles to be allocated a decent living space by the local authorities. It is not that these citizens have enjoyed beautiful living conditions. On the contrary, as Cheng has remarked: "Spatially, the urban poor . . . are concentrated in inner-city private housing areas and degraded *danwei*-managed workers' villages, characterised by dilapidated housing and facilities."[50] The author further notes that this can be historically explained by the fact that "[t]he living conditions of these old communities have therefore kept worsening due to the lack of planning and maintenance over decades. In the 1990s and early 2000s, these areas were largely overlooked by urban redevelopment plans."[51] Numerous people directly address Wang Bing and explain to him what the main issue is: the insufficient square footage of their allocated apartment or house. As the demolition of the neighborhood is fast approaching, many worry that the indemnities are not generous enough to support them in future. Others complain that the allocations should be based on the actual number of family members rather than the square footage of their current residence. Wang Bing records the reflections of these individuals and intercuts footage of men at work salvaging whatever tiles and cables they can find before the neighborhood is torn down. We see men and women selling wares on the street; trucks pass by filled with personal possessions as they make their way through narrow streets and alleyways.

"Yanfen jie" adopts a polyphonic approach weaving together several voices in what constitutes a visual treatise on poverty in urban communities impacted by the closure of SOEs and forced relocation. Wang Bing shows how urban households in industrialized cities and districts such as Tiexi were greatly transformed since the closures. An interesting bit of conversation happens when Wang Bing records a dialogue with a seventy-three-year-old retired worker whose three sons were fired when their factories went bankrupt. This is followed by a discussion between teenagers about school and what their future holds, including becoming a taxi driver, and another teenager complaining that his friend has no goals in life. As the months go by, winter sets in and the spectator witnesses the harsh living conditions of men and women who no longer have running water or electricity. They wear their winter clothes inside the house, which they swear they will never abandon until the local government gives them proper compensation or a decent house. As they face potential eviction and physical violence, Wang Bing surprises the spectator with the only bird's-eye view of the neighborhood after two hours of closely following his subjects, often in enclosed spaces. It is the only instance when the viewer gets to have some perspective on the neighborhood space and manages to see the extent of the ongoing demolition efforts. The neighborhood resembles a bombed-out landscape where few people still live. The Chinese New Year is just around the corner, and the holdouts decide to celebrate the coming of 2001 even though the new year is looking rather bleak. Just like the second part of the film began on an intriguing note with the lottery campaign at the fair, it ends with an unexpected ritual: a few people are seen moving a deceased woman's body. The spectator assumes that they intend to re-bury their mother closer to where they have been relocated. It is April 2001, and Wang Bing has shared a slice of neighborhood life in Tiexi that will remain etched in the spectator's memory for a long time.

Both "Gongchang" and "Yanfen jie" offer two sustained looks at the social totality that comprised the SOEs and the people living in one of Tiexi's neighborhoods. Compared to the first part of the film, "Yanfen jie" adopts a different approach to the problems that the end of the socialist employment system created for employees and their family members. A social issue that is not covered in "Gongchang" is the attachment that many felt for their neighborhood and, by extension, their house, however rudimentary their living conditions may have been. As we see the houses being torn down and people moving out, the large-scale demolition efforts and the frustrations associated with the forced relocation of residents become apparent in Wang Bing's film, a crucial aspect of *West of the Tracks* that has been neglected in the literature. While forcing residents to relocate is frequent in urban rejuvenation projects in China, not enough attention has been paid to the repercussions on the citizens themselves who are most likely to be poor, deprived, or old, and who are unlikely to find employment when relocated in a different part of town. Obviously, relocation implies dramatically changing one's daily routine and social network developed over years, if not decades. Wang Bing's film shows the spectator those who, in the process of shutting down factories, are equally impacted but who remain invisible. Cheng has described these individuals: "Some other urban residents outside the *danwei* system, including the disabled, elderly, retirees, chronic disease patients, self-employed and casual and informal sector workers, are also disadvantaged by social differential and enlarging income inequality with strong downward mobility among them."[52]

What emerges from Wang Bing's images is the utter confusion and chaotic state in which the neighborhood finds itself after the announcement that residents will have to relocate. This signals a crucial shift in governance whereby the *danwei* system ceased to oversee all activities: "A series of SOE reforms has led to many *danwei* to transfer their obligations regarding neighbourhood management to local governments such as local housing bureaus."[53] On numerous occasions in "Yanfen jie," the spectator bears witness to individuals who complain about the incompetence of local officials and the inadequacy of the reallocation system. The impression that the film gives is that many were left to their own devices in the process. No wonder that "the unemployed and laid-off residents from *danwei* communities have developed into one of the most deprived social groups in urban China."[54] The ultimate lesson that "Yanfen jie" teaches is that the demolition of SOEs led to the demolition of entire neighborhoods and the loss of social networks. After all, *West of the Tracks* features only one neighborhood among dozens that were impacted at the time. One can only imagine the human tragedies all over Tiexi. While the role of "Gongchang" may have been to show us the SOEs and the workers themselves, "Yanfen jie" shares the social consequences and urban impact of the end of SOEs on a neighborhood that has been completely transformed.

As the filmmaker documents this neighborhood, his role as *minjian* intellectual is to record and make visible a social issue that had not received attention before. Wang Bing's commitment to the working class extends to neighborhood life and community living in "Yanfen jie," as he reveals the social dimensions and tensions associated with the end of the SOEs beyond the representation of the factories themselves. The mistake that critics have made is to ignore the social implications of "Yanfen jie," and how they relate to the issues covered in the first part of the film. As a second variation on the communal life of a lost social totality, the second part of the film greatly adds to the portrayal of Tiexi. After all, what is lost in the English translation of the film title is the "*qu*" in *Tiexi qu*—that is to say, the *district* of Tiexi itself. As Wang Bing succinctly puts it in what may have been his first interview after shooting *West of the Tracks* in 2002: "We wanted to create a world, but in the end that world collapsed. What I filmed was the life of a group of regular people and their relationship with society."[55]

## "*Tielu*"

Entering the third part of *West of the Tracks*, the spectator wonders what story about Tiexi Wang Bing will tell next that has not been told. From a narrative standpoint, the main challenge for Wang Bing in "Tielu" is to sustain the interest of the viewer after several hours exploring the factories and adjacent neighborhood. The filmmaker employs three main strategies in "Tielu" to show yet another face of Tiexi. Firstly, regarding the human subjects themselves, Wang Bing makes a family unit his central focus. Indeed, at the heart of the third part of the film one finds Du Xiyun (aka Old Du) and Du Yang, his teenage son, who live in an extremely small, dilapidated shack on the site of a factory by the railway lines. Having documented the factories and the workers in part one of the film, and the impact of forced relocation on a marginalized neighborhood in part two, Wang turns to the microhistorical in part three to tell the story of a strained father-son relationship. Secondly, Wang Bing privileges night videography in the third part of *West of the Tracks*, and this surprising choice should give us pause. While the filmmaker documents the lively conversations between railway workers and train conductors, he participates in the revalorization of night within documentary practices, a visual gesture that he would return to thirteen years later in the long, visually striking nighttime sequence in *Ta'ang* (2016). Why would Wang Bing privilege nighttime in "Tielu"? Thirdly, the filmmaker makes a bold return to the opening sequence of the first part of the film, "Gongchang," which featured Wang's camera mounted at the front of the locomotive, penetrating industrial space after industrial space. This is a visual strategy that Wang Bing uses numerous times in the third part; in fact, the film ends on such a sequence, in the night this time, thereby connecting the ending of the film with its opening sequence.

*West of the Tracks* could be seen as providing the spectator with three points of view on the same subject matter. There clearly is a process of refinement as the filmmaker documents a lost social totality over nine hours. In "Gongchang," Wang Bing adopts a global perspective on the subject matter and records the factories and the workers themselves. In "Yanfen jie," he proceeds to narrow down the focus as he zeroes in on communal life and forced relocation in one Tiexi neighborhood. In "Tielu," the focus is even narrower as Wang settles on the family unit itself. From factory complex to neighborhood life to family relations, Wang Bing establishes a clear trajectory for the spectator to enter a disintegrating social totality. What remains to be explained is how the experience of the family unit is constructed from a visual and narrative standpoint.

Du Xiyun (aka Old Du) is introduced shortly after the beginning of "Tielu." He is seen discussing with the train workers in their break rooms. He explains to the workers that his main occupation is to collect scrap metal and coal—roughly three bags a day—for which he makes twenty yuan. Wang Bing will eventually visit Old Du's shack, where both he and his son, Du Yang, live. Their small quarters signal the two men's extreme poverty. As Old Du mentions on more than one occasion in the film, "no one would survive here." It is indeed the theme of survival that best captures the living conditions of father and son, who burn coal for heating. Old Du reveals that he has been living there for over twenty years, that he has two sons, and that his wife left him a long time ago. Equally important in the man's life story is that he was a "sent-down youth" during the Cultural Revolution who has struggled to make a living ever since he came back.

In a crucial sequence, Old Du's son, Du Yang, shares a moment alone with Wang Bing in the shack. Yang is sitting on the bed, and he proceeds to empty a plastic bag containing family pictures. He shows the filmmaker a picture of his father and then a picture of his mother. Silence weighs heavily on the scene, as the filmmaker closely observes Yang in a moment of fragility and sorrow. The son silently cries on the bed, and the spectator cannot but imagine what their family life would have been under different circumstances. Soon thereafter, the son learns that his father has been arrested by the police. This causes Yang great anxiety as he tries to get in touch with his father who has been detained. This sequence culminates in a restaurant scene where father and son reunite, but the son's disruptive behavior casts a long shadow over what should have been a celebratory moment. The last scene takes place in Old Du's new house. Both of Old Du's sons are present, and the father's ex-wife joins the family for the Chinese New Year celebrations. Wang Bing's portrait of a family unit ends with a glimmer of hope.

The second strategy that Wang Bing uses in the last part of the film concerns the decision to privilege night videography. This crucial choice participates in the revalorization of night within documentary practices. As I have discussed elsewhere,[56] the decision to work in the dark goes against the grain of most documentary practices, which have been associated with daylight and artificial light. The imperative to show, which concerns documentary media in general, is historically linked to the metaphor of light as truth in more than one way. The knowable world emerges in the light of day, as reality is said to be confirmed by the senses, especially vision, which still functions as the main conduit for sensible experience in documentary practices. What kind of phenomenological experience does night create for the documentarian, and what kind of purpose does night serve in a film such as *West of the Tracks* that addresses Chinese labor from the point of view of a lost social totality?

Ultimately, documenting in the dark serves as visual counterpoint to Wang's goal of shedding light on a family unit in the third part of the film. Indeed, footage of the father-son relationship is intercut with train sequences where the filmmaker is either discussing with the workers or positioned at the front of the locomotive, offering the spectator a chance to re-adopt the strikingly memorable point of view that opens "Gongchang." In the last part of the film, the spectator may wonder why there are recurring locomotive sequences that explore these spaces at night, night after night. It is as though Wang Bing wanted to ensure that these spaces and the crisscrossing tracks would be committed to memory, and that they would be remembered in a different kind of light and atmosphere, in which stillness, obscurity, and silence dominate. The film ends just like it began, except that the diurnal cycle of life of "Gongchang" and "Yanfen jie" no longer captures the viewer's imagination; the locomotive traverses the empty spaces, but this time it is nocturnal *inactivity* that dominates after nine hours. Lü Xinyu has poignantly captured the feeling that accompanies the final moments of *West of the Tracks* in the night: "the plants have been closed down, but the train still wanders through the empty, absurd space of their debris. The factories and people are gone, but the railroad persists like the dead soul of the ruins around it."[57]

## Conclusion

In their study of the revitalization of Tiexi district, Fan and Dai note that 254 factories were moved out after 2002,[58] leading to tremendous changes in the urban fabric. The industrial character of Tiexi had been dramatically changed, commercial and residential buildings now populating the landscape. Since 2006, local government efforts have led to the creation of the Shenyang Foundry Museum and the Shenyang Workers Village Living Museum. Writing in 2020, Dong et al. described Tiexi district as "a hot spot in Shenyang real estate market" and "the area with the fastest population growth rate in the five districts of Shenyang."[59] The rejuvenation of Tiexi district has been hailed as a complete success, and it has received numerous national and international urban design awards. Tiexi now is a symbol of how the Chinese can transform old industrial zones to make way for the commercial future. In the process, the urban fabric—and its memory—has been completely destroyed: "These buildings held a lot of the culture and memory of the Tiexi district, when this urban context was destroyed, the community culture disappeared and the industry specialty of the Tiexi district was lost and can no longer be passed on from generation to generation."[60] Documenting the heritage of China's former industrial base was not on anyone's mind, except for Wang Bing's. *West of the Tracks* remains a shard of this memory and pays homage to Tiexi district and its former workers. The description that Ross has given of the labor spaces in *West of the Tracks* aptly frames the filmmaker's intentions: "But it is all too clear from the loose tempo of work on display that this is a labor regime on its way out, underdisciplined and thus unacceptable for more demanding capitalist times. The warm sociality of the workplace that Wang Bing captures is a relic of an era when labour was not a commodity or held captive on the employer's property by the tyranny of the clock."[61]

The chapter in the history of Chinese labor presented in *West of the Tracks* is quite thought-provoking. From its representation of factories and workers to the decaying communal life of a neighborhood to the challenges faced by a father and son, Wang Bing has provided a complex portrait of a disappearing way of life after the end of SOEs. Beyond the representation of the workers themselves, it is the critical realist emphasis on the working class that makes this work memorable. I thus concur with Fiant, who has noted that Wang Bing's focus in *West of the Tracks* is exemplary: "This kind of commitment to the working class . . . is not that common in contemporary documentary film, even in the history of documentary cinema."[62] In addition to its unique place within documentary history, the 2003 film laid the foundation for what would be several of Wang Bing's preferred shooting strategies, including the handheld camera and the predilection for following in the footsteps of his subjects. Equally fundamental would be the critical realist perspective on Chinese labor and workers developed in his first film, which would find different emphases in films such as *Coal Money* (2008) and *Bitter Money* (2016). Both works examine the Chinese working class and the transformation of labor, and they reveal a different perspective on the social costs of China's economic transformations and the new orientations that Chinese governmentality took after adopting market economy principles and increasingly relying on migrant labor to support its modernizing ambitions.

Looking at *West of the Tracks* retrospectively, Wang has had harsh words for his compatriots and the Chinese nation itself: "No one talked about this most shocking, important historical event that concerned thousands of people. Why is it that in China we never try to react properly to massive historical changes? At the very least *West of the Tracks* shows what existed before this big change, as a memory. That's all I could do: show these people and wholeheartedly be with them . . . How could they have suffered such dehumanization?"[63] In the three parts of *West of the Tracks*, Wang Bing convincingly humanized the face of a vanishing industrial China, a documentary act of mourning for a lost social totality that would find alternative means of expression in his subsequent films on Chinese labor.

## Notes

1. The full-length version of the film was first shown at the Rotterdam International Film Festival in 2003 and was supported by the Hubert Bals Fund. The film received numerous awards, including the Lisbon International Documentary Festival Grand Prize and the Yamagata International Documentary Festival Robert and Frances Flaherty Prize.
2. Lu Xinyu, "*West of the Tracks*: History and Class-Consciousness," in *The New Chinese Documentary Film Movement: For the Public Record*, ed. Chris Berry, Lu Xinyu, and Lisa Rofel (Hong Kong: Hong Kong University Press, 2010), 58. In Chinese: Lü Xinyu, "'Tiexi qu': lishi yu jieji yishi," in *Xueshu, chuanmei yu gonggongxing* (Shanghai: Huadong shifan daxue chubanshe, 2015), 199–218.
3. Guillaume Morel, "Entretien avec Wang Bing," *Images documentaires* 77 (2013): 53.
4. Wang Bing, "Deuxième dialogue avec le cinéaste. Entretien avec Wang Bing réalisé par Isabelle Anselme," in *Wang Bing. Un cinéaste en Chine aujourd'hui*, ed. Caroline Renard, Isabelle Anselme, and François Amy de la Bretèque (Aix-en-Provence: Presses universitaires de Provence, 2014), 135.
5. Wang Bing, *Alors, la Chine. Entretiens avec Emmanuel Burdeau et Eugenio Renzi* (Paris: Les Prairies ordinaires, 2014), 66.
6. Zhiming Cheng, "Poverty in China's Urban Communities: Profile and Correlates," *China Report* 46, no. 2 (2010): 148.
7. Wang initially thought that the three main aspects—the factories, the neighborhood, and the trains—would have to be integrated into a meaningful whole. Unable to construct a story

with one "dramatic thread" for the three parts he had in mind, he resorted to using a tripartite structure (Wang, *Alors, la Chine*, 67) and recorded the three parts somewhat simultaneously over the next year and a half.
8. Wang, *Alors, la Chine*, 92.
9. Wang Bing, "Wang Bing fangtan: na zhong zhengti de lishi gan he mingyun gan," 2002, https://www.chinaindiefilm.org/王兵访谈：那种整体的历史感和命运感/?lang=zh-hans.
10. Barry Naughton, "The Current Wave of State Enterprise Reform in China: A Preliminary Appraisal," *Asian Economic Policy Review* 12 (2017): 287.
11. Antoine Kernen, *La Chine vers l'économie de marché: les privatisations à Shenyang* (Paris: Karthala, 2004), 142.
12. Antoine Kernen and Jean-Louis Rocca, "Social Responses to Unemployment and the 'New Urban Poor': Case Study in Shenyang City and Liaoning Province," *China Perspectives* 27 (2000): 36.
13. Mark Wang, Zhiming Chen, Pingyu Zhang, Lianjun Tong, and Yanji Ma, ed., *Old Industrial Cities Seeking New Road of Industrialization: Models of Revitalizing Northeast China* (Singapore: World Scientific Publishing, 2014), 77.
14. Wang, *Alors, la Chine*, 61.
15. Xiaojun Fan and Shanshan Dai, "Spatial-temporal Distribution Characteristics of Industrial Heritage Protection and the Influencing Factors in a Chinese City: A Case Study of the Tiexi Old Industrial District in Shenyang," *Journal of Heritage Tourism* 12, no. 3 (2017): 285.
16. Kernen and Rocca, "Social Responses to Unemployment and the 'New Urban Poor,'" 37.
17. Kernen and Rocca, "Social Responses to Unemployment and the 'New Urban Poor,'" 37.
18. Russell Smyth and Zhai Qingguo, "Economic Restructuring in China's Large and Medium-sized State-owned Enterprises: Evidence from Liaoning," *Journal of Contemporary China* 12 (2003): 204–5, emphasis in original.
19. Kernen, *La Chine vers l'économie de marché*, 38.
20. Kernen, *La Chine vers l'économie de marché*, 39.
21. Ching Kwan Lee, *Against the Law: Labor Protests in China's Rustbelt and Sunbelt* (Berkeley: University of California Press, 2007), 78.
22. Smyth and Zhai, "Economic Restructuring in China's Large and Medium-sized State-owned Enterprises," 177.
23. Jin Zeng, "Political Compromises: The Privatization of Small- and Medium-Sized Public Enterprises in China," *Journal of Chinese Political Science* 15 (2010): 268.
24. Lee, *Against the Law*, 70.
25. Wang, "Deuxième dialogue avec le cinéaste," 133.
26. For example, Lü Xinyu notes that "the true protagonist of its first part, in Wang Bing's words, is the factory itself, as an industrial reality and social ideal" ("*West of the Tracks*," 59).
27. Kernen and Rocca, "Social Responses to Unemployment and the 'New Urban Poor,'" 41.
28. Kernen, *La Chine vers l'économie de marché*, 221.
29. Titus Stahl, "Georg [György] Lukács," *The Stanford Encyclopedia of Philosophy* (Spring 2018 Edition), ed. Edward N. Zalta, https://plato.stanford.edu/archives/spr2018/entries/lukacs/.
30. Gail Day, "Realism, Totality and the Militant *Citoyen*: Or, What Does Lukács Have to Do with Contemporary Art?," in *Georg Lukács: The Fundamental Dissonance of Existence*, ed. Timothy Bewes and Timothy Hall (London: Bloomsbury, 2013), 205.
31. Day, "Realism, Totality and the Militant *Citoyen*," 209.

32. Ian Aitken, *Realist Film Theory and Cinema: The Nineteenth-Century Lukácsian and Intuitionist Realist Traditions* (Manchester: Manchester University Press, 2016), 75.
33. See Jean-Louis Comolli, "À l'ouest des rails: suite du voyage," *Images documentaires* 77 (2013): 23–34, and Manuel Ramos-Martínez, "The Oxidation of the Documentary: The Politics of Rust in Wang Bing's *Tie Xi Qu: West of the Tracks*," *Third Text* 29, no. 1–2 (2015): 1–13.
34. Morel, "Entretien avec Wang Bing," 53.
35. Wang Bing, "La memoria rimossa della Cina. Conversazione con Wang Bing," in *Wang Bing: Il cinema nella Cina che cambia*, ed. Daniela Persico (Milan: Agenzia X, 2010), 14.
36. Wang, "La memoria rimossa della Cina," 24.
37. Fan and Dai, "Spatial-temporal Distribution Characteristics of Industrial Heritage Protection and the Influencing Factors in a Chinese City," 286.
38. Diane Dufour and Dominique Païni, "Entretien avec Wang Bing," in *Wang Bing—L'œil qui marche*, ed. Diane Dufour, Dominique Païni, and Roger Willems (Paris: Le Bal / Delpire & co, 2021), 812.
39. Wang, *Alors, la Chine*, 62–63.
40. Wang, "La memoria rimossa della Cina," 22.
41. Wang, "La memoria rimossa della Cina," 23. The camera was one of the first that emerged from the mini-DV revolution. Wang borrowed the camera, as he could not afford to purchase one. The film was funded by Wang himself, his family, and he received a grant from the Hubert Bals Fund in Rotterdam in the last stages of post-production. On the topic of the importance of the DV camera, its size, and affordability, Wang has said that it would not have been possible to make the films he has made without it. Wang has now moved on to another small camera body. Since 2009, he has used Sony mirrorless cameras (Wang, "Deuxième dialogue avec le cinéaste," 141).
42. Wu Hung, *A Story of Ruins: Presence and Absence in Chinese Art and Visual Culture* (Princeton: Princeton University Press, 2012), 121.
43. Wu, *A Story of Ruins*, 121.
44. Wu, *A Story of Ruins*, 172.
45. Pascal Beausse, "The Critical Realism of Allan Sekula," *Art Press* 240 (1998): 26.
46. Hilde Van Gelder, "'Social Realism' Then and Now: Constantin Meunier and Allan Sekula," in *Constantin Meunier: A Dialogue with Allan Sekula*, ed. Hilde Van Gelder (Leuven: Leuven University Press, 2005), 85.
47. Kernen, *La Chine vers l'économie de marché*, 215.
48. Kernen, *La Chine vers l'économie de marché*, 238.
49. Lu, "West of the Tracks," 62.
50. Cheng, "Poverty in China's Urban Communities," 144.
51. Cheng, "Poverty in China's Urban Communities," 149.
52. Cheng, "Poverty in China's Urban Communities," 144.
53. Li Xin, Reinout Kleinhans, and Maarten van Ham, "Ambivalence in Place Attachment: The Lived Experiences of Residents in Danwei Communities Facing Demolition in Shenyang, China," *Housing Studies* 34, no. 6 (2019): 1011.
54. Li, Kleinhans, and van Ham, "Ambivalence in Place Attachment," 1012.
55. Wang, "Wang Bing fangtan."
56. I explore some of the philosophical ramifications of nighttime image-making in Bruno Lessard, "Shot in the Dark: Nocturnal Philosophy and Night Photography," in *Critical Distance in Documentary Media*, ed. Gerda Cammaer, Blake Fitzpatrick, and Bruno Lessard (London: Palgrave Macmillan, 2018), 45–67.

57. Lu, "West of the Tracks," 75.
58. Fan and Dai, "Spatial-temporal Distribution Characteristics of Industrial Heritage Protection and the Influencing Factors in a Chinese City," 285.
59. Dong Lijing, Wang Yongchao, Lin Jiayi, and Zhu Ermeng, "The Community Renewal of Shantytown Transformation in Old Industrial Cities: Evidence from Tiexi Worker Village in Shenyang, China," *Chinese Geographical Science* 30, no. 6 (2020): 1033.
60. Wang et al., *Old Industrial Cities Seeking New Road of Industrialization*, 91.
61. Andrew Ross, "The Filming of Deindustrialisation," in *Leaving the Factory: Wang Bing's* Tiexi qu / West of the Tracks (New York: Texte und Töne, 2009), 40.
62. Antony Fiant, *Wang Bing: un geste documentaire de notre temps* (Laval: Warm, 2019), 40.
63. Wang, *Alors, la Chine*, 93.

# 7
# *Coal Money*

## Tracking an Energy Commodity in the Chinese Anthropocene

After completing *Fengming, a Chinese Memoir* (*He Fengming*, 2007) and *Crude Oil* (*Caiyou riji*, 2008), a fourteen-hour video installation, Wang Bing was commissioned by Les Films d'Ici, ARTE, and the Musée du quai Branly to make a fifty-minute film for the series "L'Usage du Monde" headed by French filmmaker Stéphane Breton. The goal of this documentary project was to constitute "a memory of local humanity at the dawn of the twenty-first century."[1] The five films appearing on the Editions Montparnasse DVD address various socioeconomic and environmental issues pertaining to the development of the modern world, focusing on neglected geographical areas where few documentarians have ventured such as the Gabonese forest, Russia's White Sea, Nepal, and northeastern China. An investigation into the margins of modernity, the series pays homage to both Albert Kahn's "Archives de la planète" project (1908–1931) and Swiss writer Nicolas Bouvier's travel literature book, *L'Usage du monde* (1963). Wang Bing's contribution to the series, *Coal Money* (*Tongdao*, 2008), built on the foundation laid by *Crude Oil*, a video piece documenting a group of workers at an oil field in northwestern Qinghai province, which was commissioned by the Rotterdam International Film Festival.

*Coal Money* has had an intriguing critical reception within Chinese documentary studies. Indeed, based on the absence of sustained studies of this film, there seems to be consensus that it is of "relatively minor relevance in comparison to his [Wang Bing's] major documentaries."[2] Countering such hasty dismissal, this chapter argues that the distinction between minor and major work within Wang Bing's oeuvre is misleading, and that, in the case of *Coal Money*, it is neither the length of the film nor the way that it has been described in the literature that should disqualify it from being closely examined. After all, Wang Bing had experience making shorter films, having worked on the fourteen-minute fiction short *Brutality Factory* a few years before, and that film has not been dismissed because of its length. What seems to have played a greater role in the reception of *Coal Money* is Wang Bing's own comments on the production brief rather than the actual merits of the film or lack thereof.³ The rehabilitation of a film such as *Coal Money* should generate timely discussions about coal as an unsustainable energy resource in China, and how the film frames the coal-related production, transportation, and negotiation activities defining the conditions of workers within the Chinese Anthropocene.

I argue that Wang Bing's *Coal Money* makes a singular contribution to the environmental documentary genre and the representation of Chinese labor because it does not focus on the coal mines or the miners themselves, and neither does it address the transformation of coal, coal mine safety issues (including workers' chronic health problems such as pneumoconiosis), or the environmental costs of the coal industry. It is as a *transportable* and *negotiable* commodity that coal appears in the film, one toward which Chinese truck drivers, coal sellers, and intermediaries gravitate as they try to make a living in remote areas where other kinds of employment are rare. Wang Bing's film advances that, in addition to coal extraction, equally precarious labor practices come with the *movement* of coal and *negotiation* of coal prices. I show that the film signals the transition from the Silk Road of yesteryear to the Coal Road, as it were, an epochal change characterizing coal trade routes in contemporary China. While the environmental cost of the coal industry is not the focus of the film, the spectator cannot help but reflect on the multifaceted impacts of coal in a country in which it is the primary energy resource.

In the first section of this chapter, I contextualize Wang Bing's *Coal Money* using research findings on the Chinese coal industry, and I discuss a neglected aspect in the literature, which concerns the transportation of coal and its impact on the environment. Wang Bing's timely contribution to the representation of the Chinese coal industry brings to light pressing issues associated with coal transportation that merit closer attention. Second, I examine how the filmmaker represents Chinese labor through coal industry workers such as truck drivers and coal sellers and their conversations on the road. This chapter argues that Wang Bing creates a kind of relational space by emphasizing human interactions across various geographical areas and "minescapes" to understand energy resource extraction as a set of interrelated activities, including sociocultural, material, and economic exchanges, which are the focus of *Coal Money*. Finally, I reflect on the primordial role that coal plays in China, and how Wang Bing's film paved the way for the emerging genre of the Chinese environmental film in general and a work such as Zhao Liang's *Behemoth* (*Beixi moshou* 悲兮魔兽, 2015), which explicitly targets the environmental costs associated with China's overinvestment in coal.

## The Chinese Coal Industry and Its Challenges

As an energy resource, coal is located at the crossroads of various discourses on environmental politics, political economy, and labor in the Chinese Anthropocene. With respect to the political economy of coal and its related labor practices, how has coal workers' status evolved since the transition from the planned economy to the market economy? How have Chinese labor practices changed in the process? These and similar questions need to be asked to better understand Wang Bing's *Coal Money* and its representation of coal industry workers. As discussed in the previous chapter on *West of the Tracks*, industrial workers are now far more independent than they were before the economic reforms, the CCP having greatly weakened its ties to workers by establishing a new governmental regime in the post-Reform era. As noted in several studies discussed below, the socioeconomic status of the coal worker has greatly changed over the past few decades. Once some of the most well-paid workers in the country, coal workers now face precarious, contractual employment conditions in an industry that is as vital as ever.

Coal is a cornerstone of the Chinese economy and its main energy resource: it provides approximately 70 percent of the country's energy. In the post-Reform era, the Chinese coal industry has greatly increased its margin because of the thousands of small, private producers supporting what has become the largest coal-producing nation in the world in terms of output: "By the beginning of the twenty-first century, China had become the major global producer of coal, which continued to be the country's key source of energy long after most other countries had switched to oil."[4] Wright further remarks that heavy industry consumption played a great role in the total energy usage figures in the 2000s: "The iron and steel industry increased its consumption of coal from 180 to over 430 million tons between 2001 and 2007."[5] Within the next decade, it is projected that China's coal consumption will continue to increase.

In the 2000s, the CCP launched new programs that would target national space and transform it into a production resource to be exploited. One such program was the "Opening the West" (*xibu da kaifa*) campaign, and the autonomous region of Inner Mongolia acted as the foundation for this initiative. Woodworth describes the goals of this governmental program: "In Inner Mongolia, the Open the West campaign called for accelerating and increasing the scope of coal mine projects, expanding exploration and production of oil and gas, and dramatically expanding the network of pipelines to deliver these fuels to markets east and south."[6] Inner Mongolia and Shanxi are the two provinces whose important coal reserves have answered industry and consumer demands since the turn of the millennium: "Shanxi and Inner Mongolia between them account for over half of the available reserves and over 40 percent of production, while the industrial regions along the coast are the main consumers."[7] The provinces that are identified as the shooting locations at the beginning of Wang Bing's *Coal Money* are Inner Mongolia, Shanxi, and Hebei, a trio that has been at the heart of the increasing demand for coal, especially Inner Mongolia, which was "increasingly becoming the dominant player, with its production growing from under half the level of Shanxi in 2005 to overtaking Shanxi as the largest producer in 2009."[8] Inner Mongolia's unique natural resource profile is directly related to the rise in extraction activities: "Inner Mongolia is rich in resources and has the largest areas of grassland, forest and arable land per capita in China, as well as the world's largest reserves of rare earth minerals."[9]

There are notable environmental challenges associated with the growth of the Chinese coal industry in Inner Mongolia and the country's increasing consumption on a national level. One serious problem lies in the mixed messages that the CCP sends when it seems intent on developing alternatives to coal while at the same time ramping up its coal production. Writing in 2021, Ren et al. observe: "Since 2005, the Chinese government has engaged in an ambitious effort to move China's energy system away from coal and towards more environmentally friendly sources of energy . . . Paradoxically, however, China has—at the very same time—been investing heavily in a massive expansion of coal-fired thermal energy capacity."[10] The country's yearly 10.5 percent economic growth between 2001 and 2007 certainly did not help, which corresponds to the period when Wang Bing was commissioned to make *Coal Money*. Another problem concerns "water and air pollution and land degradation, and even more intractable ones in relation to carbon emissions."[11] In addition to the wastewater that coal production entails, other pressing issues relate to the storage of solid waste, as well as the pressure that the industry puts on water supplies. Finally, China's notoriously bad air quality and smog issues result in great part from coal burning, and air pollution and the discharge of methane will continue to haunt the environmental future of the nation. As the country increases its standard of living and education level and develops greater environmental awareness, carbon emissions are most likely to figure as one of the most threatening factors in the country's plans for a sustainable future considering the size of its population. The large-scale burning of coal, in addition to the burning of fossil fuels, will need to be reconsidered given the scale of the consumption patterns of Chinese consumers.

China has failed to convince the international community of its willingness to curtail carbon emissions, combat air pollution, and decrease its dependence on heavy industry such as coal-fired plants. The Chinese position has created a series of interrelated problems: "Neglect of the environmental problems caused by the production, transportation and utilization of coal leads to substantial differences between the price of coal and the actual cost of this resource. This discrepancy contributes to increasingly serious environmental pollution and ecological destruction and imposes adverse impacts on the living environment and human health."[12] It is the external costs of coal such as environmental pollution, ecological degradation, work-related accidents, and medical costs that demand immediate attention as they increase yearly. One of the critical issues for China is to think of an alternative to coal considering that it does not possess the oil reserves on which many countries rely. As Rui has argued: "Because of the lack of alternative energy sources, coal is more important for China than for almost any other country."[13] If China reduced its coal consumption nationally and ensured that it would not face a resulting gap in supply, then it would need to turn to oil or nuclear power, which presents its own set of challenges.

While the multifaceted costs of coal production serve as a backdrop to Wang Bing's *Coal Money*, the issue of transportation is the clear focus in the film. Some spectators may find it odd that the filmmaker would focus on transportation when there seem to be more pressing issues with coal production and consumption. However, transportation is clearly identified in the literature as a key logistical problem in the coal industry, and it does possess its own set of environmental challenges that may not be apparent. In China, there exist "four major modes of coal transportation: railways, trucks, inland water vessels, and seaborne ships ... Railways are the dominant transportation mode for coal with more than 60% of coal transported by rail via general and coal-dedicated lines."[14] The main issue is the great geographical distances between production and consumption sites. As Wright remarks: "the geographical distribution of the resources is poorly matched with that of consuming industries, so that transport capacity to ship coal to consumers has always been an important constraint."[15] Rui adds to this picture that "[t]he average coal transportation distance increased from 426 km in 1980 to 548 km and then to 561 km in 1995."[16] She concludes that "[t]he long distances between coal production areas and their markets, and the consequent long distances that coal has to be transported means that infrastructure bottlenecks are always a significant issue in China."[17] Both railways and highways bear the brunt of the increasing demand for coal in this expanding industry landscape, which includes "energy-intensive sectors such as steel, aluminium, glass, construction material, and cement."[18]

Transportation and distribution activities occupy the first half of *Coal Money*, and the spectator witnesses some of the challenges associated with moving coal from the northeast to the east coast. The great geographical distances between the northeastern production areas and the coastal provinces signal the need to pay closer attention to the transportation network. Surprisingly, roads, and their related logistical problems, have been neglected in the literature on the coal industry even though they play a central role in the transportation of this energy resource: "Roads are used extensively for transporting coal short distances due to the flexibility of trucking: from mines to railway loading facilities and from rail terminals or ports to consumers ... About 20% of coal produced is transported by road."[19] Truck transportation leads to traffic jams on highways and air pollution. The strain that such travels put on the highways relates to the external costs associated with transportation. Indeed, Lü et al. note that "the transportation mode that has the greatest impact on the environment and the highest external cost is highway-based transportation."[20] It is customary for shipments to travel several hundred miles before they reach their destination in port cities such as Tianjin and Qinhuangdao or farther down the coast in industrial areas. The main issue is that "[d]uring transport, major types of pollution, including total suspended particulates, sulfur dioxide, nitrogen oxides and carbon monoxide, are released by the use of different types of power fuels along railways, highways and other means of transport and cause atmospheric pollution."[21]

## Framing the Minescape and Beyond

In the preface to his collection of interviews with Wang Bing, Renzi reveals that *Coal Money*, at least in its pre-production phase, was supposed to be one of the most ambitious projects ever designed by the filmmaker. At its core, the film would have addressed the Chinese economy, "which would have been illustrated by the adventures of heroic truck drivers to greedy customs officers to corrupt cops . . . The film's structure would have borrowed the method of *Capital* from Karl Marx: describing the entirety of the circulation system of capital by following a single merchandise."[22] Admittedly, the content of Wang Bing's film does not reflect Renzi's description, but this does not mean that a Marxist reading of the work, including the tribulations of a commodity such as coal and the workers moving it, would be inadequate in this reified environment. As Fiant has noted: "It is indeed the rapport with others, entirely determined by money, that interests Wang Bing rather than the inherent solitude associated with this line of work."[23] As such, *Coal Money* demands a critical approach that looks at how China's energy commodity par excellence moves within transportation networks, is qualitatively evaluated, and then exchanged for money. As described by Wang Bing, "*Coal Money* concerns resources, coal extraction, and its use by Chinese plants. The film follows a path that goes from the south to Tianjin and Tanggu . . . then to the southern ports: for example, Guangzhou, Shenzhen, Zhejiang, Fujian, all those places."[24] Finally, the filmmaker reveals that the ultimate goal in the film is to "talk about the Chinese economy, to see what it is."[25] Such thought-provoking reflections make us reconsider the purpose of a film such as *Coal Money* insofar as it recalls a certain wish for totality, as discussed in the previous chapter, on the part of a filmmaker who wants to cover resource extraction, distribution networks, workers' interactions, and the visualization of the Chinese economy.

The life cycle of coal includes three phases: production, transportation, and consumption. The filmmaker addresses the first phase in both the opening and ending sequences of the film, thus framing the second phase—the transportation activities—with a visual record of coal production in full swing. These are the only two occasions on which the mining pit itself is shown in *Coal Money*, making the minescape a crucial element in the representation of the coal industry. In the first part, the filmmaker follows truck drivers who specialize in transporting one of the most important commodities in twenty-first-century China. Along the way, we witness drivers entering into lively conversations with mine owners, customs officers, coal buyers and sellers, and negotiators. The film begins with a minescape; it is a sequence located near an open-pit mine in Inner Mongolia. In extremely dusty and windy conditions, drivers protect themselves from the elements waiting for their trucks to be loaded. In China, most mines are still underground, but that is slowly changing as evidenced in this sequence in which Wang Bing documents the activities of an open-pit mine.

Rather than using the kind of establishing shot that would have been de rigueur in a typical film on the same subject, Wang Bing eschews such shots to privilege full immersion. Indeed, the second sequence of the film features Wang Bing sitting in the passenger seat of one of the trucks. Handholding the camera, the filmmaker does his best to maintain a stable frame, but the rough terrain makes for a rocky viewing experience. Wang's camera and wide-angle lens frame the scene in front of the moving truck. The dirty windshield filters the action, the spectator making out other trucks and excavators in the distance. Excavators continue to load the trucks in front, as the filmmaker reveals the long queue waiting to be loaded. The soundscape is composed of a mix of noises coming from the coal hitting the truck beds, machinery, and inaudible voices. After a glimpse at the driver sitting next to Wang Bing in the truck cabin, the spectator hears the incredible thuds made by the coal hitting the truck bed behind the filmmaker.

Throughout *Coal Money*, the spectator is privy to moments of less spectacular content than in the opening sequence. For example, after only ten minutes, the spectator accompanies the filmmaker into a restaurant where drivers receive their interprovincial passes. Sitting at a table, they enjoy their lunch before going back on the road. Wang Bing records various exchanges of money between the drivers, who eventually leave the restaurant. The filmmaker adopts the kind of disposition that spectators are accustomed to: he follows his subjects outside from a distance in the parking lot. The film shows other downtimes and less eventful moments. For example, the spectator witnesses a driver taking a nap or waiting for other trucks to pass by on narrow roads; a convoy of trucks makes its way to its destination in the dead of night, avoiding large crevices in the road. In another sequence, Wang Bing makes a point of showing that the movements of coal depend on the efforts of state employees who issue the passes and receipts that drivers must carry to exit the province and then enter the neighboring one with their cargo.

## On the Road: Private Ownership, Profit, and Evaluation

The transition to the market economy also impacted the SOEs that used to populate the Chinese coal industry. Changes to ownership structures resulted in a greater contribution from the private sector, as SOEs receded into the background to make room for private-sector initiatives. Wright has observed that "[t]he most dramatic change in China's coal industry after the onset of reforms was the growth of a collectively owned or privately owned small mine sector in rural areas."[26] While Wang Bing does not explicitly dwell on the differences between state-owned coal mines, state-owned mines operated by local, provincial, or county governments, and township- and village-owned enterprise (TVE) mines, which include those under private ownership, he draws the spectator's attention to the workers themselves and how they interact with the bosses and mine owners in the new capitalist environment defining the coal industry. Such interactions also play a role in the assessment of the coal minescape, which should go beyond the ravaged landscape to underline its function as a potential space for political contestation. In addition to what is visible, a minescape also includes "the structures and discourses that value and produce 'resources', and the 'already existing political landscape of forces, identities', imaginaries and power dynamics within which resource extraction occurs."[27]

A striking sequence at the beginning of the documentary illustrates some of the sociopolitical and economic issues connoting the minescape, as described above. It features a discussion between a private mine owner and a truck driver. Through their words, the spectator comes to realize that the coal industry has greatly changed since the economic reforms, and that some owners in the private sector have greatly profited from manual workers. What Wang Bing shows in a subtle manner is the increasing gap between the mine owners and the workers, which concerns the socioeconomic issues that have only recently been the subject of debate within Chinese society. Wright gives the example of the "massive social inequalities encapsulated most dramatically in the contrast between the *nouveaux riches* Shanxi coal owners and the families of the thousands of miners who die in unsafe coal mines."[28] It is in fact the growing inequality between "the private mine owners and the rural mine workers that attracts by far the most attention."[29] The disparity between the kind of money that the truck driver makes transporting the most valuable energy commodity in the country and the kind of profit that a private mine owner can expect to pocket is quite apparent in this scene, with the owner bluntly telling this stranger that he has already made 35 million yuan in profit since he purchased the mine. This discussion clearly reveals how China's market economy has generated a new type of businessman who could not have existed when state-owned mines dominated the landscape. Individual entrepreneurs like him allow Wang Bing to posit the importance of private investment and profit in the twenty-first-century Chinese coal industry, which seems to be lacking regulation after decades of state ownership.

The sequence featuring a driver named Old Meng introduces a key focus of the film: the negotiations about evaluating and selling coal. Before coal is evaluated, trucks must be unloaded. The sequence begins with a man handling a sizable piece of coal, barehanded, who proceeds to unload the truck. It is difficult to believe that the entire cargo will be unloaded by hand with the help of a simple shovel. The hands of the workers, pitch-black and dirty, make the spectator reflect on the manual labor that is still involved in the Chinese coal industry. The remainder of the sequence shows the previously featured nameless intermediary whose job consists of negotiating with truck drivers who want to sell coal. It soon dawns on the spectator that the main issue in the evaluation of coal is the impure quality of some cargos. Indeed, such cargos include too many stones unevenly distributed among the coal pieces. Obviously, the issue is that buyers do not want to purchase a mixed load of stones and coal. This sequence exemplifies why Wang Bing's film offers a unique portrait of the coal industry. As Bourgeus puts it, "*Coal Money* also provides insight into the precise procedures of work, with an impressively textural, almost visceral shot of a truck violently unloading a massive cargo of what look like pitch-black bricks. Wang keeps his camera on these objects while his subjects are discussing which are coal and which are not—encouraging us to look closer, to first hear, then see the material and decide for ourselves."[30] The spectator thus becomes enmeshed in the visual assessment of coal and, most importantly, in the appreciation of the kind of manual labor that is required to move coal from production area to delivery site.

Wang Bing closely follows the men who argue about fair prices, trailer trucks figuring in the background. From non-negotiable offers to final deals, the viewer can only speculate who is trying to make a quick profit and who is an honest worker. A similar situation occurs in the following sequence in which several manual workers unloading the trucks want to get paid by their boss, who is unwilling to do so, let alone raise their salaries. The workers often look at Wang Bing's camera, as if they were counting on the filmmaker to record the conversation in case their boss would go back on his word and fail to pay them. The film ends like it began: a long shot of the open mine pit shows dozens of red trucks queuing to be loaded. This time, Wang Bing's camera is perched on a hill overlooking this minescape, its fixed frame capturing a dusty scene where China's most valuable energy commodity is to be extracted, loaded, and transported in an apparently endless cycle.

## Coal Workers: Between Labor and Exploitation

In 1983, the Press of the Nova Scotia College of Art and Design published a book titled *Mining Photographs and Other Pictures: A Selection from the Negative Archives of Shedden Studio, Glace Bay, Cape Breton*.[31] Featuring the work of industrial photographer Leslie Shedden, the publication also includes Allan Sekula's comprehensive essay on Shedden's photographs and the history of mining practices. Offering a rich historical account of the stakes in reading a photographic archive such as Shedden's mining photographs, Sekula raises important questions about "the relationship between photographic culture and economic life" and the manner in which "photography constructs an *imaginary economy*."[32] It is the supposed transparency of the photographs that Sekula questions in assessing their production of knowledge, and the kinds of realism that the images propose to the viewers in their quest for "a unified understanding of the social workings of photography in an industrial environment."[33] At the heart of Sekula's reflections lies the importance of manual labor for mining and its perennial status in all kinds of industries.

It is instructive to extend Sekula's reflections on mining photographs into the territory of documentary film and the Chinese coal industry to ask what kind of relationship *Coal Money* establishes between documentary film and the post-Reform economic environment in which coal workers find themselves. It is the capitalist exchange relations and commodity status of coal that emerge in Wang Bing's *Coal Money*, as refracted in the representation of Chinese industrialism, manual labor, truck drivers' words, and negotiators' actions. The film creates a relational space that makes visible various sites of human labor and exploitation where workers articulate their disappointment in the Chinese coal industry and the reified relationships existing since the end of SOEs. In capturing such moments, Wang Bing opens the door to being labeled an *industrial* documentarian considering films such as *West of the Tracks* (2003) and *Bitter Money* (2016). While this label does not reflect the entirety of Wang Bing's output as a filmmaker, it does espouse the concerns of the films examined in the second part of this study. The care with which Wang has documented changing industrial environments in the twenty-first century as the country reinvented its governmental regime and implemented a mixed economy denotes great concern for the evolution of Chinese labor at a time when workers had difficulty orienting themselves in this new landscape.

In terms of documentary representation, the question that remains unanswered is what kind of industrial portrait Wang Bing paints of the coal workers. In his reflections on the politics of worker representation, Sekula has noted that the representation of the working class does not have to conform to the representation made at the hands of the elite: "Something else, something resistant and resilient and hopeful, is retrieved from the slag heap of dominant culture, from tradition, from 'popular memory,' from political struggles and from everyday experience."[34] While *Coal Money* may not have fulfilled Wang Bing's wish to offer a comprehensive treatment of the Chinese coal industry, the film does show an industry in transformation and how the workers face the challenges associated with the transportation and evaluation of coal, as they skillfully negotiate a new economic situation in which precarity and exploitation cannot be avoided. In response to an interviewer who remarked that the people in *Coal Money* were much livelier and more proactive than in his previous films, Wang Bing pointed out: "We can see that China today is not exactly the same as it was in the years when I shot *West of the Tracks*. Nowadays, you can see the hardship in people's lives, but there is also creativity, energy, and vigour among ordinary people. You can see that . . . the ordinary people are working hard to create wealth through their own labour."[35] The filmmaker's hopeful reply is quite instructive, as it implicitly constructs an image of the Chinese worker whose resilience and adaptation to new circumstances will seemingly allow for a brighter future in capitalist China. It remains to be seen if Wang Bing's future films on Chinese labor will corroborate this optimistic assessment.

## Conclusion

Zhao Liang's *Behemoth* (*Beixi moshou*, 2015) presents an alternative portrait of coal and iron production activities to Wang Bing's *Coal Money*. A hybrid film containing elements of fiction inspired by Dante's *Divina Commedia* (1321), it shows the more hellish aspects of coal and iron mines, including workers' deteriorating health conditions and pneumoconiosis patients, amid a ravaged landscape of mountains and open-pit mines. An equally important aspect of Zhao's film is to have shown the utopian desire at the heart of the Chinese economic miracle, especially what remains of the housing bubble that characterized China in the 2000s. Some of the most arresting images in *Behemoth* show ghost towns such as the infamous city of Ordos or Kangbashi New District in Inner Mongolia, a telling sign that the need for residential housing in the area had been grossly overestimated. As Woodworth notes: "In Kangbashi alone, more than 300,000 residential units were completed between 2006 and 2013. Yet the new town today has an official population of less than 50,000, a figure that is almost surely inflated."[36]

Zhao's *Behemoth* and Wang's *Coal Money* function as complementary efforts in the emerging genre of the Chinese environmental film. What a film such as *Coal Money* first addressed was the importance of transportation within the coal industry, and it showed the daily experiences of workers, including truck drivers, and their interactions with intermediaries of all sorts in the evaluation of their cargo. Zhao's film offers a more comprehensive treatment of the energy resource production sector in Inner Mongolia and its concrete, nefarious effects on workers. A more visually polished film, *Behemoth* makes of coal "an enormous evil energy," as mentioned in the director's statement, and employs a reproachful tone that is absent from Wang Bing's critical realist treatment of the same industry. Zhao admonishes the viewers for their complicity in the "catastrophic consequences of fuel politics": "We are all consumers of natural resources, so we are all accomplices of that evil that's hurting the environment. All of us are part of the monster."[37]

Zhao's and Wang's films meet in their understanding of the future of Chinese labor and the challenges that the next generation of workers will face. In his director's statement, Zhao pauses to reflect on the workers in the energy sector. He writes: "Those migrant workers, who leave their hometowns due to local scarcity of resources, and move to other places to find work, are the pivotal laborers of the modernization process in China. They don't really have any awareness or knowledge in terms of safety or protection at such a workplace. They are the most important labor force during the process of capital accumulation under a regime of centralized power. They are the victims. I hope my film can motivate the officials to protect the rights of migrant workers with legal measures."[38] What kind of "passageway" (*tongdao*), to evoke *Coal Money*'s Chinese title, is created for the next generation of Chinese (migrant) workers who may not wish to enter the heavy industry sector then? This is the topic that Wang Bing would explore in his next film on the evolution of Chinese labor in the twenty-first century: *Bitter Money* (2016).

## Notes

1. http://www.stephane-breton.com/collection-laquo-lrsquousage-du-monde-raquo.html, accessed February 2, 2022.
2. Elena Pollacchi, *Wang Bing's Filmmaking of the China Dream: Narratives, Witnesses and Marginal Spaces* (Amsterdam: Amsterdam University Press, 2021), 56.
3. Scholars have extensively relied on the following comment to dismiss *Coal Money*: "The film *Coal Money* is an incomplete project. We shot a lot at the time. But it was done for a television programme in Europe, which only gave me a fifty-minute slot. The producer, a French company, actually understood the problem. They asked me to make a complete version afterwards, but I didn't have time to go back and work on it again. Within the fifty minutes, it wasn't easy to narrate a coherent story. It is not a completed work." Wang Bing, "Filming a Land in Flux," *New Left Review* 82 (2013): 125. In a rebuttal of sorts, Stéphane Breton has claimed that, at the production stage, Wang Bing never complained about his production brief and the expected length of the film. See Fiant's account of his conversation with Breton in Antony Fiant, *Wang Bing: un geste documentaire de notre temps* (Laval: Warm, 2019), 82. It is not my attention to arbitrate between Wang and Breton in this chapter but to examine *Coal Money* on its own terms.
4. Tim Wright, *The Political Economy of the Chinese Coal Industry* (New York: Routledge, 2011), 1.
5. Wright, *The Political Economy of the Chinese Coal Industry*, 81.
6. Max D. Woodworth, "Spaces of the Gigantic: Extraction and Urbanization in China's Energy Frontier," in *Frontier Assemblages: The Emergent Politics of Resource Frontiers in Asia*, ed. Jason Cons and Michael Eilenberg (Oxford: Wiley-Blackwell, 2019), 161.
7. Wright, *The Political Economy of the Chinese Coal Industry*, 20.
8. Wright, *The Political Economy of the Chinese Coal Industry*, 28.
9. Hao-Dong Lü, Jin-Sheng Zhou, Lin Yang, Yi-Min Li, and Lu Liu, "An Accounting of the External Environmental Costs of Coal in Inner Mongolia Using the Pollution Damage Method," *Environment, Development and Sustainability* 22 (2020): 1301.
10. Mengjia Ren, Lee G. Branstetter, Brian K. Kovak, Daniel Erian Armanios, Jiahai Yuan, "Why Has China Overinvested in Coal Power?," *The Energy Journal* 42, no. 2 (2021): 113.
11. Wright, *The Political Economy of the Chinese Coal Industry*, 38.
12. Lü et al., "An Accounting of the External Environmental Costs of Coal in Inner Mongolia Using the Pollution Damage Method," 1300.
13. Huaichuan Rui, *Globalization, Transition and Development in China: The Case of the Coal Industry* (London: Routledge, 2005), 45.
14. Bertrand Rioux, Philipp Galkin, Frederic Murphy, and Axel Pierru, "Economic Impacts of Debottlenecking Congestion in the Chinese Coal Supply Chain," *Energy Economics* 60 (2016): 389.
15. Wright, *The Political Economy of the Chinese Coal Industry*, 19.
16. Rui, *Globalization, Transition and Development in China*, 62.
17. Rui, *Globalization, Transition and Development in China*, 134.

18. Max D. Woodworth, "China's Coal Production Goes West: Assessing Recent Geographical Restructuring and Industrial Transformation," *The Professional Geographer* 67, no. 4 (2015): 635.
19. Rioux et al., "Economic Impacts of Debottlenecking Congestion in the Chinese Coal Supply Chain," 390.
20. Lü et al., "An Accounting of the External Environmental Costs of Coal in Inner Mongolia Using the Pollution Damage Method," 1314.
21. Lü et al., "An Accounting of the External Environmental Costs of Coal in Inner Mongolia Using the Pollution Damage Method," 1314.
22. Eugenio Renzi, "La totalité comme forme," in Wang Bing, *Alors, la Chine. Entretiens avec Emmanuel Burdeau et Eugenio Renzi* (Paris: Les Prairies ordinaires, 2014), 11.
23. Fiant, *Wang Bing : un geste documentaire de notre temps*, 83.
24. Wang Bing, "Deuxième dialogue avec le cinéaste. Entretien avec Wang Bing réalisé par Isabelle Anselme," in *Wang Bing. Un cinéaste en Chine aujourd'hui*, ed. Caroline Renard, Isabelle Anselme and François Amy de la Bretèque (Aix-en-Provence: Presses universitaires de Provence, 2014), 134.
25. Wang, "Deuxième dialogue avec le cinéaste," 134.
26. Wright, *The Political Economy of the Chinese Coal Industry*, 93.
27. Melina Ey and Meg Sherval, "Exploring the Minescape: Engaging with the Complexity of the Extractive Sector," *Area* 48, no. 2 (2016): 181.
28. Wright, *The Political Economy of the Chinese Coal Industry*, 199.
29. Wright, *The Political Economy of the Chinese Coal Industry*, 201.
30. Camille Bourgeus, "Work/Space: Labor and Realism in the Cinema of Wang Bing," *Diacritics* 46, no. 4 (2018): 61.
31. Leslie Shedden, *Mining Photographs and Other Pictures: A Selection from the Negative Archives of Shedden Studio, Glace Bay, Cape Breton*, ed. Benjamin H. D. Buchloh and Robert Wilkie (Halifax: Press of the Nova Scotia College of Art and Design, 1983).
32. Allan Sekula, "Photography between Labour and Capital," in *Art Isn't Fair: Further Essays on the Traffic in Photographs and Related Media*, ed. Sally Stein and Ina Steiner (London: MACK, 2020), 15, emphasis in original.
33. Sekula, "Photography between Labour and Capital," 21–22.
34. Sekula, "Photography between Labour and Capital," 68.
35. Wang, "Filming a Land in Flux," 125.
36. Woodworth, "Spaces of the Gigantic," 167.
37. Grasshopper Film, "Behemoth: A Film by Zhao Liang," press kit, https://grasshopperfilm.com/wp-content/uploads/2016/01/Behemoth---Press-Kit.pdf.
38. Grasshopper Film, "Behemoth: A Film by Zhao Liang."

# 8

# *Bitter Money*

## The Spatial Politics of Migrant Labor

Shot between 2014 and 2016, *Bitter Money* (*Ku qian*, 2016) takes place in the industrial district of Zhili, located east of Huzhou in Zhejiang, a province that "is unique for its stellar record in developing the private economy during the reform era."¹ As one of the most prosperous regions in twenty-first-century China alongside Guangdong's Pearl River Delta, Zhejiang has attracted thousands of rural migrant workers who moved to manufacturing centers to find employment in textile and garment factories. It is during one of Wang Bing's stays in Yunnan where he shot *Three Sisters* (*San zimei*, 2012) and *'Til Madness Do Us Part* (*Feng ai*, 2014) that the filmmaker met three teenagers whose imminent departure for the east coast would lead him to make a film about migrant labor and the eastern textile industry. Funded by several European and Asian production companies, *Bitter Money* won the Orizzonti Award for best screenplay at the Venice Film Festival,² as well as the Human Rights Film Network Award at the Zagreb Human Rights Film Festival.

One of the central concerns at the heart of *Bitter Money* is the role of migrant labor in China's so-called "economic miracle," especially the development of the textile and garment industry on the east coast. Wang Bing has stressed on numerous occasions that what interested him in the subjects whom he followed to Zhejiang was the concrete aspects of their lives. He was particularly struck by the young generation's desire to improve their living conditions. Reflecting the governmental regime in which subjects must become entrepreneurs of the self in the post-Reform era, Wang's comments highlight how young Chinese workers feel the economic pressure to become financially independent at an early age, especially in the case of rural migrants who must support family members back home. The young workers' collective state of mind echoes the original Chinese title, *ku qian*. Used in the area in which Wang Bing shot *Bitter Money*, the colloquial expression refers to the sacrifices and hardships that rural migrants face when working in factories far away from home. The filmmaker adds: "So over the course of the shooting, I understood why they call work bitter money: all these workers have migrated to Huzhou from other regions, with the hope of making money. The word 'bitter' alludes to the discrimination that the individual has to face when he [sic] is away from his native place, the hardships and sadness a person has to face when he is away from home to earn money, working like hell all day, every day, with no personal life whatsoever."[3]

This final chapter on the transformation of labor in twenty-first-century China examines how Wang Bing frames the issues of internal migration and migrant labor through the prism of the younger generation of workers. The textile and garment industry refracts the exploitation characteristic of not only the working conditions in Huzhou, but also in most coastal cities where migrant workers have moved to find gainful employment and support China's neoliberal quest to become the "factory of the world." Wang Bing closely observes a small number of subjects in the film to paint a broad portrait of labor conditions within post-Reform China, focusing on the precarity of unskilled or low-skilled labor. These rural migrants' daily experiences are the foundation of Wang Bing's *Bitter Money* rather than the actual textile industry itself. I argue that the film privileges the *spatial politics* of migrant labor, which includes enforced mobility, labor exploitation, the dormitory labor regime, migrant subjectivity, and domestic violence. In this chapter, I focus more specifically on the representation of migrant mobility, on the two main spaces documented in the film—the workshop and the dormitory—and the interactions between workers therein, and on Wang Bing's unexpected focus on a struggling migrant couple as reflecting issues of rural migrant subjectivity and domestic violence. In addition to how Chinese governmentality operates from the point of view of spatial politics, Wang's film demonstrates that closer attention should be paid to the social production of female migrant subjectivity in terms of gender and power.

## From Yunnan to Zhejiang: The Mobility of Rural Migrants

Wang Bing ends *Bitter Money* with a title card that shares the following information: "This film was shot between 2014 and 2016 in Huzhou, Zhejiang province, where there are 18,000 textile factories. More than 300,000 people work there, having left their villages located in other provinces such as Yunnan, Guizhou, Jiangxi, Anhui, and Henan." Most Western viewers being unfamiliar with the sociohistorical and economic context of the film, they may have been surprised upon reading such impressive figures. The data demonstrate that the contribution of these migrant workers is immense, reflecting the fact that millions have sold their labor power in coastal cities such as Huzhou in the hope for better living conditions over the past decades. Historically, there are three aspects of migrant workers' labor that have made it attractive to Chinese employers: their labor is "cheap (because their reproduction can be partly complemented by the production in their home villages), easy to control (rootless, without much support from local communities) and able to be used to weaken the bargaining power of local labor."[4] Migrant labor has thus been framed and controlled over the past decades, that is, since China entered the market economy and transformed the east coast into a manufacturing powerhouse.

Branded the "factory of the world," China has drawn critical attention given its treatment of workers within factories and workshops all over the country, especially considering waves of workplace suicides such as the 2010 events at Foxconn. It is reported that more than 280 million rural migrants have left the Chinese countryside since the economic reforms to find employment in urban centers. This is the greatest internal migration wave in the history of humanity whose socioeconomic repercussions have been the subject of numerous scholarly studies. Also known as peasant-workers (*nongmingong* or *mingong*), this enormous group of people should be added to the 100 million laid-off SOE workers discussed in Chapter 6. Both groups make up the new category of the "urban poor" who are spread over the country working in all industry sectors. These workers contribute to the formation of a new working class, all of whom significantly differ from the working class of the Mao era. Wang Bing's *Bitter Money* offers a microhistorical perspective on members of this new working class in the Huzhou area. What the filmmaker thus pursues is the documentation of migrant workers after thirty years of reform and opening up to shed light on the new working class that sustains the transformation of China into the "factory of the world" because of their cheap labor, making the country the "largest apparel industry in the world"[5] and "the world's biggest producer of textiles and the number one exporter of clothing."[6] In other words, Wang investigates what price the young generation of migrant workers must pay to transform the nation into the top player in the textile industry by domestic and international standards.

Labor sociologist Pun Ngai has pointed out that a new kind of worker has been created in post-Reform China, to whom she refers as "*dagongmei/zai*, laboring girls and boys, which is a new gendered labor subject, produced at the particular moment when private and transnational capital came to China."[7] Pun adds a crucial gendered perspective to the study of Chinese governmentality insofar as it detaches labor from the revolutionary history of the country to firmly ground it in capitalist enterprises and the experience of women workers. She notes that it is under the sign of transience that the lives of migrant workers, especially women workers, take place: "A worker, especially a female worker, will usually spend a number of years working as a wage laborer in an industrial city before getting married. Upon marriage, most of the women have to return home because of the difficulty of setting up their family in the city."[8] Family, procreation, childrearing, and retirement are usually overseen in the rural community from which these women migrated. In the coastal city, there is no social safety net per se for such migrant workers who find themselves at the mercy of private or foreign-owned factories. While the CCP has loosened some restrictions on the household registration system (*hukou*), no one can claim that the gap between rural migrants and city dwellers has been bridged. Migrant workers will continue to be perceived as disposable commodities by both the government and the private sector. This is the new working class that has been deprived of protection and representation at the heart of Wang Bing's *Bitter Money*.

A unique feature in the creation of this new working class and the migrant labor market is that it was government-made rather than led by the private sector or market imperatives. This ties into the discussion of Chinese governmentality and its unique deployment in the form of, say, Special Economic Zones (SEZs) such as Shenzhen into which thousands of workers poured and laid the foundation for cheap labor practices, in addition to the laid-off workers from SOEs who had no choice but to find employment in the private sector. In other words, internal migration happened under the sign of governmentality. As discussed in previous chapters, the CCP has promoted in the post-Reform era a Chinese mode of governance resting on a unique economic model given the country's historical investment in socialist planning, going "from disciplinary regulation to a less coercive, but no less hegemonic, neoliberal governance, which aims to cultivate both durable and governable labouring subjects."[9] Discourses on the self-managing, self-enterprising, and self-governing Chinese subject abound in this neoliberal context, even though migrant workers will remain part of the "floating population" (*liudong renkou*) or known as "vagabond migrants" (*mangliu*) in the minds of many: "they were forced to undergo the process of selling their labor to the factory owners, the new owners of today's China. This is no secret. The dialectic of the reform lies in the very process of freeing rural subjects so that they can transform themselves into laboring bodies, while at the same time it severely limits their freedom in the industrial city."[10] The neoliberal conundrum for most workers was the desire—or the imperative, depending on the point of view—to transform themselves while slaving away in workshops and factories. The production of neoliberal bodies and subjectivities remains the foundation of neoliberal Chinese governmentality, and it is precisely this emphasis that Wang Bing's *Bitter Money* brings to light in its focus on migrant labor.

The CCP created the new labor market that would strengthen the rural and urban divide and result in China cementing its neoliberal agenda. The first step was to promote rural-to-urban labor migration, that is, rural workers leaving the countryside and migrating to the coastal urban centers to supply labor for industries. In this context, the notion of mobility was a sine qua non condition in China's transformation, as it is the very *movement* of migrant workers that enabled the creation of China's so-called "economic miracle" first and foremost. Recent theoretical developments within migration studies have stressed that the notion of mobility deserves closer attention in migratory waves. Indeed, migration flows have been redefined as constantly mobile, unstable, and evolving, that is, as perpetually reconstructed over time and space. Zhu and Qian's summary of how the field of migration studies has been reinvented along the lines of mobility emphasizes how it sits at the intersection of several key concepts such as "(1) rural-to-urban migration, settlement intention and the hukou system; (2) social networks and communities; and (3) mobility, identity and migrants' everyday practices."[11] Chinese migration has thus been reconceptualized as a dynamic process in which societal conditions frame the possibilities for movement within the country. This includes the *hukou* system that prevents rural-to-urban migrants from fully participating in urban life and settling where they want, which signifies the inability of being fully integrated into their new urban environment. Urban life thus is a continuously transitory flow for rural migrants, who live under the sign of precarity and contingency, jumping from city to city in search of better living conditions while evading the limitations of the *hukou* registration system. Relationships are formed and then broken in an apparently endless cycle as worker identity is split between rural citizen and urban worker and lived under the sign of stigmatization and marginalization no matter where rural migrants go.

As a master signifier within migration studies, mobility functions as an epistemological and methodological approach that has been adopted "to better theorise movements of people across different geographical scales. Mobilities involve not only physical movements but also the flow of things, ideas, emotions, and connections that traverse across different geographical scales."[12] Mobility has thus been used to question the more monolithic and rigid aspects of notions such as family, community, and identity and show how each term is constantly renegotiated as migrants move from place to place in search of better employment opportunities. As numerous migration studies scholars have shown, migration is a processual and fluid concept: "Migration is always complicated by needs, aspirations, interests, and pursuits that are situated, unpredictable and contingent on the immediate milieus of movement and encounter. Whether migrants have resources and abilities to adapt to such contingencies affect their wellbeing in profound ways. While such processual, open-ended notions of migration are well-established in migration studies, they are relatively new to studies on migration in China."[13] In the context of Chinese migrant labor practices, scholars are only beginning to conceptualize migration in such terms.

The emphasis on mobility finds an echo in Wang Bing's *Bitter Money*, which is a work that is profoundly invested in the movements of migrant labor and workers. The filmmaker adopts various strategies to show that the cinematic representation of Chinese labor and workers is unthinkable without emphasizing the movements of young bodies from the countryside to the urban center, their movements within workshops and dormitories, and, after a long day at work, their movements on the streets of Zhili in the evening.

The three sequences that open Wang Bing's *Bitter Money* illustrate various aspects of migrant mobility. The first sequence introduces the subject who will be the focus of the narrative for the first twenty minutes of the film. Adopting a low-angle position à la Ozu, the camera captures the interactions between various family members and friends in the mountainous village of Baogunao, near Zhaotong, in Yunnan Province. The gathering is a momentous occasion on which a fifteen-year-old teenager named Xiao Min[14] discusses a forthcoming journey that will take her to the east coast where she will work in a textile workshop. Based on her facial expressions, Xiao Min does not seem anxious at the thought of leaving her home in rural China for the manufacturing heart of China in Zhejiang. On the contrary, the lively tone of the conversation indicates that Xiao Min is looking forward to the trip, as she discusses the need for papers, including the possibility of acquiring fake ones, to be able to reside in the city and gain employment in the textile workshops out east. Pun has provided a rationale for teenagers to leave the Chinese countryside: "Young rural men and women alike find no way to compete with the low prices for agricultural products in the post-WTO accession era. Together with limited educational opportunities, and limited village employment opportunities . . . the rural youth have no choice but to go to work at 16 or 17 years of age. Some rural women also aspire to escape arranged marriages, familial conflicts, and patriarchal relations."[15] The second sequence takes place on the bus where we find Xiao Min and her cousin, Chen Yuanzhen. In this short sequence, Xiao Min speaks with her cousin sitting next to her, touching on various matters such as the family house being in ruin after an earthquake and the impossibility of finding a babysitter. The third sequence is the most significant before the teenager reaches her destination several hours later. Aboard a crowded train, Wang's camera documents the long journey that will take passengers from rural provinces such as Yunnan and Guizhou to the coastal province of Zhejiang, where they will arrive at their destination, Huzhou. A key scene on the train captures a conversation between two passengers in which one man, who quit his job in Yiwu, points out how dangerous it was to work within his factory because of its high levels of toxicity. The first three sequences, taking approximately twenty minutes of screen time, set the stage for the following two hours, although the film will reserve a few surprises regarding who ends up being its main subject.

This third sequence deserves closer attention as it relates to the importance of trains as a sign of modern mobility within film history and, in the Chinese context, as a sign of national progress. The sequence shot on the train paints the portrait of many passengers in their late teens and early twenties who are on their way to the coastal provinces to find employment. The inclusion of a train sequence in *Bitter Money* recalls other instances of train travel in film history in which the transitory nature of human existence is juxtaposed with the mobility afforded by the train. In an interview, Wang Bing adds a layer of complexity by explaining how train travel is associated with memory, determination, and history in the Chinese mind. Noting that the journey from Yunnan to Shanghai is 2,500 kilometers, he relates that the train they were on was fifty years old, and that it was "emblematic of all the long journeys that the Chinese embark on," and that the train "is profoundly rooted in a period of our history."[16]

In the train sequence, the spectator sees the passengers talking, sleeping, eating, and playing cards in the crowded cars. The journey is a long one, the exhaustion visible on the faces of numerous passengers. Reflecting on his own experiences shooting on trains in China, Sniadecki has noted that "[t]rains can activate or at least allow for intimacies and exchanges with strangers you might not experience in your normal living environment—ephemeral, fleeting, transient encounters."[17] There is no doubt that Wang Bing's shooting on the train allowed him to capture such intimate moments—both verbal and nonverbal—imbued with ephemerality and transience between passengers. The filmmaker carefully framed the journey of his female subject, with occasional glances at the lives of others, offering a privileged look at the journey of migrant workers who will not reappear in the film. While Xiao Min seems to be the main subject of the film after twenty minutes, the spectator will soon realize that this will not be the case. Actually, the film's narrative presents a complex structure that may not be apparent upon first viewing. As Pollacchi describes it: "the structure progressively takes the shape of a circular narrative in which the three main characters remain in focus but the many social actors surrounding them connect to one another in different ways, composing a broader mosaic of migration, relocation, and ill-paid labour."[18] Breaking down the film's complex structure is the task of the following sections, which focus on both labor and rest in the migrant experience and the representation of migrant subjectivity and domestic violence in *Bitter Money*.

## The Workshop and the Dormitory

Zhejiang Province has played a central role in China's commercial success in the textile industry. Shi Lu reports that "[i]n 2013, 15% of companies in Zhejiang Province were operating in the textile and clothing industries, making it one of China's main centres for manufacturing textile products at that time."[19] What could possibly explain Zhejiang's investment and success in the textile business? In addition to the issue of mobility, closely analyzing the spatial politics of migrant labor is imperative in this context. In the film, Wang Bing privileges two spaces in particular, the small workshop and the dormitory, that show the working and living conditions of his subjects. Capturing these spaces allows Wang Bing to document the verbal and physical interactions between employees and bosses, and it provides the viewer with a rare look inside the dormitories, which have been less represented than workshops or factories in documentary media. The filmmaker uses these two spaces to refract some of the reasons that can explain the success of the manufacturing sector in Zhejiang.

The representation of workshop spaces in *Bitter Money* occupies a central place in Wang Bing's documentation of manual labor. Xiao Min, introduced in the first sequence of the film, is seen learning on the job, asking questions of others, casually discussing familiar matters and performing daily tasks. It is noteworthy that the filmmaker does not focus on large factories in the film but chooses to capture working lives within small workshops that open onto the street where traffic noise augments the soundtrack with a sense of urbanity. Wang will return to workshop sequences midway through the film, when we expect to resume contact with Xiao Min. In an evening sequence, men are seen skillfully operating the sewing machines in the workshop, listening to loud music in the background. There is no way to tell when the workday will end. In the meantime, the workshop is bustling with activity. Wang Bing privileges scenes where employees are quite cheerful at the end of their shift. They exit the workshop and make their way to the dormitory where they wash their clothes or plan a late-night outing. The conversations between workers are quite lively and casual, which may surprise the Western viewer who would expect the employees to be exhausted after a long shift. The only occasions on which employees are critical of their working conditions is when they discuss their bosses, where pay is more generous per piece of clothing produced, or when mentioning the possibility of participating in a pyramid sale scheme to supplement their income.

In a rare on-camera intervention, Wang Bing asks a man why he did not get used to this kind of textile work and wants to quit. The man complains about the twelve-hour workdays and then is seen leaving the dormitory to return to the countryside after a stint in the city. This is as much on-camera interviewing in which Wang Bing will engage. In another telling conversation with a male employee, Wang Bing captures some of the challenges that workers face regarding the evaluation of their production. The worker, who seems quite dumbfounded, confesses that he cannot keep up with the pace of production in the workshop, and that his boss has fired him because of his slowness. He reveals that he has few prospects: he can return home; he can participate in a pyramid sale scheme; or he can get hired by one of the large factories where, he admits, he fears feeling lonely. The following morning, the worker leaves the dormitory to head to a factory where he will have a trial period of one day. He shares that if things do not work out for him in this new workplace, he will return to the countryside.

Another interaction between boss and employee takes place toward the end of the film where a female worker argues with her superior about the number of pieces that she has produced. Negotiations take place between employee and boss about a discount on a dress that the female worker herself has assembled. The wheel has come full circle in this scene, as the Chinese worker sells her labor to be able to afford pieces of clothing that she herself has made at a discount. The boss pretends that these are hard times, but the spectator cannot but empathize with the female worker whose labor is exploited to such a grotesque extent in contemporary China.

The film ends with a daytime scene, in the rain, in which Erzi, Ling Ling's husband, is seen smoking outside his shop. Wang Bing will gradually transition to an early evening exterior scene where Ling Ling prepares big bundles of clothing outside the shop, which will be loaded onto trucks later that night. Packaging and loading have not been extensively documented compared to workplace activities in documentary media. One needs to have spent some time in large coastal cities such as Huzhou to realize how preparation and transportation occupy a central place at night and in the early hours of the day when trucks are loaded. One large, tightly wrapped bundle of clothing that many workers attend to is destined to Changzhou in the neighboring province of Jiangsu. It is the playful nature of most interactions, with workers poking fun at each other while working, that strikes the Western viewer who may have expected long faces and snarky remarks. The filmmaker privileges such scenes to show the resilience and determination of Chinese workers in the night as they perform the last tasks of this daily ritual before commodities leave the shop. The film ends with Ling Ling working with her male colleagues on a rainy evening. She appears to struggle tying a bundle on her own. It is surprising that in the literature not much has been made of Ling Ling's presence in the final sequence of the film, as Wang Bing clearly wanted the spectator to remember this particular woman after two and a half hours. The filmmaker merges the workplace and the urban night to create a coda to a film that goes from abandoning its apparent main subject (Xiao Min, the fifteen-year-old girl of the opening sequence) after only 30 minutes to ending with the female subject, Ling Ling, whose resilience pays homage to the determination and labor of countless women stuck in the same position.

As the second space that Wang Bing privileges in *Bitter Money*, dormitories have played a crucial role in the economic development of twenty-first-century China. Indeed, given the inability of migrant workers to legally stay in the city, they must find accommodation close to their workplace, which is provided by the employers who rent the dormitories from the government or possess their own dormitories. Such dormitories can house hundreds and, in some cases, thousands of workers. What has been neglected is the psychosocial impact of dormitories in the story of migrant labor and transient living conditions: "Attached to the factory's collective dormitories, the workers hand over their right of abode to the space of capital and create their own transience."[20] These spaces have been so central to production needs and the emergence of the new working class that one can speak of, to borrow Pun's expression, a "dormitory labor regime," which refers to a spatialized regime of management and surveillance over workers' bodies and minds. This spatial strategy has also been part of Chinese governmentality and its "biopolitics of migration,"[21] which includes deciding where workers can live (through the *hukou* registration system) and controlling their daily activities within supervised spaces such as the workshop and the dormitory.

There are many traits that define the governmental "dormitory labor regime." First, the amalgamation of workspace and living space in the same location reveals how production and leisure have become fully integrated in the Chinese industrial complex. As previously mentioned, migrant workers do not enjoy citizenship rights within cities because of the *hukou* system, and, as a result, they must live in dormitories provided by the employer. The problem is compounded by the fact that even if they had the right to live in the city, migrant workers' wages are so low that they could never afford a decent living space. Pun adds that gender distinctions have been at the heart of the dormitory regime since the first wave of migrant workers who came into cities in the 1980s: "young and single women were among the first to be picked up by the new export-oriented industries. Often regarded as 'submissive' and 'obedient' laboring subjects with nimble fingers, young women constituted a high proportion of the factory workers, over 70 percent of the total workforce in garments, toys, and electronics industries who formed the first generation of Chinese migrant workers."[22] It soon became apparent that Chinese factories' booming activities would exhaust the pool of female workers, and, as a result, employers had no choice but to hire male workers, who were perceived as more unreliable than their female counterparts. As seen in Wang Bing's film, the current generation of migrant workers includes both men and women, who work side by side in China's vast network of workshops and factories. Wang captures the spatial ramifications of the politics of production and the political technology of the dormitory system by filming the spaces where migrant workers sleep, put their clothes out to dry, and recharge their phones. Numerous scenes show workers discussing in corridors, planning their next move, whether it be where they will spend the evening or what their next employment opportunity might be.

    The dormitory regime supports global capital with Chinese characteristics by controlling the working and non-working days of its employees. As Pun describes it, the dormitory regime at the heart of Chinese labor refracts the demands of Chinese governmentality insofar as its control over workers extends into many areas of their lives. One of the greatest challenges that migrant workers face in the city is the inability to lay down roots given the strict regulations surrounding the *hukou* system. Pun writes: "What is special about China is its particular process of proletarianization: in order to incorporate the Chinese socialist system into the global economy, rural workers are called upon to work in the city but not to stay in the city."[23] The profound disconnection between proletarianization and urbanization remains a gigantic social issue in China. This explains why the dormitory labor regime plays such an important role in China's success story and in Wang Bing's film. The spatial politics of the dormitory regime thus reveals a complex site where the extraction of labor power and the reduction of labor costs are combined.

    Improvements to the living quarters of the migrant workers have taken place over the years, but, as Pun points out, the government's intention was to invest in the migrant workers by way of improvements to their living conditions: "A cleaner living space, more private and individualized space, and better ventilated rooms are all directed to constructing a modern and industrial being—a one-dimensional person suitable for producing high-class and world-famous garment brands."[24] The urban landscape has profoundly changed in coastal cities where thousands of dormitories populate the city. While most of these buildings were supposed to be temporary, they have become a permanent sight, denoting China's long-term investment in cementing its role as the "factory of the world" and key player in global capitalism.

Under the sign of uncertainty, precarity, and liminality, internal migration reveals itself to be a spatiotemporal experience located at the intersection of governmental and institutional regimes of control, past life events and experiences, and how these are processed in the present, and the rhythms of daily life, including labor. It is noteworthy that Wang Bing does not try to individualize the migrant subject in the film. It is as if the identity of the men and women working in the workshops were not important; what seems to matter more to the filmmaker is the workers' movements within spaces of labor and rest, which are based on repetition and casual interaction with their coworkers and bosses daily. It is the experience of seeing workers in action or resting rather than hearing their personal story that takes precedence, in other words. The workshops become generic spaces where migrant workers spend long hours making, folding, and packaging clothes destined for the domestic and international markets.

Wang Bing has said of the workers in *Bitter Money*: "Age aside, the life of all the workers in my film [*Bitter Money*] is more or less the same: they work in the factory, they sleep in the factory. They have no life in the outside world. They all work endlessly, they save every penny made from sewing clothes."[25] The filmmaker's generic description of the workers' tasks captures the repetition and boredom in this kind of employment, and the repetitive nature of the activities is reflected in the viewing experience itself, which could be deemed to lack interest because of its repetitive nature. However, Wang Bing manages to sustain the interest of the viewers by varying the kinds of interaction and by shooting at different times of day. The nighttime scenes are particularly evocative of the nocturnal activities that sustain China's economy and the constant movements of the textile industry, from the noisy sewing machines to the trucks that transport packaged clothes in the night. Capturing such moments of activity and inactivity, Wang Bing continues to act as the dutiful observer in *Bitter Money*, as his camera is satisfied to record the activities of migrant workers and their verbal and physical interactions with each other. By adopting such a detached perspective, one could claim that "Wang Bing refrains from encouraging any emotional engagement when looking at the conditions of these workers. There is no judgemental stance either on whether these workers made their choice of career freely or whether society has managed to impose it on them."[26] I would concur with Pollacchi's assessment, were it not for one major exception, which the *minjian* filmmaker uses to make the spectator see beyond the working conditions to better appreciate how work and life intertwine for migrants in their quest for "bitter money."

## Migrant Subjectivity and Domestic Violence

The process of separation and isolation characterizing migrants' transition to urban life is particularly difficult because of what Pun has described has the "double alienation" produced by the dormitory regime, which, in addition to the exploitative working conditions, refers to "cutting the workers' ties with their family, their village, and their communal life."[27] In this context, it is unsurprising that most migrant workers would strike up relationships with other workers from the same province, or with those who speak the same dialect. Wang Bing emphasizes the relationships between workers throughout the film, and he focuses on a struggling couple to exemplify some of the challenges experienced by migrant workers. Wang Bing's focus on this couple could be perceived as an attempt to depart from the detached approach used throughout the film to make the spectator identify and empathize with one woman, Ling Ling, and contemplate what options she has as a migrant woman in an abusive relationship.

After about thirty minutes, Wang Bing makes the bold move of abandoning Xiao Min, the teenaged girl appearing in the first sequence of the film, to transition to another narrative thread involving Ling Ling, an experienced female worker whose hardships have received much attention in the literature on the film. Wang Bing met Ling Ling upon visiting the small shop in which the altercation between she and her disabled husband, Erzi, take places. The filmmaker relates that Ling Ling is a very competent factory worker, but what really prompted him to follow her was "a certain melancholy. I felt that she had certain problems, and she told me that she couldn't stand the noise of sewing machines, that it destroyed her nervous system. She couldn't sleep anymore. It became an illness she suffered from enormously, resulting from sleep deprivation. She couldn't work in the factories anymore."[28] Unbeknownst to the filmmaker, the decision to follow Ling Ling would lead to one of the most controversial sequences in all of Wang Bing's films.

The first time that the spectator sees Ling Ling is when she discusses domestic violence with Xiao Min, who appeared in the first sequence of the film. In the workshop, the two discuss a recent incident when Ling Ling and Erzi almost came to blows. It is the casual tone of Ling Ling's voice that strikes the spectator as she retells the troubling story. Clearly, the incident was not the first one of the sort between husband and wife. A few minutes later, after speaking with Erzi on the phone, Ling Ling will leave the workshop, and Wang Bing will follow her outside. What may be surprising after only half an hour is to witness the filmmaker abandon Xiao Min in the workshop to follow Ling Ling to an undisclosed location. Will Wang return to document the working life of the teenager, or will the narrative take the spectator to an unexpected place where Ling Ling will act as the main subject?

Wang Bing follows Ling Ling to the small shop where her husband, Erzi, is found in the company of friends. A heated argument about money lies at the heart of the shocking dispute between the quarrelling couple, which begins in violent requests for Ling Ling to leave the shop and ends with Erzi hitting her on multiple occasions. What is particularly surprising in this sequence is Ling Ling's combative spirit: she will not obey Erzi's requests to leave, even at the risk of getting hit repeatedly. She simply sits in the corner and continues to argue with her husband, being on the receiving end of numerous blows to the head.

Domestic violence (aka "intimate partner violence") sits at the center of Wang Bing's film about migrant labor. A bold move in the editing room, the filmmaker's decision to make Ling Ling such a central character reveals the intention to show the kind of interpersonal struggle female migrant workers face in the city. In patriarchal China, domestic violence was conceived as a private matter until the mid-1990s when the notion of "domestic violence" (*jiating baoli*) was first introduced in the "Program for the Development of Chinese Women" (1995–2000) and recognized as a public health matter. More recently, the "Anti-Domestic Violence Law" of 2015 reflected societal changes within China insofar as it took into account "recent demographic transitions showing an increase in nontraditional family practices such as cohabitation, divorce, and out-of-wedlock childbirths"[29] and included for the first time physical, psychological, and sexual violence. Within China, a nationwide survey conducted by the All-China Women's Federation reports that "more than a quarter of women have suffered domestic violence at least once in their lifetime, although a number of offences may go unreported."[30] Regarding domestic violence within married migrant workers, a study has shown that "as high as 45% of married rural-to-urban migrant workers experienced at least one act of physical, psychological or sexual IPV [intimate partner violence] during the last 12 months."[31]

Surveys and reports provide a broader context for the altercation between Ling Ling and Erzi, which raises the issue of intervention in the documentary production context. Based on Wang Bing's non-interventionist ethics of observation, it is unsurprising that the filmmaker would not act upon seeing the husband hit his spouse. This is compounded by the distance between the filmmaker and the couple—Wang Bing is standing outside the shop and shooting through the front window—and the fact that there are men playing cards inside who, the filmmaker may have assumed, could intervene if things escalated. Clearly, the presence of Wang Bing's camera did not prevent the husband from threatening Ling Ling with divorce and acting violently. However, many viewers would argue that it was incumbent on the filmmaker to intervene upon witnessing the violent act committed against Ling Ling. The second time Erzi hits his wife is when they are alone in the shop; however, this time the spectator can clearly notice the filmmaker taking a few steps forward, ready to enter the shop. He will not have to do so, however, as he is preceded by Lao Ye, a friend of the couple's, who decides to intervene and prevent the violence from escalating one more time. The disturbing, fifteen-minute sequence ends with a shot of Ling Ling standing on the sidewalk, most likely replaying recent events in her head.

In an interview with *Film Comment*, Wang Bing has described the relationship between Ling Ling and her husband: "As shown in the film, she also has problems with her husband. However, there are no real issues between Ling Ling and her husband, there are no major sentimental problems. It is just this anxiety that exists in the air between them and poisons their life."[32] He adds: "In *Bitter Money* it is the struggle to make a living that triggers people's anxiety: the workers have to leave their village and their families behind, move to another region, slave away in the city in order to make money."[33] Wang Bing shares that Erzi had a workplace accident in which his fingers were cut off by a machine. Then he bought the shop in which the fight took place with his injury compensation money. Wang has said that despite his obvious flaws as a husband, Erzi is also a "victim." The filmmaker proceeds to explain the Chinese patriarchal structure in which the wife is asked to move in with the husband's family, whereas, in this man's case, it was the opposite: Erzi moved in with Ling Ling's parents. Wang Bing concludes: "It's not easy for a man in China to accept this situation. They had a child, and he feels enormous financial pressure."[34]

In their study of domestic violence, Yuan and Hesketh note that "[i]n China, while women's status has improved considerably in the last few decades, traditional values around gender roles persist. These give men 'permission' to be threatening and aggressive toward their wives when they don't comply with demands or carry out what may be regarded as their domestic duties."[35] From both an ethical and a rhetorical point of view, Wang Bing's rationale differs from what is reported in the literature on domestic violence in China. There is no doubt that the filmmaker's words could easily be misinterpreted as justifying both China's patriarchal family structure and Erzi's violent behavior toward Ling Ling. However, I think that it would be a mistake to believe that Wang Bing tries to explain away Erzi's actions. While his explanation could be misinterpreted, what follows is more revealing of Wang Bing's intention: "What's most impressive in this scene is the violence perpetrated against his wife while she's absolutely unafraid of him."[36] The filmmaker will not dwell on the physical or psychological repercussions of the event, the latter including mental health problems such as depression and anxiety. Rather, it is Ling Ling's resilience and fearlessness that seem to be the focus of Wang Bing's controversial sequence.

Nevertheless, Wang's comments may be perceived as trying to diminish the importance of domestic violence by contextualizing it within a national, patriarchal frame of reference. While there is no doubt that human relationships mediated through monetary exchanges play a great role in the three films—*West of the Tracks*, *Coal Money*, and *Bitter Money*—examined in the second part of this study, it is conceivable that numerous readers will still disapprove of Wang Bing's attempt at excusing Erzi's violent behavior and reject the filmmaker's rationale for such misogynistic acts. I believe that what Wang Bing may have meant is that, while profit making has become the central goal of many Chinese workers in the post-Reform era, there has also been an undeniable deterioration in how humans interact, as shown in the troubling sequence, which points to the reified character of human bonds in *Bitter Money*. It is the gradual decline of workplace relations and family ties that sustained Chinese society for decades that the three films in the second part of this study highlight following the transition from a planned economy to a market economy in which individuals must support themselves without the help of the government. In the thirteen years that separate *West of the Tracks* from *Bitter Money*, the changes to the Chinese workplace, labor practices, and interpersonal relationships could not be more dramatic.

## Conclusion

A key question to ask at the end of this analysis of *Bitter Money* is: Does the film offer a counter-narrative to the stereotyped image of the Chinese workplace and worker that has been circulating for decades in Western media?[37] Wang Bing provides an alternative to how Chinese working bodies have been represented in the West, and he does so by emphasizing how workers are more than mere cogs in the machine of Chinese capital. While the Western spectator may have expected the film to follow one subject (as the beginning of the film famously misleads us into thinking), Wang's strategy is to privilege a small number of subjects, including a couple, and single out two spaces—the workshop and the dormitory—to show the underbelly of China's reputation as the "factory of the world," including social issues such as domestic violence that the spectator may not have expected to encounter in a "migrant labor" documentary.

As a documentary exercise in the politics of visibility, that is, making visible those who had hitherto remained invisible, the filmmaker does not focus on graphically shocking cases of labor exploitation. For example, Wang Bing does not address the kinds of grievance that factory workers face, which could lead to labor arbitration, litigation, and protests. On the contrary, Wang's goal is to balance the representation of work and leisure without privileging sensational moments of unrest or glorifying the labor of migrants either. Clearly, Wang Bing's documentary is not about the political organization of Chinese workers following workplace accidents, but the long process that takes the subject from the countryside to the coastal city, and the condition under which the process of reinventing oneself as a migrant worker may take place. Wang Bing helps to lend greater visibility and understanding to this process by focusing on workers of varying age groups and showing their respective challenges. With respect to a woman such as Ling Ling, whose lived experiences as an abused spouse and resilient worker may be the most memorable in the film, Wang Bing reveals how she is not passive but possesses agency even in the face of adversity and male brutality.

A question that Wang Bing does not address, however, concerns the kind of societal game that China has been playing with its rural migrants over the past decades and what the national endgame is. As Pun succinctly puts it: "A vicious circle has been created: the reform and the rural-urban dichotomy motivate a desire to leave the countryside; escape leads only to the hardship of factory life; the frustration of factory life induces the desire to return; however, there is no place for returning migrants—going out to *dagong* is considered the only means of survival and development."[38] Speaking of *Bitter Money*, Wang Bing has commented that he and his team shot an enormous amount of footage: "However, for *Bitter Money* I shot more than 2,000 hours. The film *Bitter Money* is only a tiny fraction of the whole shooting, about 200 hours. A seven- or eight-month work on post-production awaits me to process the whole footage. I plan to make other movies out of these 2000+ hours in the future."[39] It is expected that some of the unused footage for *Bitter Money* will appear in *Youth (Spring)* (2023), which is Wang Bing's most recent documentary on migrant labor.

## Notes

1. Zhang Qi, Mingxing Liu, and Victor Shih, "Guerrilla Capitalism: Revolutionary Legacy, Political Cleavage, and the Preservation of the Private Economy in Zhejiang," *Journal of East Asian Studies* 13 (2013): 379–80. While working in Zhejiang, Wang Bing also shot the 15-hour-long video installation *15 Hours* (*15 xiaoshi*), which documents one working day in a textile workshop. The installation was exhibited at "Documenta 14" in Kassel (Germany) in 2017.
2. Obviously, Wang Bing did not write a screenplay for *Bitter Money*. It remains unclear why he received this award at the Venice Film Festival.
3. Michael Guarneri and Jin Wang, "Interview: Wang Bing," *Film Comment*, February 22, 2017, https://www.filmcomment.com/blog/interview-wang-bing/.
4. Jingzhong Ye, Chunyu Wang, Huifang Wu, Congzhi He, and Juan Liu, "Internal Migration and Left-Behind Populations in China," *Journal of Peasant Studies* 40, no. 6 (2013): 1124.
5. Shengjun Zhu and John Pickles, "Bring In, Go Up, Go West, Go Out: Upgrading, Regionalisation and Delocalisation in China's Apparel Production Networks," *Journal of Contemporary Asia* 44, no. 1 (2014): 37.
6. Shi Lu, "Domestic and International Challenges for the Textile Industry in Shaoxing (Zhejiang)," *China Perspectives* 3 (2015): 14.
7. Pun Ngai, *Migrant Labor in China* (London: Polity, 2016), 31.
8. Pun, *Migrant Labor in China*, 33.
9. Quan Gao, "Reconstituting the Neoliberal Subjectivity of Migrants: Christian Theo-ethics and Migrant Workers in Shenzhen, China," *Journal of Ethnic and Migration Studies* 47, no. 12 (2021): 2732.
10. Pun, *Migrant Labor in China*, 73.
11. Hong Zhu and Junxi Qian, "New Theoretical Dialogues on Migration in China," *Journal of Ethnic and Migration Studies* 47, no. 12 (2021): 2688.
12. Zhu and Qian, "New Theoretical Dialogues on Migration in China," 2694.
13. Zhu and Qian, "New Theoretical Dialogues on Migration in China," 2698.

14. Noteworthy is that Xiao Min is unidentified in the film. However, the press kit does mention her name.
15. Pun, *Migrant Labor in China*, 32.
16. "Conversation entre Wang Bing et Alain Bergala," Wang Bing, *Argent amer*, DVD booklet, ARTE editions, unpaginated.
17. Scott MacDonald, "Sensory Ethnography, Part 2," in *The Sublimity of Document: Cinema as Diorama* (Oxford: Oxford University Press, 2019), 482.
18. Elena Pollacchi, *Wang Bing's Filmmaking of the China Dream: Narratives, Witnesses and Marginal Spaces* (Amsterdam: Amsterdam University Press, 2021), 120.
19. Lu, "Domestic and International Challenges for the Textile Industry in Shaoxing (Zhejiang)," 13.
20. Pun, *Migrant Labor in China*, 99.
21. Ye, et al., "Internal Migration and Left-Behind Populations in China," 1136.
22. Pun, *Migrant Labor in China*, 87.
23. Pun, *Migrant Labor in China*, 67.
24. Pun, *Migrant Labor in China*, 96.
25. Guarneri and Wang, "Interview: Wang Bing."
26. Pollacchi, *Wang Bing's Filmmaking of the China Dream*, 121.
27. Pun, *Migrant Labor in China*, 100.
28. "Conversation entre Wang Bing et Alain Bergala."
29. Hongwei Zhang and Ruohui Zhao, "Empirical Research on Domestic Violence in Contemporary China: Continuity and Advances," *International Journal of Offender Therapy and Comparative Criminology* 62, no. 16 (2018): 4880.
30. Yueping Song, Jingwen Zhang, and Xian Zhang, "Cultural or Institutional? Contextual Effects on Domestic Violence against Women in Rural China," *Journal of Family Violence* 36 (2021): 643.
31. Li Chen, Zonghuo Yu, Xianming Luo, and Zhaoxin Huang, "Intimate Partner Violence against Married Rural-to-Urban Migrant Workers in Eastern China: Prevalence, Patterns, and Associated Factors," *BMC Public Health* 16 (2016): 1232.
32. Guarneri and Wang, "Interview: Wang Bing."
33. Guarneri and Wang, "Interview: Wang Bing."
34. Guarneri and Wang, "Interview: Wang Bing."
35. Weiman Yuan and Therese Hesketh, "Intimate Partner Violence and Depression in Women in China," *Journal of Interpersonal Violence* 36, no. 21–22 (2021): NPI2033.
36. Guarneri and Wang, "Interview: Wang Bing."
37. Florence has provided an overview of how rural migrants themselves have represented their own living and working conditions. See Eric Florence, "The Cultural Politics of Labour in Postsocialist China," in *Routledge Handbook of Chinese Culture and Society*, edited by Kevin Latham (New York: Routledge, 2020), 212–30.
38. Pun Ngai, "The New Chinese Working Class in Struggle," *Dialectical Anthropology* 44 (2020): 323.
39. Guarneri and Wang, "Interview: Wang Bing."

# Conclusion

This monograph on Wang Bing's cinema has explored the two major obsessions at the heart of the Chinese documentarian's oeuvre, Maoist history and post-Reform labor practices, which reflect the bipartite division of this book. Its origins lie in my fascination with Wang's cinema, a thought-provoking practice that I have closely watched expand over the past twenty years and gain worldwide recognition. Keeping up with the secondary literature on Wang Bing over the years, I strongly believed that Wang Bing's cinema deserved a finer-grained treatment of its two main foci, and that another monograph on Wang Bing offering an overview of his career was unnecessary. What I imagined was treating Wang Bing as a *minjian* intellectual and artist whose two obsessions could serve as the foundation for investigating the labor of history, on the one hand, and the history of labor, on the other, in post-Reform China. Such a publication could help to reframe investigations into a single documentarian without having recourse to the tropes of auteur theory.

This study of Wang Bing's cinema has helped to enrich the study of contemporary Chinese documentary in several ways. The fundamental implications of this monograph concern the field of Chinese documentary studies first and foremost, but its conceptual and methodological contributions could extend into other fields within the visual arts and the humanities. In addition to the fine studies of independent Chinese documentary in our possession, this monograph has attempted to bridge the gap between social and economic history and film analysis in the form of a more focused examination of a single filmmaker. Indeed, it soon became apparent that paying justice to Wang Bing's "Anti-Rightist" trilogy would require a sustained look at social and oral histories of Maoist China before examining the films themselves. Similarly, the transformation of labor practices within twenty-first-century China would necessitate a closer analysis of the end of SOEs, the coal industry's transportation issues, and migrant labor within the textile industry, before analyzing the three films in Part Two. While I do not claim to have provided a systematic theoretical model in this study of one Chinese documentarian, I believe to have demonstrated the benefits of better contextualizing a practice such as Wang Bing's and developing both a sociopoetics of documentary film and an innovative methodology supporting original readings of the films, which could be extended to the work of other Chinese documentarians and their colleagues abroad.

Focusing on the "Anti-Rightist" trilogy, Part One contextualizes Wang Bing's obsession with the Maoist era, the Great Leap Forward, the famine of 1958–1962, and the words and life experiences of survivors. Wang Bing's artistry is examined from the point of view of three main innovations: the creation of an embodied archive, the use of techniques of repetition, and the documentation of both human and nonhuman survivors. Wang's journey takes him from the documentation of one woman survivor (*Fengming, a Chinese Memoir*), to the exploration of fiction filmmaking to recreate labor camp life (*The Ditch*), to finally return to documentary and the long-form interview to archive the life experiences of survivors, while documenting what has remained in the Gansu landscape all these years, that is to say, the life of nonhuman survivors (*Dead Souls*). It is not farfetched to claim that Wang, as a *minjian* intellectual and artist, was constantly looking for the best way to document the life experiences of survivors (both human and nonhuman) and continuously experimented with various shooting and storytelling techniques, from *Fengming* to *Dead Souls*. The "Anti-Rightist" trilogy not only attests to the struggles of famine survivors over the past decades, but it also bears witness to Wang's search for the most appropriate filmic strategies to do so over a period of ten years of experimentation.

Part Two of this study demonstrates a similar concern for the thorough contextualization of the films examined by using socioeconomic histories of Chinese labor and industry to ground the three chapters. Using two main concepts—Chinese governmentality and critical realism—the second part of the book shows how the films under study—*West of the Tracks, Coal Money*, and *Bitter Money*—greatly benefit from a thorough understanding of the CCP's investment in governmentality as a new form of control over Chinese lives (as I write this conclusion, the CCP is imposing the strictest lockdowns on the Chinese in support of its COVID-zero policy, which is yet another example of the interrelation between biopolitics and biopower on a national scale). In this analysis of Wang Bing's cinema, scholarship on Chinese governmentality is mostly mobilized to contextualize the hybrid economic model implemented by the CCP in the post-Reform era, one of its most defining traits having been to profoundly modify the social contract between the CCP and its citizens by abolishing state planning and adopting the Westernized version of the "entrepreneur of the self" who can no longer rely on the social safety net and benefits that countless Chinese workers enjoyed in the past.

Furthermore, Part Two argues that the significant transformations that Chinese labor has undergone over the past twenty years require an approach that is not only attentive to the central tenets and practices of Chinese governmentality, but that also uses "critical realism" as its principal methodological tool to make sense of the conditions of workers and the impact of neoliberalism on labor practices. As a documentary research method, critical realism challenges the social realist representation of workers in China by privileging the precarious and exploitative nature of labor in the twenty-first century. The concept of critical realism thus describes the way in which Wang Bing has reinvented what it means to observe workers and labor practices at a time when the CCP is fully invested in governing Chinese lives in an authoritarian manner unseen since the Cultural Revolution.

What the future holds for a filmmaker such as Wang Bing is difficult to predict. Will he add other chapters to his chronicle of Chinese labor practices after *Youth (Spring)* (2023)? Will he make other films such as *Ta'ang* and *Mrs. Fang* that do not directly address his long-lasting obsessions with Maoist history and labor? A promising avenue for Wang is to examine China's presence on the global stage and pursue his reflection on alternative presentation formats. For example, in September 2020, Wang Bing exhibited at the Maison des Arts in Brussels. Titled *Scenes: Glimpses from a Lockdown*, the exhibition featured an installation that combined film and performance and recreated the studio in which the artist spent the first months of the pandemic: "For the first time in his career, he will be presenting an installation in which he will be living and working 24 hours a day for the duration of the festival. He invites the audience to watch his minutely detailed audiovisual fresco reconnecting the symmetries and asymmetries in the relationship between China and Africa, where globalisation is expressed as an interconnection of visible presences and invisible forces."[1]

Wang Bing's pandemic project reminds us of the increasingly hybrid nature of his work to the point that one may argue that the documentarian has become one of China's foremost visual artists, having made documentary films, photographic series, and video installations for the cinema, art gallery, and museum spaces. Wang has clearly demarcated a unique field of artistic exploration for himself in which documentary film may well remain his primary interest, but he has also redesigned his documentary practice to make it fit other exhibition venues, which in turn has helped to generate other kinds of funding opportunities. What is certain is that the Chinese documentarian will carry on showing his work at international film festivals and that he will most likely continue to receive commissions from art galleries and museums to show video installation work that does not fit the movie theater exhibition model. Whatever is in store for him, Wang Bing will remain a key attraction at film festivals around the world for years to come because his practice has helped to redefine the political stakes of documentary film in the twenty-first century. That is no small achievement for someone who has been ostracized in his own country.

## Note

1. https://www.crousel.com/en/news/-scenes-glimpses-from-a-lockdown-2020-09-03-DEAV02, accessed May 25, 2022.

# Bibliography

Aitken, Ian. *Realist Film Theory and Cinema: The Nineteenth-Century Lukácsian and Intuitionist Realist Traditions*. Manchester: Manchester University Press, 2016.
Anheim, Étienne. "Singulières archives. Le statut des archives dans l'épistémologie historique. Une discussion de *La mémoire, l'histoire, l'oubli* de Paul Ricoeur." *Revue de synthèse* 5 (2004): 153–82.
Baecque, Antoine de. "Wang Bing, Les Ames mortes." *Transfuge* 123 (2018): 40–45.
Beausse, Pascal. "The Critical Realism of Allan Sekula." *Art Press* 240 (1998): 20–26.
Berry, Chris. "Getting Real: Chinese Documentary, Chinese Postsocialism." In *The Urban Generation: Chinese Cinema and Society at the Turn of the Twenty-first Century*, edited by Zhang Zhen, 115–34. Durham, NC: Duke University Press, 2007.
Berry, Chris, and Lisa Rofel. "Alternative Archive: China's Independent Documentary Culture." In *The New Chinese Documentary Film Movement: For the Public Record*, edited by Chris Berry, Lu Xinyu, and Lisa Rofel, 135–54. Hong Kong: Hong Kong University Press, 2010.
Berry, Chris, and Lisa Rofel. "Introduction." In *The New Chinese Documentary Film Movement: For the Public Record*, edited by Chris Berry, Lu Xinyu, and Lisa Rofel, 3–13. Hong Kong: Hong Kong University Press, 2010.
Bourgeus, Camille. "Work/Space: Labor and Realism in the Cinema of Wang Bing." *Diacritics* 46, no. 4 (2018): 56–71.
Braester, Yomi. "For Whom Does the Director Speak? The Ethics of Representation in Documentary Film Criticism." In *Filming the Everyday: Independent Documentaries in Twenty-First-Century China*, edited by Paul G. Pickowicz and Yingjin Zhang, 33–49. Lanham, MD: Rowman & Littlefield, 2017.
Bray, David, and Elaine Jeffreys. "New Mentalities of Government in China: An Introduction." In *New Mentalities of Government in China*, edited by David Bray and Elaine Jeffreys, 1–15. New York: Routledge, 2016.
Buchloh, Benjamin H. D. "Allan Sekula: Photography between Discourse and Document." In Allan Sekula, *Fish Story*, 189–200. Düsseldorf: Richter Verlag, 1995.
Cai, Shenshen. "The Chronicles of Jiabiangou (Jiabiangou jishi): An Analysis of Contemporary Chinese Reportage Literature Using the Theory of Totalitarianism and Power." *Modern China Studies* 23, no. 1 (2016): 121–34.
Caillet, Aline. *Dispositifs critiques. Le documentaire, du cinéma aux arts visuels*. Rennes: Presses universitaires de Rennes, 2014.

Chan, Andrew. "Fengming: A Chinese Memoir." December 3, 2008. http://www.reverseshot.org/reviews/entry/571/fengming_chinese_memoir.
Chen, Huei-Yin. "Interview with Chinese Documentary Filmmaker Zou Xueping." August 10, 2022. https://www.asiancinemablog.com/interviews/interview-with-chinese-documentary-filmmaker-zou-xueping/.
Chen, Li, Zonghuo Yu, Xianming Luo, and Zhaoxin Huang. "Intimate Partner Violence against Married Rural-to-Urban Migrant Workers in Eastern China: Prevalence, Patterns, and Associated Factors." *BMC Public Health* 16 (2016): 1232.
Cheng, Zhiming. "Poverty in China's Urban Communities: Profile and Correlates." *China Report* 46, no. 2 (2010): 143–73.
Comolli, Jean-Louis. "À *l'ouest des rails*: suite du voyage." *Images documentaires* 77 (2013): 23–34.
Day, Gail. "Realism, Totality and the Militant *Citoyen*: Or, What Does Lukács Have to Do with Contemporary Art?" In *Georg Lukács: The Fundamental Dissonance of Existence*, edited by Timothy Bewes and Timothy Hall, 203–19. London: Bloomsbury, 2013.
Deleuze, Gilles. *Difference and Repetition*. Translated by Paul Patton. New York: Columbia University Press, 1995.
Delisle, Jacques, and Avery Goldstein. "China's Economic Reform and Opening at Forty." In *To Get Rich Is Glorious: Challenges Facing China's Economic Reform and Opening at Forty*, edited by Jacques Delisle and Avery Goldstein, 1–26. Washington, DC: Brookings Institution Press, 2019.
Derrida, Jacques. *Mal d'archive. Une impression freudienne*. Paris: Galilée, 1995.
Didi-Huberman, Georges. *Images in Spite of All: Four Photographs from Auschwitz*. Translated by Shane B. Lillis. Chicago: University of Chicago Press, 2008.
Dikötter, Frank. *Mao's Great Famine: The History of China's Most Devastating Catastrophe, 1958–62*. New York: Vintage, 2010.
Domenach, Jean-Luc. *Chine: l'archipel oublié*. Paris: Fayard, 1992.
Dong, Lijing, Wang Yongchao, Lin Jiayi, and Zhu Ermeng. "The Community Renewal of Shantytown Transformation in Old Industrial Cities: Evidence from Tiexi Worker Village in Shenyang, China." *Chinese Geographical Science* 30, no. 6 (2020): 1022–38.
Dubow, Jessica. "The Art Seminar." In *Landscape Theory*, edited by Rachael Ziady DeLue and James Elkins, 87–156. New York: Routledge, 2008.
Dufour, Diane, and Dominique Païni. "Entretien avec Wang Bing." In *Wang Bing – L'œil qui marche*, edited by Diane Dufour, Dominique Païni, and Roger Willems, 811–16. Paris: Le Bal / Delpire & co, 2021.
Dutton, Michael, and Barry Hindess. "Governmentality Studies and China: Towards a 'Chinese' Governmentality." In *New Mentalities of Government in China*, edited by David Bray and Elaine Jeffreys, 16–29. New York: Routledge, 2016.
Edwards, Dan. *Independent Chinese Documentary: Alternative Visions, Alternative Publics*. Edinburgh: Edinburgh University Press, 2015.
Edwards, Dan, and Marina Svensson. "Show Us Life and Make Us Think: Engagement, Witnessing and Activism in Independent Chinese Documentary Today." *Studies in Documentary Film* 11, no. 3 (2017): 161–69.

Ens Manning, Kimberley, and Felix Wemheuer. "Introduction." In *Eating Bitterness: New Perspectives on China's Great Leap Forward and Famine*, edited by Kimberley Ens Manning and Felix Wemheuer, 1–27. Vancouver: UBC Press, 2011.

Ey, Melina, and Meg Sherval. "Exploring the Minescape: Engaging with the Complexity of the Extractive Sector." *Area* 48, no. 2 (2016): 176–82.

Fan, Xiaojun, and Shanshan Dai. "Spatial-temporal Distribution Characteristics of Industrial Heritage Protection and the Influencing Factors in a Chinese City: A Case Study of the Tiexi Old Industrial District in Shenyang." *Journal of Heritage Tourism* 12, no. 3 (2017): 281–95.

Fiant, Antony. *Pour un cinéma contemporain soustractif*. Paris: Presses Universitaires de Vincennes, 2014.

Fiant, Antony. *Wang Bing: un geste documentaire de notre temps*. Laval: Warm, 2019.

Florence, Eric. "The Cultural Politics of Labour in Postsocialist China." In *Routledge Handbook of Chinese Culture and Society*, edited by Kevin Latham, 212–30. New York: Routledge, 2020.

Foucault, Michel. "Governmentality." In *The Foucault Effect: Studies in Governmentality*, edited by Graham Burchell, Colin Gordon, and Peter Miller, 87–104. Chicago: University of Chicago Press, 1991.

Gao, Er Tai. *In Search of My Homeland: A Memoir of a Chinese Labor Camp*. Translated by Robert Dorsett and David E. Pollard. New York: Ecco Press, 2009.

Gao, Quan. "Reconstituting the Neoliberal Subjectivity of Migrants: Christian Theo-ethics and Migrant Workers in Shenzhen, China." *Journal of Ethnic and Migration Studies* 47, no. 12 (2021): 2725–44.

Grasshopper Film. "Behemoth: A Film by Zhao Liang." Press kit. https://grasshopperfilm.com/wp-content/uploads/2016/01/Behemoth---Press-Kit.pdf.

Greenhalgh, Susan, and Edwin A. Winckler. *Governing China's Population: From Leninist to Neoliberal Biopolitics*. Stanford: Stanford University Press, 2005.

Guarneri, Michael, and Jin Wang. "Interview: Wang Bing." *Film Comment*, February 22, 2017. https://www.filmcomment.com/blog/interview-wang-bing/.

Guha, Ranajit, and Gayatri Chakravorty Spivak, ed. *Selected Subaltern Studies*. Oxford: Oxford University Press, 1988.

He Fengming. *Jingli: wo de 1957 nian*. Lanzhou: Dunhuang wenyi chubanshe, 2000.

He, Fengming. "Les lettres de Jingchao. Extraits de *Année 1957, Mon vécu*." In *Actualités critiques. Capricci 2012*, edited by Thierry Lounas, 62–69. Paris: Capricci, 2012.

Helsinger, Elizabeth. "Blindness and Insights." In *Landscape Theory*, edited by Rachael Ziady DeLue and James Elkins, 323–42. New York: Routledge, 2008.

Housset, Emmanuel. "L'objet du témoignage." *Philosophie* 88 (2005): 1–10. https://hal.archives-ouvertes.fr/hal-01878462/document.

Hurst, William. *The Chinese Worker after Socialism*. Cambridge: Cambridge University Press, 2009.

Jeffreys, Elaine, and Gary Sigley. "Governmentality, Governance and China." In *China's Governmentalities: Governing Change, Changing Government*, edited by Elaine Jeffreys, 1–23. New York: Routledge, 2009.

Kahana, Jonathan. "Introduction: What Now? Presenting Reenactment." *Framework: Journal of Cinema and Media* 50, no. 1–2 (2009): 46–60.

Kernen, Antoine. *La Chine vers l'économie de marché: les privatisations à Shenyang*. Paris: Karthala, 2004.
Kernen, Antoine, and Jean-Louis Rocca. "Social Responses to Unemployment and the 'New Urban Poor': Case Study in Shenyang City and Liaoning Province." *China Perspectives* 27 (2000): 35–51.
Koehler, Robert. "Ghost Stories: Wang Bing's Startling New Cinema." *Cinema Scope* 31 (2007), https://cinema-scope.com/cinema-scope-magazine/interviews-ghost-stories-wang-bings-startling-new-cinema/.
Lee, Ching Kwan. *Against the Law: Labor Protests in China's Rustbelt and Sunbelt*. Berkeley: University of California Press, 2007.
Lessard, Bruno. *The Art of Subtraction: Digital Adaptation and the Object Image*. Toronto: University of Toronto Press, 2017.
Lessard, Bruno. "Shot in the Dark: Nocturnal Philosophy and Night Photography." In *Critical Distance in Documentary Media*, edited by Gerda Cammaer, Blake Fitzpatrick, and Bruno Lessard, 45–67. London: Palgrave Macmillan, 2018.
Li, Xin, Reinout Kleinhans, and Maarten van Ham. "Ambivalence in Place Attachment: The Lived Experiences of Residents in Danwei Communities Facing Demolition in Shenyang, China." *Housing Studies* 34, no. 6 (2019): 997–1020.
Lü, Hao-Dong, Jin-Sheng Zhou, Lin Yang, Yi-Min Li, and Lu Liu. "An Accounting of the External Environmental Costs of Coal in Inner Mongolia Using the Pollution Damage Method." *Environment, Development and Sustainability* 22 (2020): 1299–321.
Lu, Shi. "Domestic and International Challenges for the Textile Industry in Shaoxing (Zhejiang)." *China Perspectives* 3 (2015): 13–23.
Lü Xinyu. "'Diceng' de zhengzhi, lunli yu meixue." In *Xueshu, chuanmei yu gonggongxing*, 244–57. Shanghai: Huadong shifan daxue chubanshe, 2015.
Lü Xinyu. *Jilu Zhongguo: Dangdai Zhongguo xin jilu yundong*. Beijing: Sanlian shudian, 2003.
Lü Xinyu. "'Tiexi qu': lishi yu jieji yishi." In *Xueshu, chuanmei yu gonggongxing*, 199–218. Shanghai: Huadong shifan daxue chubanshe, 2015.
Lu, Xinyu. "Rethinking China's New Documentary Movement: Engagement with the Social." In *The New Chinese Documentary Film Movement: For the Public Record*, edited by Chris Berry, Lu Xinyu, and Lisa Rofel, 15–48. Hong Kong: Hong Kong University Press, 2010.
Lu, Xinyu. "*West of the Tracks*: History and Class-Consciousness." In *The New Chinese Documentary Film Movement: For the Public Record*, edited by Chris Berry, Lu Xinyu, and Lisa Rofel, 57–76. Hong Kong: Hong Kong University Press, 2010.
Lukacs, Georg. "Critical Realism and Socialist Realism." In *The Meaning of Contemporary Realism*, 93–135. Monmouth, Wales: Merlin Press, 2006.
Lukacs, Georg. *History and Class Consciousness*. Cambridge, MA: MIT Press, 1971.
MacDonald, Scott. "Sensory Ethnography, Part 2." In *The Sublimity of Document: Cinema as Diorama*, 451–94. Oxford: Oxford University Press, 2019.
Margulies, Ivone. *In Person: Reenactment in Postwar and Contemporary Cinema*. Oxford: Oxford University Press, 2019.
Mitchell, W. J. T. "Preface to the Second Edition of *Landscape and Power*: Space, Place, and Landscape." In *Landscape and Power*, Second Edition, edited by W. J. T. Mitchell, vii–xii. Chicago: University of Chicago Press, 2002.

Mitchell, W. J. T. "Realism and the Digital Image." In *Critical Realism in Contemporary Art: Around Allan Sekula's Photography*, edited by Jan Baetens and Hilde Van Gelder, 12–27. Leuven: Leuven University Press, 2010.

Montrose, Louis. *The Purpose of Playing: Shakespeare and the Cultural Politics of the Elizabethan Theatre*. Chicago: University of Chicago Press, 1996.

Morel, Guillaume. "Entretien avec Wang Bing." *Images documentaires* 77 (2013): 49–54.

Mühlhahn, Klaus. "The Concentration Camp in Global Historical Perspective." *History Compass* 8, no. 6 (2010): 543–61.

Naughton, Barry. "China's Domestic Economy: From 'Enlivening' to 'Steerage.'" In *To Get Rich Is Glorious: Challenges Facing China's Economic Reform and Opening at Forty*, edited by Jacques Delisle and Avery Goldstein, 29–53. Washington, DC: Brookings Institution Press, 2019.

Naughton, Barry. "The Current Wave of State Enterprise Reform in China: A Preliminary Appraisal." *Asian Economic Policy Review* 12 (2017): 282–98.

Nichols, Bill. *Speaking Truths with Film: Evidence, Ethics, Politics in Documentary*. Berkeley: University of California Press, 2016.

Pernin, Judith. "Filmed Testimonies, Archives, and Memoirs of the Mao Era." In *Popular Memories of the Mao Era: From Critical Debate to Reassessing History*, edited by Sebastian Veg, 137–60. Hong Kong: Hong Kong University Press, 2019.

Pernin, Judith. *Pratiques indépendantes du documentaire en Chine: histoire, esthétique et discours visuels (1990–2010)*. Rennes: Presses universitaires de Rennes, 2015.

Phay, Soko. "L'archive-oeuvre à l'épreuve de l'effacement." In *Un art documentaire: enjeux esthétiques, politiques et éthiques*, edited by Aline Caillet and Frédéric Pouillaude, 273–80. Rennes: Presses universitaires de Rennes, 2017.

Pickowicz, Paul G. "A Hundred Years Later: Zou Xueping's Documentaries and the Legacies of China's New Culture Movement." *Journal of Chinese Cinemas* 10, no. 2 (2016): 187–201.

Pickowicz, Paul G. "Zou Xueping's Postsocialist Homecoming." *Filming the Everyday: Independent Documentaries in Twenty-First-Century China*, edited by Paul G. Pickowicz and Yingjin Zhang, 69–83. Lanham, MD: Rowman & Littlefield, 2017.

Pickowicz, Paul G., and Yingjin Zhang, ed. *From Underground to Independent: Alternative Film Culture in Contemporary China*. Lanham, MD: Rowman & Littlefield, 2006.

Pickowicz, Paul G., and Yingjin Zhang. "Introduction: Documenting China Independently." *Filming the Everyday: Independent Documentaries in Twenty-First-Century China*, edited by Paul G. Pickowicz and Yingjin Zhang, 3–18. Lanham, MD: Rowman & Littlefield, 2017.

Piketty, Thomas, Li Yang, and Gabriel Zucman. "Capital Accumulation, Private Property, and Rising Inequality in China, 1978–2015." *American Economic Review* 109, no. 7: (2019): 2469–96.

Pollacchi, Elena. *Wang Bing's Filmmaking of the China Dream: Narratives, Witnesses and Marginal Spaces*. Amsterdam: Amsterdam University Press, 2021.

Pun, Ngai. *Migrant Labor in China*. London: Polity, 2016.

Pun, Ngai. "The New Chinese Working Class in Struggle." *Dialectical Anthropology* 44 (2020): 319–29.

Ramos-Martínez, Manuel. "The Oxidation of the Documentary: The Politics of Rust in Wang Bing's *Tie Xi Qu: West of the Tracks*." *Third Text* 29, no. 1–2 (2015): 1–13.
Ren, Mengjia, Lee G. Branstetter, Brian K. Kovak, Daniel Erian Armanios, Jiahai Yuan. "Why Has China Overinvested in Coal Power?" *The Energy Journal* 42, no. 2 (2021): 113–33.
Renzi, Eugenio. "La totalité comme forme." In Wang, Bing. *Alors, la Chine. Entretiens avec Emmanuel Burdeau et Eugenio Renzi*, 7–19. Paris: Les Prairies ordinaires, 2014.
Ricoeur, Paul. *Memory, History, Forgetting*. Translated by Kathleen Blamey and David Pellauer. Chicago: University of Chicago Press, 2004.
Rioux, Bertrand, Philipp Galkin, Frederic Murphy, and Axel Pierru. "Economic Impacts of Debottlenecking Congestion in the Chinese Coal Supply Chain." *Energy Economics* 60 (2016): 387–99.
Robinson, Luke. *Independent Chinese Documentary: From the Studio to the Street*. London: Palgrave, 2013.
Ross, Andrew. "The Filming of Deindustrialisation." In *Leaving the Factory: Wang Bing's Tiexi qu / West of the Tracks*, 38–45. New York: Texte und Töne, 2009.
Ruchel-Stockmans, Katarzyna. "Loops of History: Allan Sekula and Representations of Labor." In *Critical Realism in Contemporary Art: Around Allan Sekula's Photography*, edited by Jan Baetens and Hilde Van Gelder, 28–39. Leuven: Leuven University Press, 2010.
Rui, Huaichuan. *Globalization, Transition and Development in China: The Case of the Coal Industry*. London: Routledge, 2005.
Sekula, Allan. *Fish Story*. Düsseldorf: Richter Verlag, 1995.
Sekula, Allan. *Photography Against the Grain: Essays and Photo Works 1973–1983*. Second edition. London: MACK, 2016.
Sekula, Allan. "Photography between Labour and Capital." In *Art Isn't Fair: Further Essays on the Traffic in Photographs and Related Media*, edited by Sally Stein and Ina Steiner, 13–80. London: MACK, 2020.
Sekula, Allan, and Benjamin H. D. Buchloh. "Conversation between Allan Sekula and Benjamin H. D. Buchloh." In *Allan Sekula: Performance under Working Conditions*, edited by Sabine Breitwieser, 21–55. Vienna: Generali Foundation, 2003.
Shabtay, Talia. "The Art and the Politics of 'The Forgotten Space.'" *Oxford Art Journal* 38, no. 2 (2015): 263–82.
Shedden, Leslie. *Mining Photographs and Other Pictures: A Selection from the Negative Archives of Shedden Studio, Glace Bay, Cape Breton*, edited by Benjamin H. D. Buchloh and Robert Wilkie. Halifax: Press of the Nova Scotia College of Art and Design, 1983.
Sheehan, Jackie. *Chinese Workers: A New History*. New York: Routledge: 2002.
Shen, Rui. "To Remember History: Hu Jie Talks about His Documentaries." *Senses of Cinema* 35 (2005). https://www.sensesofcinema.com/2005/conversations-with-filmmakers/hu_jie_documentaries/.
Silberberg, Jerome. "Landscape Theory from a Chinese Space-Time Continuum." In *Landscape Theory*, edited by Rachael Ziady DeLue and James Elkins, 277–81. New York: Routledge.
Smyth, Russell, and Zhai Qingguo. "Economic Restructuring in China's Large and Medium-sized State-owned Enterprises: Evidence from Liaoning." *Journal of Contemporary China* 12 (2003): 173–205.

Song, Yueping, Jingwen Zhang, and Xian Zhang. "Cultural or Institutional? Contextual Effects on Domestic Violence against Women in Rural China." *Journal of Family Violence* 36 (2021): 643–55.
Stahl, Titus. "Georg [György] Lukács." *The Stanford Encyclopedia of Philosophy* (Spring 2018 edition), edited by Edward N. Zalta, https://plato.stanford.edu/archives/spr2018/entries/lukacs/.
Tchen, Jack (John Kuo Wei). "Interview with Allan Sekula." *International Labor and Working-Class History* 66 (2004): 155–72.
Thaxton, Ralph A. Jr. *Catastrophe and Contention in Rural China: Mao's Great Leap Forward Famine and the Origins of Righteous Resistance in Da Fo Village*. Cambridge: Cambridge University Press, 2008.
Van Gelder, Hilde. "'Social Realism' Then and Now: Constantin Meunier and Allan Sekula." In *Constantin Meunier: A Dialogue with Allan Sekula*, edited by Hilde Van Gelder, 71–91. Leuven: Leuven University Press, 2005.
Van Gelder, Hilde, and Jan Baetens. "A Debate on Critical Realism Today." In *Critical Realism in Contemporary Art: Around Allan Sekula's Photography*, edited by Jan Baetens and Hilde Van Gelder, 120–37. Leuven: Leuven University Press, 2010.
Veg, Sebastian. "The Limits of Representation: Wang Bing's Labour Camp Films." *Journal of Chinese Cinemas* 6, no. 2 (2014): 173–87.
Veg, Sebastian. "Literary and Documentary Accounts of the Great Famine." In *Popular Memories of the Mao Era: From Critical Debate to Reassessing History*, edited by Sebastian Veg, 115–36. Hong Kong: Hong Kong University Press, 2019.
Veg, Sebastian. *Minjian: The Rise of China's Grassroots Intellectuals*. New York: Columbia University Press, 2019.
Walker, Janet. "Rights and Return: The Perils of Situated Testimony after Katrina." In *Documentary Testimonies: Global Archives of Suffering*, edited by Bhaskar Sarkar and Janet Walker, 83–114. London/New York: Routledge/AFI Film Readers, 2010.
Wang, Bing. *Alors, la Chine. Entretiens avec Emmanuel Burdeau et Eugenio Renzi*. Paris: Les Prairies ordinaires, 2014.
Wang, Bing. "Deuxième dialogue avec le cinéaste. Entretien avec Wang Bing réalisé par Isabelle Anselme." In *Wang Bing. Un cinéaste en Chine aujourd'hui*, edited by Caroline Renard, Isabelle Anselme, and François Amy de la Bretèque, 133–44. Aix-en-Provence: Presses universitaires de Provence, 2014.
Wang, Bing. "Filming a Land in Flux." *New Left Review* 82 (2013): 115–34.
Wang, Bing. "La memoria rimossa della Cina. Conversazione con Wang Bing." In *Wang Bing: Il cinema nella Cina che cambia*, edited by Daniela Persico, 13–34. Milan: Agenzia X, 2010.
Wang, Bing. "L'image comme preuve du réel. À propos d'images des camps." In *Wang Bing. Un cinéaste en Chine aujourd'hui*, edited by Caroline Renard, Isabelle Anselme, and François Amy de la Bretèque, 147–50. Aix-en-Provence: Presses universitaires de Provence, 2014.
Wang, Bing. "Past in the Present. Director's Statement." 2012. https://www.sabzian.be/article/past-in-the-present.
Wang, Bing. "Premier dialogue avec le cinéaste. Entretien avec Wang Bing réalisé par Isabelle Anselme." In *Wang Bing. Un cinéaste en Chine aujourd'hui*, edited by Caroline Renard,

Isabelle Anselme, and François Amy de la Bretèque, 19–43. Aix-en-Provence: Presses universitaires de Provence, 2014.

Wang Bing. "Wang Bing fangtan: na zhong zhengti de lishi gan he mingyun gan." 2002. https://www.chinaindiefilm.org/王兵访谈：那种整体的历史感和命运感/?lang=zh-hans.

Wang, Bing, Dominique Château, and José Moure. "Documentary as Contemporary Art—A Dialogue." In *Post-cinema: Cinema in the Post-art Era*, edited by Dominique Chateau and José Moure, 355–65. Amsterdam: Amsterdam University Press, 2020.

Wang Hui. *Dongxi zhijian de "Xizang wenti."* Beijing: Shenghuo, dushu, xin zhi sanlian shudian, 2011.

Wang, Mark, Zhiming Chen, Pingyu Zhang, Lianjun Tong, and Yanji Ma, ed. *Old Industrial Cities Seeking New Road of Industrialization: Models of Revitalizing Northeast China*. Singapore: World Scientific Publishing, 2014.

Wang, Ning. *Banished to the Great Northern Wilderness: Political Exile and Re-education in Mao's China*. Vancouver: UBC Press, 2017.

Wang, Qi. *Memory, Subjectivity and Independent Chinese Cinema*. Edinburgh: Edinburgh University Press, 2014.

Wang, Xiaobo. "The Silent Majority." https://media.paper-republic.org/files/09/04/The_Silent_Majority_Wang_Xiaobo.pdf.

Wemheuer, Felix. *A Social History of Maoist China: Conflict and Change, 1949–1976*. Cambridge: Cambridge University Press, 2019.

Williams, Philip F., and Yenna Wu. *The Great Wall of Confinement: The Chinese Prison Camp through Contemporary Fiction and Reportage*. Berkeley: University of California Press, 2004.

Woodworth, Max D. "China's Coal Production Goes West: Assessing Recent Geographical Restructuring and Industrial Transformation." *The Professional Geographer* 67, no. 4 (2015): 630–40.

Woodworth, Max D. "Spaces of the Gigantic: Extraction and Urbanization in China's Energy Frontier." In *Frontier Assemblages: The Emergent Politics of Resource Frontiers in Asia*, edited by Jason Cons and Michael Eilenberg, 155–70. Oxford: Wiley-Blackwell, 2019.

Wright, Tim. *The Political Economy of the Chinese Coal Industry*. New York: Routledge, 2011.

Wu, Hung. *A Story of Ruins: Presence and Absence in Chinese Art and Visual Culture*. Princeton: Princeton University Press, 2012.

Wu, Wenguang. "DV: Individual Filmmaking." In *The New Chinese Documentary Film Movement: For the Public Record*, edited by Chris Berry, Lu Xinyu, and Lisa Rofel, 49–54. Hong Kong: Hong Kong University Press, 2010.

Wu, Wenguang. "Opening the Door of Memory with a Camera Lens: The Folk Memory Project and Documentary Production." *China Perspectives* 4 (2014): 37–44.

Wu Wenguang, ed. *Xianchang*. Tianjin: Shehui kexueyuan chubanshe, 2000.

Wu Wenguang, ed. *Xianchang 2*. Tianjin: Shehui kexueyuan chubanshe, 2001.

Wu Wenguang, ed. *Xianchang 3*. Tianjin: Shehui kexueyuan chubanshe, 2005.

Yang Jisheng. *Mubei: 1958–1962 nian Zhongguo da jihuang jishi*. 2 vols. Hong Kong: Cosmos Books, 2008.

Yang, Jisheng. *Tombstone: The Great Chinese Famine 1958–1962*. Translated by Stacy Mosher and Guo Jian. New York: Farrar, Strauss and Giroux, 2012.

Yang Xianhui. *Jiabiangou shiji*. Guangzhou: Huacheng chubanshe, 2008.
Yang Xianhui. "Wenxue, zuowei yizhong zhengyan—Yang Xianhui fangtan lu." *Shanghai wenxue* 12 (2009): 91–96.
Yang, Xianhui. *Woman from Shanghai: Tales of Survival from a Chinese Labor Camp*. Translated by Wen Huang. New York: Anchor Books, 2010.
Ye, Jingzhong, Chunyu Wang, Huifang Wu, Congzhi He, and Juan Liu. "Internal Migration and Left-Behind Populations in China." *Journal of Peasant Studies* 40, no. 6 (2013): 1119–46.
Yu, Kiki Tianqi. *'My' Self on Camera: First Person Documentary Practice in an Individualising China*. Edinburgh: Edinburgh University Press, 2020.
Yuan, Weiman, and Therese Hesketh. "Intimate Partner Violence and Depression in Women in China." *Journal of Interpersonal Violence* 36, no. 21–22 (2021): NPI2016–NPI2040.
Zeng, Jin. "Political Compromises: The Privatization of Small- and Medium-Sized Public Enterprises in China." *Journal of Chinese Political Science* 15 (2010): 257–82.
Zhang, Hongwei, and Ruohui Zhao. "Empirical Research on Domestic Violence in Contemporary China: Continuity and Advances." *International Journal of Offender Therapy and Comparative Criminology* 62, no. 16 (2018): 4879–87.
Zhang, Qi, Mingxing Liu, and Victor Shih. "Guerrilla Capitalism: Revolutionary Legacy, Political Cleavage, and the Preservation of the Private Economy in Zhejiang." *Journal of East Asian Studies* 13 (2013): 379–407.
Zhang, Yaxuan. "Je suis un conservateur. Entretien avec Wang Bing." In *Actualités critiques. Capricci 2012*, edited by Thierry Lounas, 70–81. Paris: Capricci, 2012.
Zhang, Zhen. "Bearing Witness: Chinese Urban Cinema in the Era of 'Transformation' (*Zhuanxing*)." In *The Urban Generation: Chinese Cinema and Society at the Turn of the Twenty-first Century*, edited by Zhang Zhen, 1–45. Durham, NC: Duke University Press, 2007.
Zhao Xu. *Jiabiangou can'an: fangtan lu*. Washington, DC: The Laogai Research, 2008. Foundation. https://d18mm95b2k9j1z.cloudfront.net/wp-content/uploads/2019/01/25-夹边沟惨案访谈录.pdf.
Zhou, Xun. *Forgotten Voices of Mao's Great Famine, 1958–1962*. New Haven, CT: Yale University Press, 2013.
Zhou, Xun, ed. *The Great Famine in China, 1958–1962: A Documentary History*. New Haven, CT: Yale University Press, 2012.
Zhu, Hong, and Junxi Qian. "New Theoretical Dialogues on Migration in China." *Journal of Ethnic and Migration Studies* 47, no. 12 (2021): 2685–705.
Zhu, Shengjun, and John Pickles. "Bring In, Go Up, Go West, Go Out: Upgrading, Regionalisation and Delocalisation in China's Apparel Production Networks." *Journal of Contemporary Asia* 44, no. 1 (2014): 36–63.
Zhuang, Jiayun. "Remembering and Reenacting Hunger: Caochangdi Workstation's Minjian Memory Project." *TDR: The Drama Review* 58, no. 1 (2014): 118–40.

# Index

*15 Hours*, 3, 159n1
*1966—My Time in the Red Guards*, 11, 51

adaptation. See *The Ditch*; *Fengming, a Chinese Memoir*
affect, 44, 47, 56, 81, 84, 86
Ai Weiwei, 11
Ai Xiaoming, 11, 12, 38, 77
Aitken, Ian, 115
Akerman, Chantal, 61
Anhui, 145
Antelme, Robert, 50
Anthropocene, 97, 132. See also *Coal Money*
Anti-Rightist Campaign, 3, 7, 27, 34–35, 43, 61, 64, 77, 78–79, 80, 81, 83, 85, 90, 92. See also *Brutality Factory*; *Dead Souls*; *The Ditch*; *Fengming, a Chinese Memoir*
Antonioni, Michelangelo, 5, 116
archive, 4, 16–17; access, 28, 43–44, 58; audiovisuality, 29, 38, 43, 52; embodiment, 44, 45, 53, 57, 77, 162; famine, 28, 37, 39; Great Leap forward, 28; photography, 139; reenactment, 72–73. See *Fengming, a Chinese Memoir*; Ricoeur, Paul

Baecque, Antoine de, 89
Bahar, Robert, 77
*The Battle of Chile*, 80
*Beauty Lives in Freedom*, 3
Beijing Film Academy, 5

Bergman, Ingmar, 5
Berry, Chris, 4, 6, 30
biopolitics, 100, 152, 162. *See also* Foucault, Michel
*Bitter Money*, 3, 18, 19, 20, 97, 98, 104, 107, 127, 140, 142, 144–60, 162; domestic violence, 155–58; gender, 146, 153, 155–58; internal migration, 145–47, 154; mobility, 147–50; space, 145, 150–54
Bourgeus, Camille, 139
Bouvier, Nicolas, 131
Braester, Yomi, 15
Breton, Stéphane, 131
*Brutality Factory*, 61, 131
Buchloch, Benjamin H. D., 105
*Bumming in Beijing—The Last Dreamers*, 8, 10. *See also* Wu Wenguang
Burch, Noel, 104

Cai, Shenshen, 31
Caillet, Aline, 62, 73
camera technique. See *Fengming, a Chinese Memoir*; *West of the Tracks*
Cannes Cinéfondation, 45
Cannes Film Festival, 3, 43, 45, 61, 77
Caochangdi Workstation, 39–40. *See also* Folk Memory Project; Wu Wenguang
Carracedo, Almudena, 77
censorship, 5, 8, 49
Chan, Andrew, 56–57
Chen Kaige, 7
Cheng, Zhiming, 121, 122

China, education, 29–30, 103, 134; environment, 2, 11; environmental documentary, 19, 132, 141–42; Five-Year-Plan, 34, 113; Hundred Flower Campaign, 34, 56; industry, 97–98; inequality, social / economic, 1–2, 4, 108n20, 123; 138; market economy, 8, 13, 99, 101–3, 110, 112-13, 120, 127, 133, 137–38, 146, 158; mixed economy, 1–2, 18, 140; neoliberalism, 2, 18, 105, 110; penology, 16, 32–34; postsocialism, 102, 115; poverty, 114; rural-urban divide, 2, 159. *See also* Anti-Rightist Campaign; Cultural Revolution

Chinese Communist Party, 2, 7, 9, 13, 18, 19, 28, 31, 32–35, 37, 52, 55–57, 79, 98–103, 112, 133, 134, 146–47, 162–63

Chinese documentary studies, 10, 12, 13, 15, 31, 102, 131, 161. See also *xianchang*

coal, 18, 20; commodity, 132; consumption, 136; industry, 132–33; production, 136; transportation, 4, 132, 136; workers, 3, 133. See also *Coal Money*

*Coal Money*, 3, 18, 19, 20, 97, 98, 104, 107, 127, 131–43, 157, 162; critical reception, 131–32, 142n3; environment, 132–35; resource extraction, 97; transportation, 134–39; workers, 138–40

collective memory, 7, 29, 57, 69, 81

Costa, Pedro, 61

creative repetition. *See* repetition

critical realism, 18, 98, 104-7, 108n21, 126, 127, 162–63. *See also* Sekula, Allan

*Crude Oil*, 3, 77, 131

Cultural Revolution, 29, 37–38, 39, 43, 54, 61, 62, 125, 163

Dai, Shanshan, 112, 117, 126

Dante, Alighieri, 141

*danwei*, 18, 19, 98, 99, 102, 112, 121, 122–23

Day, Gail, 115

*Dead Souls*, 3, 6, 7, 16, 17, 27, 28, 29, 34, 43, 63, 64, 66, 69, 73, 74, 77–93, 162; *The Ditch* compared to, 82–84; landscape, 18, 77, 84–92; mise-en-scène, 80; nonhuman, 78, 85–90, 92; oral testimony, 79; soundtrack, 86; temporality, 80–82; treatment for, 78, 82. *See also* Mingshui

Deleuze, Gilles, 17, 62, 70–72. *See also* reenactment; repetition

Delisle, Jacques, 2

Deng Xiaoping, 1, 4, 43, 102

Derrida, Jacques, 45

*diceng*, 12, 13–15. See also *minjian*; *ruoshi qunti*; vulnerability

Didi-Huberman, Georges, 58, 68–69

Dikötter, Frank, 28, 80

displacement. See *Bitter Money*; *West of the Tracks*

*The Ditch*, 3, 7, 16, 17, 27, 28–29, 33, 38, 43, 45, 47, 55, 59, 61–76, 77, 78, 80, 85, 162; adaptation, 62–66, 68; *Dead Souls* compared to, 83; desert, 83–84; ethics, 64–65; indexicality, 67–69; landscape, 82–84; photography, 66–69; soundtrack, 84. *See also* reenactment; repetition

documentary cinema. *See* Chinese documentary studies; independent Chinese documentary

Domenach, Luc, 33

domestic violence, 20. See *Bitter Money*

Dong, Lijing, 126

Du Haibin, 11

Duan Jinchuan, 8

duration, 6, 80–81, 90. *See also* slow cinema

Dutton, Michael, 101

editing, 38, 116, 118, 156

Edwards, Dan, 11, 12, 14

embodiment. See *Fengming, a Chinese Memoir*

energy, 18, 132–35, 136, 138, 139, 141. See also *Coal Money*

environment (documentary). *See* China
ethics of documentary, 14–15, 62, 156. See also *minjian*; *xianchang*
experience. *See* He Fengming

factory space. See *Bitter Money*; *West of the Tracks*
famine, 3, 4, 16, 27–40, 43, 45, 49, 51, 53, 56, 62, 64, 65, 77, 80, 81, 90, 162. See also *Dead Souls*; *The Ditch*; *Fengming, a Chinese Memoir*; Great Leap Forward; Jiabiangou labor camp
Fan, Lixin, 111
Fan, Xiaojun, 112, 117, 126
*Fengming, a Chinese Memoir*, 3, 7, 16, 17, 27, 28, 29, 34, 38, 43–60, 61, 62, 63, 64, 65, 66, 69, 73, 74, 77, 78, 79, 80, 83, 85, 131, 162; adaptation, 51–53, 59n2; becoming-archive, 53, 55–58; cinematography, 46–47; mise-en-scène, 47, 55–57; performance, 55–57; *suku*, 57. *See also* archive; Jiabiangou labor camp
Fiant, Antony, 6, 86, 126, 136
fiction. *See* Yang Xianhui
Fifth Generation filmmaking, 7
Folk Memory Project, 12, 39–40, 77. *See also* Wu Wenguang
forced labor camp. *See* Jibing; labor camp
Foucault, Michel, 100–102. *See also* governmentality

gallery space, 47, 77, 163
Gansu, 32, 38, 43, 45, 53, 54, 63, 65, 66, 71, 77, 85
Gao Ertai, 3
gender. See *Bitter Money*; *West of the Tracks*
Gobi Desert, 47, 65,73, 74, 84
Godard, Jean-Luc, 5
Goldstein, Avery, 2
governmentality, 18, 98; China, 101–3, 111, 116, 127, 145, 152–53, 162. *See also* Foucault, Michel
grassroots. See *minjian*
Great Famine. *See* famine

Great Leap Forward, 3, 4, 12, 16, 17, 27–40, 43–45, 56, 57, 61–62, 162. See also *Dead Souls*; *The Ditch*; *Fengming, a Chinese Memoir*
Greenhalgh, Susan, 101
Guangzhou, 97, 136
Guizhou, 145, 149
Guzmán, Patricio, 6, 77

He Fengming, 16–17, 34, 39, 43–48, 62, 63, 66, 80, 83; biography, 27–28, 45, 47, 54–55, 58; experience, 51–52, 54, 56, 58; memoir, 17, 32–34, 38, 44, 45–46, 51–52, 54, 55, 59n11, 69; performance, 44, 47, 56–57, 69. *See also* archive; *Fengming, a Chinese Memoir*; Wang Jingchao
Hebei, 133
Helsinger, Elizabeth, 91
Henan, 145
Hesketh, Therese, 157
Hindess, Barry, 101
historicity (textuality), 30
history. *See* China
Holocaust, 49
Hu Jie, 11, 13
*hukou*, 146–48, 152–53
Hundred Flowers Campaign. *See* Great Leap Forward
Hurst, William, 99
Huzhou, 18, 144, 145, 149, 152. See also *Bitter Money*; textile industry

independent Chinese documentary, 1, 3, 4, 8–11, 14–15, 161
indexicality, 67, 69–70. See also *The Ditch*; photography
inequality. *See* China
Inner Mongolia, 133–34, 136, 141. See also *Coal Money*
intellectual. See *minjian*
intertextuality, 16–17, 44, 66
intimate partner violence. See *Bitter Money*

Jeffreys, Elaine, 101, 103

Jia Zhangke, 9, 111
Jiabiangou labor camp, 16, 27, 28, 32, 33, 45, 54, 64, 66, 74, 77–79, 83, 89, 91–92. See also *Dead Souls*; *The Ditch*; *Fengming, a Chinese Memoir*
*Jiabiangou Elegy*, 12, 38, 39, 51, 77. See also Ai Xiaoming
*Jiabiangou jishi*. See Yang Xianhui
Jiang Yue, 8, 11
Jiangsu, 152
Jiangxi, 145

Kahn, Albert, 131
Kernen, Antoine, 113, 114, 119
Kierkegaard, Søren, 70

labor. See *Bitter Money*; *Coal Money*
labor camp, 3, 12, 14, 16, 17, 27–32, 34–35, 39, 43, 45–47, 55, 56, 57, 63–65, 67–68, 77, 83, 85, 162. See *Dead Souls*; *The Ditch*; *Fengming, a Chinese Memoir*; Jiabiangou labor camp
laid-off workers. See *West of the Tracks*
landscape. See *Dead Souls*; minescape
Lanzhou, 43, 45
Lanzmann, Claude, 6, 50. See also *Shoah*
*laogai*, 16, 29, 31, 32–34, 35. See also *The Ditch*; *Fengming, a Chinese Memoir*; Jiabiangou labor camp
*laojiao*, 16, 29, 32–33, 53–54. See also *The Ditch*; *Fengming, a Chinese Memoir*; Jiabiangou labor camp
Lee, Ching Kwan, 113
Levi, Primo, 50
Li Wenhan, 63–64. See also Yang Xianhui
Liaoning, 19, 97, 119
Lü, Hao-Dong, 135
Lu, Shi, 150
Lü Xinyu, 8–9; self-ethics, 15; *West of the Tracks*, 120, 126; *xianchang*, 15
Lu Xun Academy of Fine Arts, 5, 97
Lukács, Georg, 98, 106, 108n21, 108–9n28, 114–15, 117

*Man in Black*, 3

*Man with No Name*, 3, 43
Mao Zedong, 1, 7, 28, 29, 79, 102; Great Leap Forward, 34–37. See also Anti-Rightist Campaign; Cultural Revolution
marginality, 1, 7–9, 12–14, 54, 124, 148
Margulies, Ivone, 62, 72, 85
Marx, Karl, 136; Marxism, 13, 102, 104, 136
memory. See collective memory
microhistory, 7
migrant labor, 2, 18, 127. See also *Bitter Money*
migration. See *Bitter Money*
minescape, 20, 132, 136–39
Mingshui, 17, 54, 63–65, 77, 78, 79, 81–82, 85–90, 91, 92. See also *Dead Souls*
*minjian*, 8, 16, 17, 18, 62, 78, 92, 101–2, 103, 115, 154; ethics, 14–15; etymology, 12–13; intellectual, 12–14, 46, 47, 51, 53–54, 58, 73, 123, 161–62; Wu Wenguang, 39–40
Mitchell, W. J. T., 86, 91–92, 106
Mongolia, 65
Montrose, Louis, 30
*Mr. Zhang Believes*, 12, 38
*Mrs. Fang*, 3, 118, 163
Mühlhahn, Klaus, 31
Myanmar, 3

neoliberalism, 2, 18, 105, 110, 162
New Chinese Documentary Film Movement, 8–11
New Left, 13
Nichols, Bill, 6, 62; reenactment, 69–70, 71–72
Nietzsche, Friedrich, 70
*No. 16 Barkhor South Street*, 8
nonhuman, 17, 28, 74, 82, 103, 117–18, 162. See also *Dead Souls*

observational cinema, 6, 38
Oppenheimer, Joshua, 69

oral history film, 16, 27, 30, 38–40, 44, 57, 62, 74, 79, 85. See also *Fengming, a Chinese Memoir*
*The Other Bank*, 8
Ou Ning, 10
Ozu Yasujiro, 148

Panh, Rithy, 44, 69
participatory filmmaking, 38
performance. See *Fengming, a Chinese Memoir*
Pernin, Judith, 39, 57
Phay, Soko, 44, 57
photography. See *The Ditch*
Pickowicz, Paul, 4, 9
poetics. See sociopoetics
Pollacchi, Elena, 65, 67, 71, 85, 150, 154
post-Reform era, 2, 13, 133, 115, 144, 147, 157, 162
prison camp. See *laogai*; *laojiao*
Pun, Ngai, 146, 149, 152–53, 155, 159

Qian, Junxi, 147
Qinghai, 131
Qinhuangdao, 135
Qiu Jiongjiong, 12, 38

realism. See critical realism; Sekula, Allan
reeducation, 7, 30, 31; labor camp, 32–34
reenactment, 17, 28, 29, 61, 62, 69–73. See also archive; *The Ditch*
Reform and Opening (*gaige kaifang*), 1–3, 38, 146
refugee, 3, 12
Reggio, Godfrey, 116
reification, 2, 136, 140, 158
relocation. See *Bitter Money*; *West of the Tracks*
Ren, Mengjia, 134
Renzi, Eugenio, 136
repetition, 17, 28, 62–72, 74, 77, 83. See also Deleuze, Gilles
Ricoeur, Paul, 17, 48–51, 58. See also archive
Rocca, Jean-Louis, 113, 114

Rofel, Lisa, 4, 30
Ross, Andrew, 126
Ruchel-Stockmans, Katarzyna, 105
Rui, Huaichuan, 134–35
*ruoshi qunti*, 12–13. See also *diceng*; vulnerability

*Scenes: Glimpses from a Lockdown*, 3, 163
Sekula, Allan, 18, 98, 104–6, 115, 119, 139–40. See also critical realism
Shaanxi, 1
Shanxi, 133, 138
Shabtay, Talia, 105
Shanghai, 37, 63, 66, 83–84, 149
*shanshui*, 89
Shedden, Leslie, 139
Sheehan, Jackie, 99
Shenyang, 3, 5, 18, 19, 97, 99, 110–14, 126. See also *West of the Tracks*
Shenzhen, 97, 136, 147
*Shoah*, 50, 77, 80
Sigley, Gary, 101, 103
silent majority, 2, 12. See also Wang Xiaobo
Sixth Generation filmmaking, 9
slow cinema, 5–6
Smyth, Russell, 113
Sniadecki, J. P., 150
social history, 16. See also sociopoetics
social totality, 19, 111, 114–18, 122–25, 127. See also *West of the Tracks*
socialism, 1, 34, 35, 98, 100, 102–3, 110
socialist realism, 8, 10, 19, 105–7, 108n21, 119. See also critical realism
sociopoetics, 3, 4, 6–8, 30, 161
*The Sorrow and the Pity*, 80
space. See *Bitter Money*; *West of the Tracks*
Special Economic Zone, 147
*The Square*, 8
Stalin, Joseph, 33
Stanislavsky, Konstantin, 71
state-owned enterprise (SOE), 2–3, 4, 18–20, 46, 97, 98, 99–100, 104, 110–16, 119–20, 122–23, 126, 137, 140, 146–47, 161. See also *West of the Tracks*

state studio, 5, 14, 117. *See also* censorship; Wang Bing
subaltern intellectual, 13–14
Svensson, Marina, 11–12

*Ta'ang*, 3, 124, 163
Tanggu, 97, 136
Tarkovsky, Andrei, 5
testimony, 17, 38–39, 44, 46, 48–51, 56, 58, 62–64, 69, 78, 80–81, 86–89, 91. See also *Dead Souls*; *The Ditch*; *Fengming, a Chinese Memoir*
textile industry, 3, 4, 20, 144–46, 150, 154, 161. See also *Bitter Money*; Huzhou
textuality, 30
*Three Sisters*, 3, 144
Tiananmen, 6, 13
Tianjin, 97, 135, 136
Tiexi district, 18, 19, 97, 110–17, 119–24, 126. *See also* Shenyang
*'Til Madness Do Us Part*, 3, 144
*Traces*, 74, 85
trauma, 16, 17, 27, 28–29, 32, 33, 37, 39, 40, 45, 48, 50–51, 52, 77, 78, 80, 82, 85, 90, 91

Van Gelder, Hilde, 106, 119
Veg, Sebastian, 8, 12, 14, 54, 62, 64, 65, 71. See also *minjian*
violence. See *Bitter Money*
Visconti, Luchino, 5
voice-over, 9, 10, 15, 85
vulnerability, 12. See also *diceng*; *ruoshi qunti*

Walker, Janet, 39
Wang Bing, awards, 3–4; biography, 1; education, 5, 7, 29; funding, 5, 163; gender, 54–55; history, 6–7; The Image as Proof of the Real, 66–67; reputation, 3–4, 163; retrospectives, 3–4; slow cinema, 6; work experience, 5. See also *specific films*
Wang Hui, 4

Wang Jingchao, 28, 44–45, 54. See also *Fengming, a Chinese Memoir*; He Fengming; Yang Xianhui
Wang Xiaobo, 12
Wang Xilin, 3
Weerasethakul, Apichatpong, 61
Wemheuer, Felix, 30–31, 34, 35, 55
Wen Hai, 111
*West of the Tracks*, 3, 6, 9, 18, 19, 20, 21n9, 46, 61, 65, 69, 77, 80, 83, 97–99, 104, 106, 107, 110–30, 133, 140, 157, 158, 162; digital camera, 117–18, 129n41; forced relocation, 120–23; gender, 119–20; *Gongchang*, 116–20; night, 124–26; poverty, 112–14; *Tielu*, 123–26; workers, 110–14; *Yanfen jie*, 120–23. See also Shenyang, social totality; Tiexi district
Williams, Philip F., 32, 52
Winckler, Edwin A., 101
Wiseman, Frederic, 15
witnessing, 1, 3, 10, 27–29, 34, 38, 39, 43, 44, 47–48, 50–57, 58, 77, 80–81, 86, 88, 101, 118, 122, 123, 156, 162
Woodworth, Max D., 133, 141
Wright, Tim, 133, 135, 137–38
Wu Hung, 118–19
Wu Wenguang, 8, 9–10, 11–12, 14–15, 22n39, 51. See also Folk Memory Project; *xianchang*
Wu, Yenna, 32, 52

Xi Jinping, 2, 11, 103
Xi'an, 1
*xianchang*, 10, 14–15, 22n39, 46; ethics, 15; etymology, 14
Xintiandun, 79
Xu Cenzi, 71, 83, 84. See also *The Ditch*
Xu Tong, 11

Yang Jisheng, 32, 38, 80
Yang Xianhui, 16, 17, 33, 44, 45, 46, 51, 53–54, 58, 62–64, 66, 83–84. See also *The Ditch*; *Fengming, a Chinese Memoir*; He Fengming

*Youth (Spring)*, 3, 159, 163
Yuan, Weiman, 157
Yunnan, 3, 46, 144, 145, 148, 149

Zhai, Qingguo, 113
Zhang Mengqi, 11
Zhang Xinmin, 9
Zhang Yimou, 7
Zhang, Yingjin, 4, 9
Zhang Yuan, 8
Zhang Zhen, 10, 14

Zhao Liang, 11, 132, 141
Zhejiang, 20, 97, 136, 144, 145, 149, 150
Zhou Enlai, 5
Zhou Xun, 80
Zhu, Hong, 147
Zhu Rongji, 112
*zhuantipian*, 9
Zou Xueping, 11; *Zoujiacun* series, 12, 38, 40, 51